"The Gold Club"
The Jacklyn "Diva" Bush Story

How I Went From
Gold Room To Court Room

Jacklyn "Diva" Bush

Milligan Books   **California**

Published and Distributed by:
Milligan Books, Inc.
An imprint of Professional Business Consultants

Cover Design
Clint D. Johnson

Formatting
Alpha Desktop Publishing

First Printing, January 2003
10987654321

ISBN 0-9725941-2-4

Milligan Books, Inc.
1425 W. Manchester Ave., Suite C
Los Angeles, California 90047
www.milliganbooks.com
(323) 750-3592

Dedication

I dedicate this book to my three beautiful daughters, Breanna, Brittany and Bethany. You give me the strength and courage to keep striving forward in this cruel, sadistic world that we live in. You are my angels and without you, there is no me!

And to my Mom, I am grateful to have you next to me for the rest of our days. I will work hard to make you proud.

To all of the victims and their families of the September 11th tragedy, my thoughts and prayers are with you. And to all of the men and women who serve in the armed forces, the fire and rescue units, and the police departments, "thank you for protecting our freedom."

To my aunt Barbara Young and Kim Owens, for believing in me and giving me supporting words that kept me going, "I love you."

To my cousin Clarence Young, Jr., I know you are watching down on me. Rest in Peace!

And to Ernest Hardy, Sr., you are my favorite member of the family, you have kept very quiet about a lot of things. You have worked so hard all of your life and I hope I can make you proud. I love you with all my heart.

Acknowledgments

First, I would like to thank God, for without His love and His blessings I could not have made it this far, I praise Him! I believe in Divine Intervention and, through it, God has brought some special people into my life.

Dana Harrell, you are my friend as well as my confidante, I appreciate all that you do for me, thanks "Baby Girl!"

To Randall and Donnis, for not only being my business partners and my management, but my friends. Through God's grace, we will go far. To my good friend "Miss Sib," you are an inspiration to me, I admire your creative instinct, you're a beautiful person inside and out, thanks so much.

To my daughters, thank you for your courage in this challenging time. I know it's been hard but the worst is behind us!

To Steve Kaplan, for being like a father to me and "papa" to the girls, I love you and will always be here for you. I thank you for my freedom, and for peace of mind, you are my hero.

To Stanley B. Lackey, you are not just my friend, you are my other half. Thank you for your persistence and your patience and for being understanding. You stood by my side when I needed you the most. I truly love you!

To Richard Rubin, you are truly a phenomenal person. Thank you for allowing me to help you with the charity projects and for being an uplifting friend to me and my children. You and I have a deep bond, I will cherish you always.

Thank you to my best friend Nicole Schug, we've been through so much and have both suffered great losses but through prayer and friendship we have prevailed. I love you!

To Renata Denayo, "Mulan," Elisa Corujo, thanks for being my friends and sticking by my side through everything.

To my sisters and brothers for believing in me, I love you!

To all of the Gold Club employees, I extend my deepest apologies. All those who got to know me, know that my heart is good and I meant well.

To all of those who read this book, I hope it makes a difference in your life and shows you that no matter how bad things may get, there is a silver lining, you just have to pray and go after your dreams.

About the Author

Jacklyn "Diva" Bush gained national attention for her role in the infamous Gold Club Trial, which was reported around the globe. Jackie has worked as a car sales associate, parent leader, administrative assistant, and a wedding coordinator.

Ms. Bush attended Milwaukee Public Schools where she began her life-long community service, supporting such causes as the Special Olympics and devoting herself to disabled athletes.

As an adult, Ms. Bush attended the nationally renowned Creative Nail Design School in Virginia Beach. She modeled at the age of eighteen and was Miss Teen Queen Wisconsin Pageant at nineteen. She has continued working with non-profit organizations such as Project Open Hand, and the Make-a-Wish Foundation.

Ms. Bush began dancing at the world famous Atlanta Gold Club in 1997, where she quickly gained power and recognition. Her ability to connect with people, along with her innate leadership qualities made her the number one entertainer. In 1998, Ms. Bush was crowned Miss Gold Club. Her incredible life tells of many more such lives—from celebrities and millionaires to young women who she turned out in the stripping industry.

As a means to process her experiences, Ms. Bush has taken her inborn talent for storytelling and written her first book—The "Gold Club" The Jacklyn "Diva" Bush Story: How I Went From Gold Room to Court Room.

"I wrote this book for both men and women, to reveal a side of life that most people don't even dare to dream about. In short, I intend this book to stand as a testament to the human condition."

Currently Ms. Bush is a public speaker who tells her story as a means to entertain and to help others. She is working on her second book and lives in Atlanta with her three daughters, Breanna, Brittany and Bethany.

Chapter One

Some people say that I was the Michael Jordan of the stripping industry. Well, maybe I was. My name is Jacklyn Bush, a.k.a. Diva. I started dancing in Milwaukee at the age of 18 and ended in what was arguably the most prestigious, high-dollar, high-class strip club in the United States—the world famous Atlanta Gold Club.

Now outside of the city, in the sticks, backwards judgmental assholes will gladly tell you Atlanta is the Sodom & Gomorrah of the South. Maybe that's true, too. It's the city where the adult entertainment industry is second only to Coca-Cola. It's the city that never sleeps—except on Sundays when we all need a break from the hustle, the big boobs, the blow jobs, the threesomes and oh my God, the champagne. Champagne Diva. That's me.

The Gold Club was a haven for men of means, high rollers, guys who thought nothing of dropping a $4,000 tip. Women who thought nothing of a lesbian sex show and two well-placed fingers. GHB. Ecstasy. Cocaine. Chicks with kids and boyfriends at home. College girls looking for an easy way to get through school. Nothing to it.

Maybe I thought it was easy, too.

If you're reading this book, I'm guessing you want to know something about me and the people who frequented the

Gold Club. And after you hear all that, maybe you'll want to know, what a nice girl like me was doing in a place like that. I have no regrets for anything I did, none whatsoever. I mean, it's not illegal to make money, is it?

Corporate America is neck and neck with the adult entertainment industry for hustling. When I was a kid, I learned street sense. The Gold Club is the other side, the corporate level of that. For a woman to put on a suit, shoes and handbag and go into a strip club and come out with five Gs, she's hustling her ass off.

Having conquered and devoured the strip club industry, I was in 1998 officially crowned "Diva," Miss Gold Club. I had made it to the top of the top. You can't get any higher than that.

I did not get where I was on this particular night by letting the stripping world make me over. I made myself into what they wanted me to be.

Tonight, my hair is down, straight and silky, like an Asian's. I have on a sparkly gray evening gown that shimmers under the club lights. The fabric shakes with my body as I walk, like a second skin. There is a slit up the side that exposes my perfectly sculpted right leg and ends just at the top of my hip. I walk like a panther in my seven-inch heels. I'm not wearing any underwear. I never do.

When I first started at the Gold Club I would work from four in the afternoon until four in the morning. Now I come in whenever I damn well feel like it. Tonight, I feel like arriving at 9 o'clock, in time to make my money but not so early as to greet the deadbeat crowd.

Inside the front door I see Arthur, my favorite floorman. He's a big dark black guy and a very sharp dresser. All the floormen wear tuxedos but Arthur is wearing his own trademark Derby hat. Every night he has a different one on and it always matches his cummerbund; orange, lime green, yellow, black and royal blue. His tie always has a rhinestone.

"Good evening, Diva," Arthur greets me with a distinguished smile—not suck up, not happy. Detached.

The night is young. I put on my game face—no mom, nobody's neighbor. I set my mind like a clock: I am at the witching hour, one of the sexiest women in the world. I'm Cinderella in a G-string.

Arthur's job was to keep the guys happy. He was so good at it he made as much money as some of the dancers.

At the Gold Club the first person you met was a floorman. He was the point guy who notified everybody else by radio a new customer was in the house. Then another floorman would come down and escort the customer from the main floor to wherever he wanted to go—the VIP Lounge, the Gold Mine, the Viper Lounge, even straight to a Gold Room. The floormen got the guys comfortable. On any given night, there were 25 of them on the clock to take care of an average of 1,000 men.

They were there for protection, pretty much as bouncers, but Steve Kaplan, the millionaire owner of the club from New York, didn't call them bouncers. He called them floormen. They were there to protect the girls but at the same time make the customers feel like kings—two jobs in one. If the customer asked a floorman to go get a particular girl, he marched his ass over and got that girl. He was at the beck and call of the patrons.

In addition to the 25 floormen, there were five managers on duty every night, about 120 dancers, waitresses and shooter girls.

The club is getting full, fast. One after the other, guys pulled up to the front door. A valet opened their doors and parked their expensive cars. Two floormen out front greeted them, friendly. "Welcome to the Gold Club. Come on in."

The cover charge was only 10 bucks, paid at the same time the ID was checked.

The VIP lounge was downstairs and had a mammoth bar, as well as a raw bar with oysters, clams, lobster tails and crab legs the size of miniature baseball bats. The kitchen was always open, steaks, burgers, salads, sandwiches—whatever anyone wanted.

Past the main floor on the left was the dressing room with mirrors, lockers, a make-up artist. It's where the girls snorted a line or changed for a skit. It's where we showered off after we poured honey all over our D-cup breasts up on stage.

In spite of the five managers and 25 floormen on duty every night, half the time management didn't know what was going on because the place was so big. They couldn't be everywhere in a club which was sprawled out 5,000 square feet.

The upstairs was U-shaped and circled around the entire downstairs, a big massive open floor. Upstairs was where Gold Rooms one through twelve were located. This coveted area was connected to downstairs by two staircases, which met at the main stage, a Vegas-style structure with mirrors as a backdrop. There was a state-of-the-art lighting system and a full-time DJ in a booth upstairs. A couple of steps down from the upstairs was a balcony that held the champagne area, called the Viper Lounge. That means if you want to sit there, you buy champagne. Former Atlanta Mayor Bill Campbell used to like to stand there at the balcony because you could look out over the whole club. There wasn't anything you couldn't see. It was the place movie stars and athletes liked to go to first. They'd have a drink, pick the girls they wanted and go to a Gold Room.

Gold Club girls were classy—real ladies. They didn't

have to make the walk after a dance to get tips from the customers. When they weren't naked, they wore expensive evening gowns instead of teddies or mini-skirts or whatever. The main stage and the other two smaller ones were used to showcase everything we had on the menu. Big breasts. A perky butt. Blond hair. Red hair. Tall. Short. Exotic. Kinky. Sweet. Any flavor girl a guy could possibly dream up, we had. Better than Baskin Robbins. Girls didn't make money on stage. They drummed up business.

On this night that I'm telling you about, I didn't have time to bullshit around. I knew I had to get in there and make my money. Fact was, if I didn't, some other girl was going to make it for me. Two hundred women who are professionals at turning guys on is a lot of competition.

So I was walking around the main floor, checking on the early arrivals, and a smelly fat guy stopped me. Even a guy like that—I gave them all a chance. I didn't size up customers by their suits or watches or shoes. That was a bad way to do business. A lot of the guys who just wear sweats and tennis shoes—like Steve Kaplan—are the ones with the fat wallets.

This fat guy stops me and wants a dance. Except for the skits, I never went on stage. By 1998, I didn't have to. I was making all my money sitting on my butt in the Gold Rooms. God bless whatever gift He gave me for the gab but I could talk my way into making a lot of money.

The customer leans back in his cushioned chair, swirling the ice in his glass with a swizzle stick. He's watching me—my crotch is right up there in his face—how can he help but watch me? Ten bucks for a completely nude dance. He'll probably tip me another ten because that's what they think it's worth to take a peek.

The song playing is "The Most Beautiful Girl in the World."

While I'm dancing I start thinking that I need to go to a

Gold Room. I need to make a thousand dollars. I'm calculating in my head, trying to figure how to get this fat slob to a Gold Room. Every man is different and you have to approach each one differently. Some men you could catch on the main floor. Most of the men who came in had either heard about Gold Rooms from a friend or been to one before so they knew what it was all about. All of them wanted to experience a Gold Room just to say they did.

Thinking of the Gold Room makes me feel sexier. I'm not looking at this guy caring if he's sexy or not. I'm wondering if I'm sexy to him and how that will translate.

My dress goes back on, dropping over my near-perfect body like a curtain. I sit down and he offers to buy me a drink. "Champagne," I say automatically. I look two guys down and see the waitress. She's taking another order.

I hear the girl say, "Gold Club Martini." She's a college student, a nice white girl putting herself through Georgia Tech. The waitress knows what she's talking about. I know what she's talking about. Gold Club drinks don't have any alcohol in them and I think it's real shystie to pretend like you're getting drunk when the guy's drinking real alcohol. This chick is giggling and swerving her head but she's as sober as a Judge in the courtroom.

That wasn't me. If a guy was paying for my drink, I drank it. I got into the evening, every evening. Like most of us—the customers, the employees—just hammered every night. You got the music going, the drinks are flowing and you can't help it. Besides, getting drunk wasn't detrimental to my business. I could be totally inebriated but when it came to my money, I was on point. I knew to the dollar how much money I had every night.

My guy is an asshole anyway. He starts talking shit—a smooth operator. I'm smiling, so interested, listening to how cool he is, how many women he's got and how much money he has and what it can do for me. I'm listening until all I hear is noise. I see his lips moving, see the zits on his chin. All I'm thinking is, "Shut the fuck up. I don't need you. You ain't shit. Bragging about these so-called women you have—why the hell are you here? When can I get up and leave? You ain't spending shit."

Then I hear the DJ announce my name from upstairs. "Diva to the main stage. S&M."

"Sorry baby, I gotta go on. Can I send someone else over to keep you company?" I say, relieved.

"Yeah, someone with bigger tits, how 'bout?" The asshole sneers.

"Sure," I say. I look across the room and see a new girl with blonde hair and tits spilling out of the top of her dress like watermelons. I nod to her and ask if that's the type he's looking for.

"Yeah, she looks good. Send her over."

The asshole slips the tip slowly into my garter, copping a feel at the same time, then slaps me on the ass as I leave to get Miss Watermelon and make for the dressing room beside the main floor.

My girl. Diva. Nobody can fuck with Diva. Steve's words ring in my ears. I could have had that asshole thrown out if I wanted. I could have anyone thrown out and that thought gives me a rush. This guy wasn't worth it, though. It was still business. As long as he was spending, he could stay. As long as he didn't piss me off too bad, I'd leave him to his big attitude and big tits. They were lopsided anyway because this girl obviously didn't massage them when they got put in. Some of these girls were stupid.

Shaney, my favorite S&M partner, is already in the dressing room. She's beautiful, a sweet kind of girl. She's putting on her white little-girlie outfit for the role of the submissive. As for me, I'm the enforcer. My costume is seven-inch boots that come up to my thighs, chains, patent leather bottoms and top, a mask and a whip.

The lights on the main stage go down and we take our places, Shaney at the top of the steps and me on the stage. The DJ announces us and then the lights slowly come up with the music, "I Want to Fuck You Like An Animal" by Nine Inch Nails. There's a long heavy chain hooked to Shaney's neck. I control her, bringing her down the steps. She looks frightened, naïve, like a little girl.

Me and Shaney love doing this skit together. It makes us both hot. Everyone in the room can feel the bass in the music, thudding in their guts, pumping their blood. Shaney looks so innocent. I grab her by her brown hair and slam her face between my legs. I Want to Fuck You Like An Animal...

The audience goes wild. I push her away until she is on all fours like a dog, her round ass facing the audience, showing her clit, the oval shape of pink. I slap her on the butt and it's so loud it rings through the whole place. It doesn't really hurt her. There's an air pocket and trick to slapping. If you do it wrong, you leave a welt.

Shaney lets out a gasp of pain. The enforcer has no sympathy. I start smacking her around and hitting her with the whip. You get me closer to God ... She's so flexible, there's nothing I can't do with her or to her. I'm all but fucking her on the stage and it's legal. No penetration. I'm loving it. Working in the only state in the country that allows nude dancing and alcohol. I suck her tits and grab between her legs. I get off on being in control. As the song nears the end, I slap Shaney across the face and make her go up the steps.

I'm exhilarated.

It's 10 o'clock when I return to the dressing room. The housemom, Rose, is kneeling by Joy, who's flat out on the floor. She's one of the chicks known for doing GHB.

As I'm changing out of my S&M clothes, I say, "Hold on, Rose. I'll give you a hand." I hate this shit.

"Diva, she's out."

I jumped down on the floor and started pumping Joy's chest to get her heart going. Rose is talking to her, saying anything.

"Come on, baby. We're right here. Come on back."

Joy flat-lines, just dies right there. I keep pumping.

G is a natural chemical in your body. You buy this stuff over the counter called Blue Nitro and it enhances the G you already produce in your body. If you take too much of it, though, it can kill you instantly. It can stop your heart, it can shut your brain down, you can have a stroke. It stops you from breathing. It attacks the nervous system.

Steve always thought drugs destroyed life and they do. He hated the fact that he'd come into town and see girls in his club all fucked up on whatever they're doing, GHB, coke and stuff. I was glad he wasn't in the club that night to see Joy.

A moment later, Joy gasps for air and her torso pops up like a car seat. "Get off me!" she screams.

Then she falls back, out again. I'm thinking, there's no way I'm going to let this chick die. I'm thinking about my mother. I'm six years old and she's bouncing on the floor. Me and my brother Jimmy get a spoon to hold her tongue down. Me and Rose do twenty minutes of CPR waiting for the ambulance. The paramedics take Joy out the back way. Nobody's the wiser.

After going out four times, Joy makes it. She lives to come back and do the same thing all over again.

When I finally get out of the dressing room I see Chuck No Last Name, you'd think it was a national secret. The average spender is between five and ten thousand. Anything above that is above average. Chuck came in once every three weeks or so and blew thousands of thousands of dollars, like $60-70,000 in one night. Therefore, Chuck's platinum card put him in the above-average category.

Arthur was taking care of Chuck, roping off a section of the Viper Lounge. I went to say hello. Everyone is going to do well. But I'm the girl who knows how to handle the situation.

I put on a big smile and flirt with Chuck for a moment to relax him. He's not ugly but a little dorky looking. His hair is wild as usual, pupils dilated with coke and he's got white stuff around his nostrils. Chuck is about 38 years old, medium height and you can tell he works out from the muscles, plus he always winds up half naked by the end of the night.

Chuck is looking around, shopping. He sees a girl he likes. She's a little exotic with long dark hair. She's wearing Chinese red. "Diva," he smiles, "see her? Could you tell her to come down here?"

I see the girl, round her up and eventually have three. When you spend Chuck's kind of money you're allowed to have rules and it was my job to make sure they are followed to the letter.

Like I said, we roped off an area in the Viper Lounge for him and then nobody was allowed to cross that line without his permission. That's how he was.

The dark-haired girl came over and started to cross the line, like a bull in a china shop. I looked at her. "Look, Tiffany. These are the rules: get naked. He wants you naked at all times. He wants you drinking, dancing and having a good time, not sitting on your ass. Do not ask for one thin dime. He will tip you very well. Do not ask for anything. Dance with him and have a good time and drink and party. That's all you should do over here. Don't come over here asking how much by the hour. Just enjoy."

Tiffany nodded her head. Chuck ordered $10,000 worth of Gold Bucks for openers. He was starting off in his usual way all around: big trays of crab legs and shrimp. It was Chuck's party.

What can you get for $60-70,000 besides a Jaguar or a small house? At the Gold Club, that kind of money would buy you seven girls, all naked for six hours; thirteen bottles of champagne at $2,000 a pop; large platters of extravagant food—$50 per lobster tail. It was the Royal VIP treatment.

By the end of the evening, I would have maybe $5,000 in Gold Bucks just for handling everything. The other girls could expect a couple of thousand and a hell of a good time.

While I'm getting Chuck set-up, I notice there's a celebrity in the house. How do I know? Norbie Calder, one of the general managers, is running around with his head stuck up his butt.

I go upstairs. The girls are lined up against the rail outside Gold Room 7—the preferred room of celebrities.

I pass Gold Room 5 and one of the girls is getting raked over by one of the floormen. Some of these girls give them $50 or $100 to keep putting them in Gold Rooms. It pisses me off. I lose it. "Look, you fucking moron asshole, you're already getting tipped and getting commission on memberships, getting tipped for seating guys. Then just because you come and put her in a room, she's suppose to tip you out of her money and you hold your hand out for more? You shit head. We work on tips alone. We don't get paid per shift. You've got to be kidding me, shaking her down like that."

It worked. Most of the floormen were terrified of me because they knew the label that I had, Steve's girl, meant that I got whatever I wanted. They were afraid if they didn't do what I told them, back off or whatever, they were going to get fired.

"Look, you motherfucker, don't you even look at me like you got anything to say, but 'Yes ma'am, Jackie.' That's all you got to say."

Then I went over to Arthur and took control. Celebrity or no, I never relied on floormen to set me up. And I didn't need anybody's permission to manage a big room. My list of regulars alone, 60-70 guys on any given month, was such that I had somebody that I knew in the club every night. No question, I was going to a Gold Room.

I immediately connected with the money man, the guy who was paying for the room. He had two friends—so that meant at least three girls, depending on what they wanted. Norbie and Arthur were selling him the membership, getting his license and credit card and all the paperwork signed.

He opts for the Platinum VIP membership for $5,000. It's set up so the bonus is, he actually gets $6,000 back in F&B Bucks (food and beverage). The customer can use the F&B Bucks to buy anything he wants; food, beverage, Gold Rooms, girls. The customer doesn't know it but the floorman makes a commission on the membership. They sell a $1,000 membership, they get $150 commission. A $2,500 membership they get $300. A $5,000 was $500. Then the guy tips the floorman just for selling it to him. Going into the Gold Room, the VIP manager had a form for the customer to sign saying, "These are the girls that are in your room. You are okay for them to be there. This is how much they're making an hour," and the guy would have to sign it before getting even remotely intoxicated.

I negotiated the cost of the room and the hourly rate for the girls, taking my cut off the top, my fee. The room is $500 an hour and each girl is another $1,000 plus whatever tip. Not bad. If they got $500, I would get $600 and so on.

I walk with the money man and his guest, a little scrawny guy, and look over the selection. Kendall, a blond with blue eyes, and brown-haired Hayley are both magazine model types, average B cup. There was Dina, a beautiful black girl, and Nurse Cindy, so-called because of her costume. I choose Dina and Cindy.

The two friends are nervous. I organize the room. Dina in the corner with the little guy and Nurse Cindy with the other.

The music in the background was Alliyah's "One in a Million." That song always put me in a sexy frame of mind and reminded me of my boyfriend, Elliott. It was our song about being completely in love and uninhibited.

My clothes come off and then before the song is over the other girls have their clothes off, too. When the music stops, the guy is happy. I sit with my legs over his lap and he's rubbing my thigh.

These guys are so tense and scared, almost petrified. Nurse Cindy loosens her guy's tie, straddles his lap and smacks him in the face with her boobs to loosen him up. I can't see what Dina is doing but I know the conversation is starting to wane. What do you do when you're alone with three naked girls anyway?

"Let's get a Gold Club Sundae," I say, swirling the tip of my fingernail ever so lightly against the money man's temple.

Nurse Cindy and Dina respond like cheerleaders, high pitched, Please Daddy may I have? voices.

Within minutes the Gold Club Sundae arrives—strawberries, chocolate syrup and whipped cream served with champagne.

I started. You take the strawberry and dip it in the chocolate and rub the chocolate on your nipple. Then you take the whipped cream and add it on. Nurse Cindy and Dina make their sundaes at the same time.

"Okay, gentlemen," I smile. "We're going to have a contest to see who can eat the chocolate and whipped cream off our tits faster."

The guys get all gung-ho. This wasn't sucking our tits—it's a contest! "Okay, one ... two ... three ... go!" We girls count together.

The guys immediately race to see who can eat the Sundae off faster. The little guy is the winner. "I'm done!" he congratulates himself, in spite of the fact that there isn't actually a prize.

Dina says, "No, you're not! You missed a spot!" So he goes back down to get a smidge off of her milk chocolate Double-D breast.

The Gold Club Sundaes relaxed the guys. The rule is that they're not allowed to touch but then again, we entertainers were more than happy to break the rules, to be a little more lenient when it suited us. You can grab my butt or you can hold onto my boob. To us it's just a titty. Go ahead, squeeze it, I don't care. Other people might look at it like I was selling myself short. But when you're making $3,000 in an hour or two it's hard to look at it like that.

By the time our customers are on their fourth or fifth drink they're all half-naked. The guys have their shirts off, ties around their heads. Their two hours are up and they pay us: a thousand to each girl, a thousand apiece in tips and then I got an extra thousand on top of that for putting it all together.

Two in the morning and I've already made $5,000. But it's not enough. I have Fat Garter Syndrome. I wonder who else is around.

I go back downstairs and watch Sherry, one of the five shooter girls, giving this college student a body shot. She climbs up and straddles the guy like she's fucking him, then she places a shot tube between his legs and she starts moving her head as if she was giving him a blowjob. Somewhere in her act, she deep-throats the tube which is about the size of her thumb.

Most tricks were passed down—like the body shot, because they were already so sexy, you'd want to do it that way, though each girl had her own style about doing it.

The shooter girls were a different breed from strippers. They figured why should they have to take their clothes off, when they could make just as much money as we could. They would go into Gold Rooms if guys asked them and some of them like Sherry and Tabitha, gave real blowjobs on a regular basis. For my purposes, if I had a sexually active guy, I'd call on a shooter girl cause I knew that they would do anything for money!

Next to Sherry and her college student, I see this sweet old man. He's white and looks like a high-class business-man—very corporate.

Within one glass of champagne I talk him into getting a Gold Room. I pick up Frederique along the way. We worked together a lot because there was nothing she wouldn't do. I figured, why should I do that shit if I can get Frederique to do it for me?

We were old friends from my stripping days in Milwaukee and I felt comfortable having her in a room. The three of us set up in Gold Room 6 and right away the businessman guy is like, Whatever you guys want you can have. Music to my ears.

There's a couch upholstered in navy blue and burgundy that wraps the room in a U-shape, a red velvet curtain hanging from the ceiling like a chandelier and mirrors everywhere. To the left is dark smoked glass so you can't see in from the outside but you can see out. It's very intimate and pretty. The carpeting matches the upholstery.

Me and Frederique make our gentleman sit against the far wall. We get drunk and then drunker. We get to talking about bisexuality and sex in general. What it was like to be bisexual. The old gentleman is curious because he had never known that side of life. He was a straight guy who had been married a long time. To him, doggy style was being adventurous. We listened to him talking and found out he hadn't been promiscuous as a young man and had never really experienced the wilder side of life.

21

Frederique asks, "So you've never seen two women together?"

"No."

By this time we've been in the room almost two hours.

"Do you want to see what it's like for two women to be together?" I venture. He looks at me as if to say, Are you serious?

I nod, emphatic yes.

I look at Frederique and she looks at me because we were both horny at this point since we'd been talking about sex for two hours.

With Frederique, this was somebody I knew. She and I could French kiss and touch each other all night long and it didn't bother me because I knew her. It wasn't like she was a stranger.

We put on an exhibition and showed him what it's like for two women to be together. He was fascinated. He doesn't want to touch us. He just wants to watch. We get so into each other that at one point we forget he's there.

We begin kissing and caressing each other as if we were a man and woman together. We kiss each other's neck and breasts. We don't have dildoes so we use our fingers and tongues as we sixty-nine each other, moaning, and then both of us climax at the same time.

Our gentleman businessman says, "That is the most beautiful thing I've ever seen in my life."

I loved having sex with Frederique. She was everybody's best sexual experience—men and women. Give credit where credit is due.

At the end of the night I cash out my Gold Bucks— $10,000 and some change. I pay my taxes, thirty percent, so I don't end up owing at the end of the year.

I take one of the Gold Club limos without even stopping for the breathalyzer. I know I'm too drunk to drive. I'm always too drunk to drive. The white stretch Lincoln limos all had a plate on the front that said "Gold Club."

As I watch the lamp posts go by on the highway on the way out to the suburbs, I think to myself, My God, everybody wanted me tonight. What was it? The dress? The way I wore my hair? That I was in a good mood and had a glow and people saw it and wanted it?

It's six a.m. by the time I arrive home and pay the all night babysitter. My kids are up at 7:30 for school so I stay up cooking breakfast, pressing clothes, fixing hair. When I know my kids are on the bus, I'll go to bed for four or five hours and wake up about 1:00 p.m. In the afternoon, I'll run errands and come back in time for the afternoon school bus to drop off my three daughters. Just like a regular Mom, I make dinner, get homework and baths taken care of until it's time to go back to work.

Chapter Two

I only talk about my past as a way to shed light on my past. My mother's maiden name was Karen Muir and she was beautiful with long red hair and milky white skin. She grew up one of four children in a Catholic household in Brampton Canada and was descended from Scottish royalty. I hear they even have a crest to go with the blue blood.

The family later moved to Milwaukee. My mother's childhood was fairly run of the mill with the exception of her brother, Ricky, who was murdered with his best friend. The killers took them to this lake and their bodies were never found.

My father's name is James Edward Lewis, Sr.—a smooth-talking Creole from Shreveport, Louisiana. He was an All-American in male gymnastics and finished high school with a B average. Looking at his picture, his Louisiana-red clay colored skin, people might think he was just a black man, but he isn't. Not really. Not if you want the truth and not some ancient law about one drop and all that. No, my father is a Creole from a family that spoke patois. He's a mix of French, Irish, Cherokee, Chickasaw and Jamaican.

So, while my birth certificate says I'm white, my tea-stained skin has always posed a question mark to those I meet. My smooth reddish brown hair is long, but like what? Thick, like who? Hard to tell. I'm a little like a chameleon. Just about whatever culture I stand next to is what I look like. I am a mixture of many people. I am a member of none.

My parents met at a popular Milwaukee restaurant, Stouffer's. Mom was a waitress and Dad worked in the kitchen as a prep cook. He used to flirt with her all the time but she didn't pay him any mind at first. Still, he was so handsome and smooth, she thought he was the greatest thing in the world and eventually gave in to his advances. They fell in love and she got pregnant or vice versa. It was then that she discovered that he'd lied to her about his age. Dad told her he was twenty when he was only seventeen. My mother was eighteen and her parents didn't like the fact that she was with a black man. In spite of the few times we saw our Canadian grandparents in early childhood, they ended up cutting off the relationship with all of us kids because of the color of our skin.

Not that that matters. Just saying. So my parents met, my mother got pregnant and they had my brother, Jimmy. Six weeks later, my Mom was pregnant with me. That makes Jimmy and I eleven months apart. No wonder we look so much alike.

I have a very long memory. I grew up in the heart of the ghetto. And in Milwaukee, that pulse beats loudest at the corner of Eleventh and Hadley. Our house was gray and white, probably built around the turn of the century, wooden clapboard, infested with roaches and rats. The front room was the main living room and then the dining room housed a guest bed. Just around it on the other side was another room big enough for a bunk bed and a closet, where my big brother, Jimmy, slept and where I slept after I was too big for the crib in the dining room. There was also a cramped hallway that led to a dark and dusty basement with creaky narrow stairs. Beyond that, there was a bathroom, a small kitchen and pantry, and a back door that led out onto a spacious porch and a big yard. We lived downstairs at first. My father's mother Ann Hardy lived upstairs.

In my earliest memory, my mother would buy tangerines and oranges, my favorite wintertime fruits. She'd display them in a big bowl on the table and dole them out conservatively. This particular day is one of my oldest surviving memories. Mom had just returned from the grocery store and sat the tangerines and oranges on the floor by the refrigerator. I didn't walk until I was almost three because I was so roly-poly, I looked more like a beach ball, not at all ready to rise up and walk on two feet. So I crawled into the kitchen, grabbed the bag of oranges and put them under my crib. Then I went back, got the tangerines, and hid with them underneath, too. Finally, I peeled every last orange and tangerine and ate them all.

By the time I crawled out, I was sick to my stomach and looked like death warmed over. My Mom kept asking me what was wrong. I was looking up at her but I couldn't talk to tell her what I'd done. Like a dream. She keeps smelling the strong citrus odor and follows it to its source—the mound of peels under my bed. When she returns I'm sitting under the dining room table and my guts come up all over her feet. She's furious—red hair blazing, seeping into the white of her face. She pops my hand until I feel a sharp sting like a hornet. "You don't go in the kitchen and touch anything!"

Even then, that early, Mom was big on corporal punishment. Or maybe it was just a release for her.

Besides, I was a big frustration for a mother so young. Not only was I a thief, but I was a storyteller, a troublemaker and a prankster. I would bump my head to go to sleep. The bumping made my crib dance across the dining room floor. About a week after I ate the Christmas oranges and tangerines, I bit open the mattress in my crib to make a place to hide from

26

my Mom. I climbed down in the mattress and pulled the blanket over my tubby self. Of course when she came in, she couldn't see me and she started freaking out, thinking I'd climbed out of the crib. I laid under the blanket listening to the commotion I had caused. I was like a ghost, giggling from nowhere, from out of the walls, from thin air. She could hear my sinister baby giggle but she couldn't see me. Finally Mom pulled the crib cover back. I just stared at her.

Truth is, maybe my memory is too good. Maybe I remember too much. Like the day my brother swallowed a cup full of bleach when he was three and I was two. How he puked up his guts and he had to go to the hospital to have his stomach pumped.

My mother was always the only white lady on the block. Throughout the nine years I lived with my mother—the first nine years of my life—she was a drug addict. My father, her "doctor," dealt marijuana and ran crap games out of our house. He was also a womanizer and a wife-beater.

He ran the streets with different women very boldly. We'd see him drive by in our car with another woman in the passenger's seat. His MO was to leave whenever he wanted and to come home whenever it suited him. I think he came home mostly to beat our mother. He'd choke her. Beat her with his fists, a baseball bat, whatever was close at hand.

To deal with the beatings, the cheating and fear, the lack of money and family estrangement, Mom smoked weed and took pills. She was hooked on uppers, downers, and Cadillacs, a kind of an upper with a hallucinogen. If she was too far up, my father gave her something to bring her down. If she was too far down, he'd give her something to bring her up. If she was convulsing, her body would start bouncing off the floor, and we would hold her and put a spoon in her mouth to keep her tongue down so she wouldn't gag on it.

In addition to being a drug dealer, and a sometimes shade-tree mechanic, our father, as I said, ran a crap operation out of our house. At night, the place would fill with smoke, R&B, and the sound of 10-20 men throwing dice, talking shit, the calls of the bids rising higher. While he did have the basic concept of commerce, my father broke the cardinal rule of gambling. What little money he made, he gambled away. Everyone knows, you can't win against chance.

Chapter Three

The first time I came to beautiful Atlanta was in February of 1997. It was 12 degrees in Milwaukee and 74 here. 'These people here are living large,' I said to myself. I came down with a turtleneck and a sweater and had to start shedding clothes. Milwaukee is like the North Pole. Snow to your waist and wind chill to 50-60-70 below. Wind cutting you like a knife. You had to put Vaseline on your skin and a scarf on to keep from getting frostbite. People skiid to the grocery store. Dogs pulled sleds. But then it was beautiful for Christmas, the snow blanketing the eaves and the lights on the houses.

Milwaukee is real pretty in the spring and summer when the flowers are in bloom and the leaves are in the trees. But in the winter, it was the most depressing city I've ever been in in my life. You get tired of minus 75 degrees wind chill. Tired of having the tears freeze in your eyes. You hibernate and get fat. I'm a free spirit. I like to be where it's warm, sunshine, blue sky, trees.

I'd been dating Elliott Henderson, a professional basketball player overseas, for one year by 1997. We'd met in a nightclub in Milwaukee. At the time, shortly after my divorce, I was working during the day as a salesperson at a car dealership and picking up even better cash at night dancing at Encore, an upscale Milwaukee strip club. Elliott was gone most of the year, either playing the season or at basketball camp, but he came home every May and stayed through August, and then back for Christmas. We spent all our time together.

His best friend, Henry James, was an NBA player for the Atlanta Hawks. When he went to visit Henry in Atlanta, Elliott fell in love with the city and decided to stay. Shortly after, he planned a trip for me to come down.

When I came down to Elliott's place, his pager was constantly blowing up. I later learned that he was playing the open field with every slut who would give him the time of day. But at the time, I really loved Atlanta. I stayed two weeks, extended my trip to three. Finally I said, I do hate Milwaukee and I do want to start a new life. So I went back to Milwaukee and talked to my ex-husband Joe, told him that I wanted to go and asked if he could keep our three daughters while I found a job and an apartment. Joe agreed.

As it went, I kissed my kids good-bye, packed up and moved down, ready to start fresh. I got my own apartment but spent a lot of time with Elliott and Henry, who suggested that I get a job at the Gold Club—the hottest strip club in the country. I had heard about the Gold Club back home, and thought, Holy shit, maybe I'll give it a shot.

It took two months sitting around the pool at the apartment complex to get up enough nerve to go in and ask for an audition.

One night, when my best friend, Nikki, was in town, I asked her to go with me for moral support. She said, "I can't stay and watch."

"Why?"

"What if you don't get the job? You are going to come out of there so irate."

But I was gonna do what I was gonna do. I'd heard that

it was very difficult to get in the Gold Club. I wanted to try just to see if I could make it.

So I went in, looked around, and was immediately knocked off my feet by everything I saw—the stage, the decor, even the naked women—it was a beautiful club. I stood up straight, took a deep breath and told the first person I met I was there to audition. My hair was about an inch long and slicked straight back. No makeup except a little lip gloss and an almost sheer floor-length sun dress.

A floorman took me to the dressing room to wait for the General Manager. The procedure was simple. Denise, the housemom on duty, explained, "All you have to do is take your dress off and turn around. He'll look at you and say whether or not you can work here."

"I don't have to get up on the stage and dance?"

"No, you don't have to do that here," she said, patting my back.

The General Manager, Norbie Calder, walked in and looked me in the face. Without ceremony, he said, "Pull your dress down."

I dropped it to the floor and turned around for the manager who just stood there staring. I thought the answer was no when Norbie turned to the housemom and said, "This woman is so beautiful. Give her any night she wants."

They gave me directions to City Hall East where I would get my $30 adult entertainment permit. I started the next night. In the city of Atlanta, permits are required to dance or work in an adult entertainment club. Even if you're a floorman—whatever.

The housemom, Rose Marie Ward, kept the permits in a book and two file boxes. There was also a permit calendar posted on the dressing room mirror. A month before a renewal was due, Rose pulled the girl aside and gave her a heads up. If someone screwed around and didn't get legal, she couldn't work. It was a great incentive to keep your paperwork current.

On my first day I showed up for work at 2 o'clock in the afternoon, nervous, and armed with some of my costumes from Wisconsin. I got dressed. Rose gave me a tour of the upstairs, all the Gold Rooms. She explained the procedures ending with, "You can sit downstairs on the main floor and just watch the girls until you feel comfortable enough to get up and go mingle. Take your time and if you get nervous just find one of us. We'll help you."

I sat on the main floor for a while, watching how things worked. One of the girls saw me alone and asked me to come join her and the two guys she was sitting with. It was then I did my first table dance.

I was so uncomfortable standing right in front of the guy where he was right up close and in person. With my 7-inch heels, his eyes were tight between my legs. In spite of the fact that I'd danced plenty before, I was nervous. The 3-1/2 minute song finished, the end of an eternity. I did it! I breathed a sigh of relief.

The next stinking thing I hear, comes over the PA system, "Jackie! Come to the main stage."

I went up to the DJ booth and said "Did you call me?"

"You're next up on the main stage," the DJ said in a generic mid-western voice. He was about 6'1" with big square-rimmed gold glasses and sandy blond clean cut hair.

"But I just started tonight!"

"Doesn't matter. Everybody goes in rotation. Get used to it. Didn't you dance before?"

"Yeah."

"Same thing."

"No, it's not the same thing," I corrected him. "I have to

32

get naked up there." At home, strippers only went down to their G-string.

"Go have a drink, then," he said. His name was Steve Shades and I could tell right off he was a funny guy.

I had two and then told Steve the DJ what kind of music I liked. When I got on the stage, there was sweat pouring down my whole body. The song started and I began to psyche myself. This is the same thing you used to do back home. You're just gonna take your bottoms off. Big friggin' deal.

I put myself into a place where I zoned everything else out and put on the best performance I could. Guys started coming up, kissing my hand as they tipped me. Like the starlet at the Oscars, inwardly I was gushing: They like me! That was when I knew I could do it. I could dance at the Gold Club.

No sooner had I started than I went back home to Milwaukee, got my kids and brought them back with me to Atlanta. There was a girl at work named Shelby who had a dark tan, dyed blonde hair and blue eyes. She was a main floor girl. Her roommate baby-sat part time. Great. Shelby said, "I'll introduce you and see if you like her." Her name was Kiki. She was a young girl, 20 years old, in school trying to earn extra money. My kids liked her on sight—she was small with childlike features. It was a done deal. I agreed to pay Kiki $600 a week along with extra cash to go places and, of course, for the all important pizza outings. Not bad wages for a young girl to keep three kids who were asleep most of the time.

I went back to my job.

Work started at 4 o'clock in the afternoon and went until 4 o'clock in the morning. Getting into the swing of things was very hard for me. To begin with, I was very intimidated by the women there. They were beautiful. And then, while I saw others making money, I couldn't figure out how they were doing it.

One night we were doing one of our revues where we sold Gold Club hats, sunglasses and T-shirts just before the skits went on. We would do two songs for twenty dollars and the customer got to keep the merchandise. All the girls lined up on stage so the guys could look at them.

When I came down this guy asked me to dance for him. When I pulled my dress down, he snapped, "Put your dress back on. Your boobs are too small." I was devastated. I went in the back and started crying. I was so embarrassed, I didn't want to go back on the floor. It planted a negative seed and made me very self-conscious going forward.

A couple of times in those first weeks I broke down in the dressing room and Norbie sat back there and comforted me. Norbie was Cuban with slick jet black hair, a boyish face, the kind that grow old. His smile was enchanting, soothing. Even with Norbie there to console me, I felt I couldn't do it. I was frustrated. There were so many girls. I didn't know how to compete.

Norbie said, "You have to find your way. You have to be determined in the business." The Gold Club philosophy that was repeated to all of the new girls was repeated to me then: If you can make it through the first four weeks, you can make it.

"You gotta be a little more outgoing and personable," Norbie added. "You just gotta get out there and go for what you want. You can't sit around with your arms folded thinking money is just going to come to you here cause it doesn't work like that. You've got 120 other girls to compete with." He was right.

There was a group of money-making girls in the club who motivated me to want to work harder—Banks, Levi, Tyler, Mercedes, Hanna and Raven. I would watch them coming in the dressing room with $2,500 tucked under their garters. I was afraid to speak to them because I thought they'd just blow me off.

One night Banks was standing upstairs on the rail and I walked up to her. I said, "I know you don't know me and I'm new, but if you don't mind I would like to work with you."

She must have known I was nervous and needed a friend. "I really don't work with anybody but if I get a Gold Room and there's enough people, I'll cut you in," she said.

I was so grateful. Banks kept her word and included me a few times when she had rooms. Each time, I made a nice sum of money.

I watched Banks and learned. She knew how to talk to a man, get him in a room for two-three hours and dance naked maybe only two or three times. The rest of the time she would have her clothes on and she'd just be sitting there talking. Banks showed me a whole other side of entertainment. She'd walk out with $2000 for talking.

Once I figured it out, that most of the time guys just wanted someone to talk to, it was all over. I thought, Wow, men are so simple. It was crazy. Money started flowing like water.

From May to November I was pretty regular on the stage. There were a couple times I put on such a hard-driven show that guys would throw money and the stage floor would be filled with bills. All the dancers had to pick up their money before leaving the stage which was tedious ... depending on what they were throwing. But for the most part I learned you don't want to spend your time going through all that just to make a little bit of money when you could be upstairs chilling in a Gold Room.

On the main floor of the club, you had your tourists, the guys the girls called the "deadbeats." Students, guys who could afford a couple beers and a couple dances and they were done for evening.

The main floor girls danced all the time. Whatever money they got was because they were constantly moving, dance after dance.

That first seven months, I was a main floor girl and I still wasn't making the kind of money the girls like Banks did. Only a few hundred dollars a night. It took me six months before I got my first Gold Room and I made $900 that night. I was dumbfounded.

For a guy to get a Gold Room he had to buy champagne and then pay a minimum of $200 per hour per girl. He had to pay an hourly rate for the room too, costing $150 to $500. During the Super Bowl, VIP rooms booked by movie stars, athletes, musicians and dignitaries would go for a thousand dollars an hour.

But for a girl to get a guy into a Gold Room was a whole other art.

The first objective was to get a guy that you could sit with and start a conversation. A lot of guys would turn you down, saying, "No, not right now," and brush you off.

But once you got a guy to talk, the second objective was to get him out of his jacket and loosen up his tie. If you could do that, you had established some trust and made him feel like he could relax around you. It took at least three drinks to accomplish this.

The whole time you were with him, you wanted him to think, "It's all about you, baby." Everything he said, you had to be in tune to. Even if it's the worst joke you ever heard, you giggled. That was the idea of entertainment, to make that man think he was the king for that night. As long as you were very attentive and complimentary, the guy would fall right into your hands.

The night I got my first Gold Room, I was sitting with this guy named Terry who was very uptight. So I made a joke about how uptight he was. At first he was taken aback, thinking

I was criticizing him, and asked, "Are you being funny or are you just being rude?"

"That's what I'm talking about right here," I said. "Look at you. You took that so personal."

He looked at me, and said "What did you mean by it?"

"What I meant was, you're like a stuffed shirt the buttons are about to pop off of. It means you're just so uptight and tightly wound I can't get comfortable. I better go."

"No no no. Sit down. Don't leave," he caught himself.

I had put it off on him, like he was one fucked-up individual making me leave, that I didn't want to be with a sourpuss. So he got to thinking he should relax a little.

Next, our waitress Heather came over and said, "Hi, I'm Heather. I'll be your waitress." The waitress's job was to make sure he orders you that first drink. She asked pleasantly, "What will you be drinking tonight and will it be cash or credit?"

"I'll put it on my credit card."

Heather took the card and license, made a copy of it, went to the bar to get a yellow form they kept track of the drinks with, put all that together in a nice little package and gave it to the bartender. The bartender kept the card and license while the customer was running his tab. Then Heather returned and had Terry sign the yellow ticket so that he could start his tab.

Once the waitress had her package, she went to a manager to get authorization to start the tab. The waitress comes back and asks what she can get for the guy and if he'd like to buy the lady a drink. Nine times out of ten a guy's not going to want to look like a schmuck.

Terry and I sat on the main floor for an hour talking and drinking. He had pulled his jacket off and he asked me to dance for him. So while I was dancing, I undid his tie and took it off. I said, "Do you want to see a neat trick?"

"Sure."

I tied his tie on like a G-string and he was just fascinated.

Next, I asked him if he'd like to go upstairs in the VIP area where it was a little bit more intimate and not so wide open. "I'm not feeling comfortable down here," I said. "I don't like the fact that I'm sitting here with you and all these other guys are staring at us." When you throw something like that out to a guy, odds are, he's going to say Yes, because then he thinks on that level with you: I don't want all these people staring.

So we went and sat upstairs in the VIP area and we were drinking and I did a couple more dances for him. He was getting loose by this time. So I said, "Terry, it's going to be cheaper if you get a room instead of you trying to average out in your head how many dances I do. We can do it by the hour and we can square away how much you want to spend tonight. That way you can have me all to yourself. We'll have our own private waitress. We'll sit in our own room together and we can talk in there where it's not as loud. You can hear each other without screaming. It's a little more intimate."

Terry looked at me, and said, "I hadn't really planned on spending that much money tonight. How much is it?"

I was ready. "To be honest with you I get a minimum of $200 an hour. I don't know what they're charging for rooms right now—that you have to take up with the VIP room manager. He'll explain everything to you. Everything can go on your credit card. Everything shows up as MSB Incorporated. It does not show up as the Gold Club." As soon as a guy heard that, he was all for it. Terry canceled out his VISA card and threw out the corporate American Express.

We used to joke about it, MSB, Inc., saying it stood for Mike's Sports Bar.

It's good to tell a guy you're saving him money and being discreet.

The way it worked was at that point, the VIP room manager says he has a membership he can sell the guy starting at $1,000, but the club gives back $1,000 in F&B (Food and Beverage) bucks, i.e.

The floor manager came over and explained everything to Terry. "There's a 20% surcharge if you order Gold Bucks for the lady. If you'd like to pay her cash, there's an ATM downstairs."

Terry opted for his AmEx and we got a room for an hour. We got in the room and they brought him his membership and $1,000 in F&B Bucks. I asked him, "Do you mind if I order some champagne? I think this calls for a celebration—your first Gold Room."

"Sure, sure," he said holding out his newly purchased F&B Bucks. "I can pay with these, right?"

So we ordered a bottle of Dom and we were sipping away and I did not do one dance in that room. Terry sat and talked the whole hour and when the waitress came in to take his Gold Buck order for me, he said, "I would really like to give her a nice tip." He looked at me and looked at the waitress and said, "Does $600 sound okay for an hour?"

I was flabbergasted but after he ordered the Gold Bucks he decided he wanted to stay another half-hour.

"I thought you were leaving," I said.

"I'm just not quite ready to go yet," he said.

"Okay. Not a problem. Whatever the cost of the room is, the VIP manager will just break that in half for you. Tell the waitress when she comes back to get another bottle of champagne."

We were in there talking for another 45 minutes. When Heather came back for the Gold Bucks order, she said, "Do you two want to stay the full hour or are you ready to close out?"

"No, I'm ready to close out," he said. We stayed 40 minutes.

"Since I stayed over the half hour, can you just order her 300 more dollars?"

I had just made $900 in an hour and forty minutes. Not to mention the time I spent out on the floor with him, just about an hour.

There was not a night that went by that somebody famous didn't walk through the front door of the Gold Club from Leonardo DiCaprio to Aerosmith. And it was busy to over-flowing every night except Sunday. With the bible belt Blue Laws, there was no stripping allowed in Atlanta on the seventh day. We kept our clothes on on Sunday. The rest of the time, we were shaking our asses just for you.

But, like I said, at first I wasn't making that much money. There were nights I'd come home with sixty bucks. I'd have to cash out, pay the housemom, tip the DJ, pay my taxes and that would leave me with nothing. I'd start with $200 and end up with sixty.

Twenty dances—if you were lucky—could amount to $200 with tips. The actual cost of the dances were, only $10 and then there was the fact that you had to get them. You had to sit down, talk to somebody, and have a drink, get to know them, and see if they wanted you to dance.

There was one main floor where girls would walk around asking for dances all night long. A lot of times the guy would say No, and then she'd go to the next guy, and the next guy and that's all she did all night.

I couldn't do it. Just walk up to a guy and ask for a dance. I would have to sit down, talk to this guy for a little bit, find out who he was, and then ease into it, like, Are you ready for a dance? By then the guy had already invested time and he felt like he owed me something.

In the stripping industry, you get your feelings hurt three times out of five. Some guys are just rude and say, "I don't want you to dance for me." Or, "you're not what I'm looking for, your boobs are too big or not big enough or your butt's too big." Guys say crazy shit like that and you're looking at them like: Did he just open his mouth and say that to me?

In that first year, I had a guy come up to me and say, "Can I ask you a question? What is your nationality?"

"Why?"

"I'm just curious," he continued. "I can't figure out what your background is because you look so exotic."

So I told him.

He said, "So you're mixed. African-American and white, but just kind of mixed up in there with the Indian, right?"

"Yes," I nodded, waiting for the punch line.

Then it came. "How much can I pay you to fuck you on a Confederate flag, you stinking black bitch?"

I stood there a minute and looked him over. He was a white guy with a cowboy hat and suspenders, a typical redneck farmer. He was young, probably 35, with a scruffy beard and dirty dishwater blond hair. His teeth were crooked and rotten from tobacco chewing and he had dandruff flaking out of his eyebrows. I looked at him and these were the things I saw.

Maybe there was some pity but the anger outweighed any sympathy I might have felt. I did not mince my words. "It's really sad that people like you exist in this world," I began. "Racism left a long time ago as far as I'm concerned because it never existed in me. You gotta be a racist to open your mouth and say something like that to a lady—and I am a lady—because if I wasn't, my foot would be so far up your fucking ass they would need a search party to find it." I walked back to the dressing room and started crying.

Rose was by my side immediately. "Sweetheart, you will experience all walks of life in this building," she said, taking me in her arms. "You will come across the nicest people in the world and the most nasty, disgusting men you'll ever meet in your life. Take the good with the bad but don't let them get you down. Don't let them make you cry."

Sammy Sosa was the celebrity version of the biggest asshole you'd ever want to meet. He was an arrogant, cocky, something-to-be-desired type of person. He came in and went straight upstairs to the Viper Lounge. The floorman grabbed me immediately. I was his type of girl. My hair was long then.

I sat down and Mr. Sosa ordered a bottle of Cristal. The waitress poured two glasses and I went to reach for my glass when he stopped me, "I didn't say we were drinking just yet."

"Okay, you're in my establishment now and I don't do what you tell me to do. This is my job. Now if we were on the baseball field, it'd be a different story."

Having passed the hurdle of basic manners, Mr. Sosa began asking me questions about myself. Why are you doing this? Don't you think you're better than this? Why are you here? Don't you think you're better than being here? He finished the moral berating and, as if a brand new thought had just popped into his mind, he said, "You know, you're a feisty one."

"I'm not feisty," I said, point blank. "I'm real."

So I learned to walk away, to be confident enough in myself to recognize flat-out ignorance and how little of me I was willing to give to it. Besides, nobody is worth your tears except your children. No other human being should make you that upset over saying something stupid that you should cry over it.

Steve Kaplan was a business genius. He brought Russell Basile, the consultant known as the 'Champagne King' whose philosophy was that you can't just pour champagne, you have to serve it. If you had no champagne experience, the Gold Club management would put you through a short training course: How many glasses were in a bottle, how to serve it, the whole champagne mystique.

Russell was a nut whose every other word was fucking. But he was a smart business man. Everyone Steve worked with was—like Larry Gleit, the accountant for the corporation.

At the Gold Club, they kept track of champagne sales with pink slips that were good for twenty dollars. At the end of the night the waitresses rang them into the computer to keep count of how much champagne everyone sold.

Later, in 2001, in the courtroom during the Gold Club trial, when the lawyers distributed my champagne numbers, the jurors were fascinated. They were looking at me like: How in hell did she do that? In a six-month span I had sold 169 bottles of champagne, costing from $350 to $2,000 a bottle, and, for the most part, I was a Cristal drinker. That went for $800 a pop. A lot of times I sold the $2,000 bottles, the ones that stand waist-high.

One little trick I did with the bottles might have been responsible for my healthy sales. I would take all the foil off the top and put the neck in my mouth like I was giving the bottle a blowjob. I would really get into it. I would take the cork in my teeth and pop it and then the cork would be sitting in my mouth and just a little bit of foam would come off the top of the bottle. Guys loved that. She can make the bottle cum!

At the Gold Club, there were separate classes of girls. Girls who strictly worked the main floor, the dancing girls. They did not like to go to the Gold Rooms. There were the in between girls who worked the floor, the stages and tried to work the VIP rooms at the same time. Then there were the strictly VIP girls.

The VIP girls were Banks, Frederique, Angelique, Dina, Mercedes, Raven and eventually me.

Then, in addition to the different classes, there were four distinct cliques under the VIP girls. The Banks group was called The Vultures. They were the money-hungry, conniving scheming girls who had a little credit card scam going with the Gold Bucks lady where they double-billed customers.

Once I became "Diva" at the end of 1997, the girls under me became known as The Sluts. I knew I had made a bad name for myself but I didn't care. My attitude was always, "Fuck you guys! You don't pay my bills and you don't take care of my kids so I don't care what you call me." Not that I was getting paid by anybody to do it—it was just when I talked, girls listened.

If there was a good customer in the building, I knew which girls to call to go in that room. I knew which girls were going to touch. I knew which girls would perform oral sex. I knew which girls would do lesbian sex shows. I knew which girls to call for each individual situation.

The third group was called The Drugheads. These girls did coke and Ecstasy and GHB but they were money-makers. That was Tina, Torrey, Shaney, Shania, Shawna, TJ, and Jordan who did more coke than anybody I've ever seen in my life. Jordan would get so high some nights that she would have shit coming out of her nose. We would have to turn her around and walk her back to the dressing room, clean her up. She was fired over and over but Steve always hired her back out of sympathy.

And finally, you had the Skit Girls, forty-five of us who came in to practice every Wednesday afternoon. We did Las Vegas style shows. The shows were choreographed and Wendy O's, a place that caters to the strip club industry, made costumes in sizes 1-10 for almost every skit.

The skits included: Hot for Teacher; En Vogue; Queen of the Night; YMCA; Country; Smooth Criminal; Thriller; Beat it; Pajama Party; Spice Girls; Genie; Mickey; Dirty Bird; Dude; Vogue; Material Girl; Like a Virgin; and Pink Panther.

They would stop everything in the Gold Club for us to come on stage to do our skits four times a night. It was just a break to liven up the place. It worked. Steve knew exactly what he was doing when he started that. We worked hard and we were tight. The girls took pride in what they did and it was a good show. Before the skit started the DJ announced, "Stand on your feet, guys!" It was the job of entertainers and floormen to go around, get the guys to stand up and cheer these girls on. If dancers didn't support the skits, they got fined $25.

We also did a chorus line once a night, every night, as further advertisement. It was mandatory for every dancer in the building except for the VIP girls who were champagne sellers and usually had high rollers in the club at all times.

And then, there were the twice-a-year employee motivational meetings.

My children always came with me to these Sunday afternoon company meetings. There was a room set up with a sitter for all the kids, ranging from babies and infants to 17, an average of twenty kids each time bringing their little dogs with them.

The Gold Club was more or less like a family. At the meetings, congratulations went out to the people who were selling lots of champagne, or customer service from the floormen, or memberships being sold. They were always boosting you up, making you feel good about what you were doing instead of down talking you.

The drug problem was talked about at every meeting. They would point out the girls who were notorious for getting fired for drug use but then they let them come back after a clean test.

Although Steve Kaplan was out of town a lot, he always returned to run the motivational meetings with Ziggy Sicignano, the so-called CEO of the Gold Club. It was them, along with the lesser management personnel.

They'd go through role-playing for the dancers on how to greet men instead of just walking up and saying, "Do you want a dance?" They talked about how to present yourself like a lady instead of a stripper. In fact, we didn't even call ourselves strippers. At the Gold Club, we were called entertainers.

Usually the role-playing would be acted out by Steve and Ziggy. Ziggy would call himself Ziggarina. It was funny because he was this big Italian guy who bore a striking resemblance to Spock.

Steve would be the customer. Zig would walk up to Steve and say, "I'm Ziggarina. How are you? Can I sit with you and chat?"

Steve would say, "Sure, have a seat. Can I get you a drink?"

"Sure."

Then they'd role-play the waitress. "Hi, I'm Heather. I'll be your waitress this evening. Whatever I can get for you just let me know. Are you going to be paying with cash or credit?" She would go on explaining how the club worked.

As Steve and Ziggarina continued, Ziggarina began with the chitchat, "Where are you from? What are you doing in town? What do you do for a living?" That was their definition of how to be a lady instead of walking over and saying, "Want a dance?" and if the guy said No, the girl says, "Well fuck you!"

The Gold Club wasn't like that. If you walked over and the customer didn't want you, you said, "You have a wonderful evening. Is there a certain type of girl you're looking for? Do you prefer blondes or brunettes? We have every type of girl that there is." Then the customer would say what he wanted, maybe that he preferred brunettes with a heavier butt. We were trained to deal with that. "Fine, I know a couple of girls. Do you mind if I send them over for you to see if you like them?"

That was how we conducted business. As ladies, we would never present ourselves in any other manner.

The role-playing would then show bad examples of how some girls would talk to a customer and go off on them. Ziggarina cussing the customer out and how Steve as the customer calls over a manager to complain. And then, of course, how management reprimands the girl and tells her she's going to be sent home if it happens again. They would show us how everything was supposed to work.

One night in late October of 1997, I got to work about eight o'clock and was sitting with one of my regulars, Ralph, a sweet old guy, about 62, who came to see me twice a week. Right off, Ralph handed me my usual $900 in cash in one hundred dollar bills which I tucked away in my garter.

Ralph liked to drink wine so he always asked if he could just have it for the price of the champagne. He was a multimillionaire so he really didn't mind being charged out the wazoo.

We were on our first glass of wine for the evening. Shelby, the girl who lived with my babysitter, Kiki, was working that night. She had a bunch of friends that she worked with and one, Justin, walked up and tapped me on my shoulder. I had my glass in my hand and turned around, "Yeah?" Shelby came wailing past me on the other side. Ralph was occupied talking to his business partner.

I started talking to Ralph, drinking my wine. All of a sudden the room got extremely loud, blaring inside of my head. Everything got distorted. Ralph's head expanded three feet before my eyes.

I was shaking my head, "Ralph, something's wrong. Nothing looks right. Go get a manager." I stood up and the floor was moving. Norbie was coming up the ramp and I grabbed him and slurred, "I think somebody slipped something in my drink. I was on my first glass ...."

That's all I could get out. That was all I remembered.

Later Norbie told me that I just dropped to the floor. My skin got pasty and cold. They took me in the dressing room and threw me in the shower which sent my body into shock. My heart stopped beating and I was foaming at the mouth. They called an ambulance. On the way to the hospital, I went into cardiac arrest. I was DOA.

I remember being at the top of the hospital room and seeing the people below working on me. Doctors working on my chest, a nurse squeezing an oxygen bag, hitting me with an IV, yelling out Give her this! Give her that!

I can remember watching them do this to me, looking at myself lying on the bed. The doctor hit me with the fibrillator to get my heart going. Okay everybody stand clear. Pow! My body flew up off the bed. At that moment I heard a voice say to me, You need to fight. It's not time yet. Your kids need you. You need to fight.

I looked around to see who was talking to me. The doctor zapped me again. Nothing happened. The third time that was it. I lucked out. Four days later I woke up.

I had been in a coma and still heard everything around me, felt everything around me. I had violent reactions to the drugs and could hear the nurses tell me to lie down: Miss Bush, calm down, we understand.

The toxicology report from the hospital said I had a combination of Ecstasy, Cocaine, GHB and Rufenol mixed in a liquid form in my bloodstream. It is apparent someone tried to kill me.

Chapter Four

    In the beginning of my childhood, there was only me and Jimmy. The house next to us was called The Corner Store and the family that ran it—the Vezeys—lived upstairs. Like everyone else in the neighborhood except my Mom, they were black and would give me and Jimmy free junk food and whatever we wanted.

    Both of my parents had children outside of marriage and put them up for adoption. My mother had a son, and so did my Dad with this lady named Sue Dagey, a platinum blonde with blue eyes, an hour glass figure and a sweet disposition.

    So there are these two brothers out there. What are you supposed to think about something like that? We also have one lost sister. Other women, secret lives, sidelines, children.

    My parents actually only had three children together—Jimmy, me, and Marquita—in that order. But before Marquita and after Marquita, my father continued to see Sue Dagey and my parents were always fighting about that fact. Ironically, they still see each other to this day.

    In retaliation, my mother turned to another man for comfort—Harold Abernathy. Everyone called him Rock. Rock was 6'1", about 175 pounds, dark brown hair in a short afro. Very handsome. He floated when he walked, smooth and debonnaire. His basic livelihood was pimping about 12 or 13 girls. It didn't bother my mother though. No matter how many women were in Rock's stable, she knew she was his number one girl. That was their lifestyle—dealing drugs, gambling and pimping. My Mom's best friend was a whore—Tanja. She was loud, outspoken, but a pretty woman. Tanja was bigger than most, nearly six feet tall, built like a shit brick house. She had golden brown skin and long hair that was probably a wig. Tanja was so adamant about kids getting into grown folk's business, she'd pull my tongue out of my mouth and slap it. "Now go outside and play with the other kids and get out of grown folk's faces," she said.

But the best thing about Tanja was that she loved my mother to death and wouldn't let anybody in the neighborhood bother my Mom—no small feat considering she could beat up most of the men in the neighborhood. In the end, though, her pimp killed her.

So you see, my parent's marriage was pretty fucked up. Who knew who was coming or going? Who knew when it would finally fold in on itself? Certainly not me or Jimmy. For all we knew, the hell our parents created was heaven.

We were on Welfare and never got off of it my whole childhood. Sometimes my Mom would sit on the front porch and cry because we didn't have enough. In the early fall of 1974, my Dad had been gone for a few days. When he came home, my mother didn't know he was leaving again. So she left. Then he left while we were at school. When me and Jimmy came home, nobody was there.

An empty house, however, wasn't unusual. We knew what to do. We let ourselves in, did our homework, whatever cleaning needed doing. I could cook a decent meal at six years old. We had dinner, and as the day drew to a close, no Mom or Dad.

The next day we got up and they still weren't home. We got ready for school, went to school, and came home again to an empty house. Our food stamps arrived in the mail. Me and

Jimmy went next door to the Vezeys' store and bought lunch meat and snacks. It was our little secret. We didn't tell anybody our parents weren't home because we thought if we did, we'd be taken away. This went on for a week.

Finally Dad came home and discovered us alone. If he had guilt pangs, I don't remember seeing them in his face, just amazement at his kids' resourcefulness. Hell, we'd been practicing taking care of ourselves all along. We were already on our own. His notice of us was short lived. Five minutes later, he was on the phone, dialing everyone in the book tracking down our mother. When he found her camped out at her parents' in Canada, he dropped us with his mother and went to fetch Mom.

A couple of months later when the weather turned cold, and Dad had been gone for a few days, again Mom took off to see Rock. When Dad got home, he was so mad he beat Mom with my brother's Louisville Slugger bat and then hung her out of the closet window by her ankles. She was pregnant with Rock's baby, our little sister, Tina. When neighbors threatened to call the police, Dad pulled her back in and disappeared for another week.

The sound goes off at times like these and all you have left is a black and white photograph of your mother hanging out of a second story window.

We were living in an upstairs apartment. It was cold and dreary and we hardly had any food. While Mom slept, me and Jimmy put on our snow suits and walked five miles through the nasty weather to our aunt's beauty salon to get some money for groceries. Then we shopped, carried the bags home, put the food away and later prepared a meal.

Without our father and with something to eat, the week passed in relative peace. Mom saw Rock a couple of times. Then late one night, my father returned. He must have thought we were asleep and that we couldn't hear what was going on. People make that mistake about children.

Children are like heavy duty paper towels, for lack of a better image. They see and hear better than older people. And me and Jimmy heard the fighting and the screaming. Then we heard and saw our father give our mother the order to take off all of her clothes and bend over. "I want to see if anyone's been with you!" he sneered in a drunken Louisiana drawl. Quietly, silently, maybe again in black and white, we saw our mother's long red hair falling to the floor, her legs spread and bare bottom raised for inspection, the opening from which we came pried apart with our father's dark fingers. We felt the slow constant death he was dealing her.

Most of all, I remember the Louisville Slugger bruises that colored almost every part of my mother's white body. Dad was so comfortable with beating her that he would send us next door to the Vezeys' so he could beat my Mom in private, like some parents probably send their kids down the street so they can have sex.

Sure, Mom called the police plenty of times. They said it was domestic and if she didn't like it, she should leave him. She was terrified and drugged out of her mind and Dad told her if she left, he'd kill her. It's easy to tell some people what they should do when you don't have any idea what it's like. I still get angry when I hear pious sons-of-bitches giving advice, like they've ever been through this shit.

My mother tried to take control by killing herself before Dad did. The life you save may be your own. Isn't that the truth?

Close to Christmas time, Mom left again, she'd had enough of the other women and the beatings. That year Sue Dagey bought me and Jimmy Christmas presents. Sue was scared of our father, too. You could tell she didn't want to be there.

Chapter
Five

Some people let you see certain things in life, experience certain things that help you along your path to what you're supposed to be. I believe that everything happens for a reason, you gain and you lose and it's all about gaining as much knowledge as possible while you're here on earth.

When I was waking up in the hospital, the first thing on my mind was my kids, if they were okay. The hospital had notified the Department of Family and Children's Services (DFCS) and called my ex-husband back home. Joe and my brother, Jimmy, now a grown man, got in the car and drove down to Atlanta. The kids were at my aunt's house until Joe and Jimmy arrived. Two days after I came out of the coma, they went back to Milwaukee.

I knew exactly what had happened. Just not who had drugged me.

In the hospital, Shelby and Kiki brought me balloons, a get-well card, pajamas, and a curling iron. I had been wearing jewelry; a four-carat emerald-cut diamond ring; a five-carat ruby; a diamond tennis bracelet, diamond earrings and a Movado watch. The housemom had put the $900 from Ralph in my purse before the ambulance took me away. There was also a checkbook and credit cards—my entire financial life.

The nurse told Shelby and Kiki that she'd appreciate it if they would take the valuables home so that the hospital wouldn't be held responsible. I agreed and asked them to put the now pricey purse in the closet next to my safe.

The next three weeks while I was in the hospital, these girls took the safe and emptied not only my purse but my checking and savings accounts as well. It was like the Grinch that Stole Everything Jackie Had. While my daughters watched, before they dropped them at their great aunt's house, Shelby and Kiki told my girls they were taking the TVs and VCRs from each room to keep them safe while I was away. They even took all of my CDs.

The final insult was that I'd asked Shelby to write a check for rent and a few more for utilities. The day she was to pick me up from the hospital, after hours of re-dialing her number, Shelby simply never showed up. A sympathetic nurse finally drove me home at 9 o'clock, after her shift.

I got home on November 15th with no house keys, it didn't matter—my door was wide open and there was an eviction notice on it.

When I walked in, the place looked as if they'd thrown a huge party. There was garbage in the kitchen and all my stuff was gone. The nurse walked me through the rest of the house. My kids' rooms were trashed. The TVs and VCRs were gone, my stereo, my purse and the safe were gone. "What did these girls do to me? I was devastated. I knew it had to be them because they were the only ones with access.

I called their home. Nobody was there. Nobody had seen them at work. I called Henry, Elliott's best friend, and told him what happened. He said I could stay at his place. He was getting ready to move anyway because he had been traded to the Cleveland Cavaliers.

I felt good enough to go back to work just before Thanksgiving and contacted the bank to begin an investigation. My credit cards were all maxed out. At that point everything I owned, I had lost.

An ex-boyfriend, Terence Ward from Chicago, came into town to see his son and was staying at the Embassy Suites Hotel in Buckhead, the ritzy part of town. I stayed with Terence for three days, catching up on old times. His last night in town I was working, and planning on seeing him afterwards. At the same time, a dancer named Sapphire was having problems with her boyfriend who had kicked her out while she was at work and told her not to bother coming home. Sapphire came to me and said she needed a place to stay for the night.

She knew I was good for taking girls home drunk and letting them come back the next day to get their car. I told her I wasn't going home but to Terrence's hotel. It was my best offer to bring her along. One of the other girls, Lisa, who was known for meeting customers outside of the club, dropped me off because I was drunk.

Twenty minutes after I arrived at the hotel, Jeff Johnson, another club manager, called, asks for me, then went off. "Why are you trying to take girls up out of here to prostitute over at the hotel??" he screamed. "I'm on my way over there and if I come over there and find Lisa ...."

I cut him short. "First of all, you're not coming anywhere. Secondly, this is totally disrespectful of you to call my boyfriend's room like this. What is your problem?"

"You're suspended for two weeks," he said and slammed the phone down.

Sapphire had told Jeff Johnson that I asked her to come to the hotel to prostitute with me. She didn't bother to mention the part about she just needed a place to crash for the night.

Maybe I'm biased, but if you want my opinion, Jeff Johnson was a lowlife piece of shit. He was like a miniature ape with big black lips that stuck out and long stocky arms. He was also bald, and scary, because he had been known to rape women. I used to hear stories about him from the girls in the dressing room that he was always coming on to them.

When I first started, Jeff Johnson worked the upstairs podium. Then he became the assistant manager.

Jeff was just a bully. If a girl didn't tip him for a Gold Room, he'd find a reason to suspend her for a couple days to think about it. That was the way he talked to the girls. Rather than using even their stripper names, he preferred words like bitch, whore, cunt, slut, or any type of derogatory statement to make a woman feel less than what she was.

I figured Jeff calling the hotel room was just another one of his ploys to get something he wanted down the line.

The next day I called the club looking for Norbie but he was on vacation. I said, "Well, let me speak to the owner," not knowing whom the owner was at the time. The response was, "Mr. Kaplan is in New York."

In the end, I was told I'd have to wait for Norbie to get back. When he returned ten days later, he said, "Come up here right now. Mr. Kaplan is in the building. That's the owner, Jackie." Norbie sounded cold.

Jeff Johnson apparently had already told him his side of the story. I walked into the office and Steve Kaplan, this seemingly forty-something guy with a coffee stain on the front of his old t-shirt, started cussing me out. "I don't fucking allow prostitution in my club and you don't leave here to see customers!"

I stood there listening without saying a word, just taking it all in.

I was getting angrier by the second. When it appeared that Steve Kaplan had finished, I said calmly, "Are you done yet?"

"Yeah, I'm done."

"First, take that tone out of your voice with me," I spat with equal venom. "Secondly, don't curse at me because you don't know me and is that any way for you to talk to your employees? Thirdly, you got the whole frigging story messed up. Jeff Johnson didn't know what he was talking about and I don't know why Sapphire lied and told him that story, but if you'd like, I can get Terrance Ward on the phone and he'll explain exactly what the situation was. So, no, I did not leave your club to be with any frigging customer nor would I and the next time you swear at me and talk to me like that, I'm pressing charges. Now, do you want to talk to me like a normal adult?"

I guess no one had ever stood up to Steve Kaplan. They were always too afraid.

I wasn't afraid of taking up for myself but I was afraid I'd lost my job. I was wrong. "I like this girl," he smiled. His teeth were so white in contrast to his olive skin. "Now, everybody get out of here except you."

Then the great man sat down and talked to me. "I'm really sorry. On behalf of everybody, I apologize."

I was feeling brave. I had his attention. "Oh, and by the way, why didn't I get a fucking phone call at the hospital that I was in for three weeks after being drugged up in your club?"

He had no idea. I told him everything. How Joe had taken the kids back home. How I had lost everything. Then Steve blew his stack and called Norbie back into the office.

"Why didn't anybody tell me what happened?" he demanded.

Norbie hadn't seen this coming. He stammered, "We didn't want you to worry. It was under control."

"What's under control? Do you know I could be faced with a lawsuit? Who's paying her medical bills?"

We didn't have medical insurance. Steve Kaplan paid every last dime of my hospital bills.

After the drugging, I didn't get the kids back for another eight months. I had to save money all over again, find another place to live, buy furniture, the works. So it was a huge relief not to have to see what three weeks in a private room at the hospital cost.

I never found out. Steve called the hospital and told them he'd take care of it, not to send me any bills.

After that, we bonded. I really got to feel him out. He could tell when people told half-truths about business, but deep down, there was something more, something really good about this man.

"I'm going to show you the ropes around here and teach you to make good money," he said. And that's just what he did.

Steve gave me some extra money and on Christmas Eve, I loaded up the car with toys and presents and drove to Wisconsin, straight through a blizzard, to be there in time for the kids to wake up. There was hope on the horizon, but too, everything seemed bleak. The girls had just moved in with Joe's mother because he had gone to jail two weeks earlier for a domestic violence case left over from 1995. It was one of the fruits of our marriage.

I started going home every two weeks to see the kids. I knew it depleted the money I would need to get us started again but I couldn't help it. I needed to see them and they needed to see me. I had a big surprise in store. I was saving for a down payment on a house, a nice house, in a nice neighborhood. That's what I wanted for my girls.

*   *   *

Steve continued to check on me when he was in town. On Mother's Day, I got flowers from him at work. I was stunned. My daughter's birthday came around and he gave me $400 to go shopping for her.

Before Steve began to take an interest, people used to step over me and dog me out like I was nobody. After my friendship with Steve kicked off, I became very popular.

That's when the animosity started. Every girl in the club was trying to ride the Steve Kaplan Express and they hated me for being on board. Anybody would try to get close to anybody who was close to him. He was one of those people you can't help but want to be around. They thought because he was this millionaire they could get something out of him.

Girls came onto him all the time even though he was married. There was Debbie Pinson, who later testified during the trial. There was Dina, the voluptuous Barbie doll-looking black girl. There was trailer trash Tyler who was Miss Gold Club one year and also ran the skits. There was a girl named Amanda whose dance name was Storm. And then Michelle who we called Summer.

My stage name in Milwaukee was Jackie—my real name. I believed if you were a dancer, you should be proud of what you do and not be embarrassed by covering up your name.

In December of 1997, shortly after I became friends with Steve, a couple of the girls got together and came up with the name Diva for me. They said it was very independent and strong and it suited me because they looked to me as a leader. I was uncomfortable with Diva though because back in Milwaukee, it was Frederique's stage name at Heartbreaker's. Her real name was Jana Pelnis. When Jana came down to Atlanta a couple of months after me, she asked what my stage name was down here and I told her Diva. She laughed and said,

"Isn't that ironic?"

A lot of times, however, girls took on a stage name to cover up their identity. You go somewhere to be with your kids and somebody's yelling out Diva! It can get weird.

At the Gold Club, the housemom kept a list of all the girls. If you wanted your name to be Destiny and there already was one, you couldn't have that name. A good stage name had to fit who you were. If you were petite and cute and small, a name like China would work.

Jana's new name, Frederique, suited her because it was a strong name and she was a big girl—about six feet tall. It was noticeable and any smart girl wanted her name to stand out, unlike the Champagnes of the world. The smart girl didn't want to be average. Average like Princess, Justin, Jordan, Hillary, Lindsay, Mica and Strawberry, names you could hear in any club in the United States. Cocoa at the black clubs. Vanilla. Isis.

Then the customers always asked what your real name was out of curiosity, just to see if you'll tell them.

I used to tell guys my real name all the time. I was developing these relationships with these gentlemen and anticipating seeing them again. That's how I built my clientele.

That's also how I made one of my closest and dearest friends, BP, a sweet guy who came into my life as a one-time customer. We started out chatting on the phone, went out for few meals and found that we had a lot in common that had nothing to do with sex. We went to hockey games and to each other's work Christmas parties—all because we truly enjoyed each other's company. BP could have been my prince charming—only problem was—I didn't realize how much he meant to me until I was facing jail time with the trial. It wasn't the time to let him know.

In any case, once you get involved in a strip job, it's like selling cars. I sold cars during the day, after my divorce. But I wasn't just selling cars. I had to check on my customers three or four months down the road and say, "Hey, it's time for an oil change." People appreciated that. You can't just sell the car and let that be it. You have to keep moving, get involved in your job. That was why I became a skit girl and why I later took part in the Miss Gold Club contest.

At the Gold Club, even on the main floor, girls danced with each other. Not actually touching but simulating it. The average man everywhere thinks about sex every six to eight seconds. At the Gold Club, with the deadly combination of music, alcohol and drop-dead gorgeous women, hormones were raging.

In a way, taking up the lesbian sex shows was like taking more interest in my job—a promotion of sorts. Added to the fact that there is nothing sexier to a man than two women doing each other. When a man is looking at two women getting it on, he's thinking he wants to participate. Other than the gay population, there isn't a man alive that doesn't want two women in the bed. If he can't have that, the next best thing is watching.

At the Gold Club, if Steve needed something done, he could call me at three o'clock in the morning and I would jump out of bed. On the other hand, he was also one of those people who, if he called you and you were busy with your children, he would not interrupt. He didn't believe in taking away from family time.

I've never slept a lot anyway. I figured then as I figure now, there will be time enough for sleeping when I die.

A lot of times I would wonder why certain girls were dancers, especially the ones that looked like the girl next door.

I'd be thinking that they needed to be in school. Many of them were, at the local colleges and universities: Georgia State, Georgia Tech, Emory, Spellman, and Clark-Atlanta. It was a way for them to make extra money.

These sweet schoolgirls thought they were out to make extra money but then got caught up. Stripping is not an easy task. At first, if you're a strong one, you don't drink. You come in, do your job and go home. Then the drinking starts and for some, the drugs, and then you get caught up.

The industry turns you out. You're around famous people. When you go out, the club owners recognize you. Next thing you know you're on the VIP list at every club in town. Your life is a whirlwind. You can't comprehend what's going on. It's not peer pressure. It's the atmosphere.

I've been around people like Bill Gates and Ted Turner. Bill Gates is such a pleasant and humble man. Mr. Turner came in with his two sons and some businessmen one evening. He seemed like the most laid back kind of guy. He was laughing and smiling and just really nice. He introduced me to his sons and then said, "You can sit and have a drink with us." I did. We had a drink called Blue Motherfucker, which was like a Long Island Iced Tea but blue. Then I got called to do a skit.

But still, that's about as high as you can get. It's easy with people like that around to get star struck, to want to live the life of a millionaire's wife. The realization is, unfortunately, that it might not ever happen. You can't set yourself up for such big disappointment.

For me, when I first moved down South, Atlanta was like Hollywood. After a couple months though it got old. Girls would break their necks to see Denzel Washington walk through the door. Girls would run up squealing, "Denzel's upstairs!" I'd say, "Yeah? Let Denzel be upstairs. Denzel don't pay my bills."

* * *

That was the beginning of 1998. When things started rolling for me. It was then I got to know more about Ziggy Sicignano, Steve's right hand man. He might have been helpful to Steve Kaplan in some way but he was an arrogant loud-mouth who used to run around screaming he was protected like he had connections to the mob. A lot of the girls were afraid of him but I knew better. I could read people because that was my job.

In fact, the first time I met Ziggy I told Steve, "I do not trust him. He's a bad element. You do not need that man in your life. He's going to bring you down."

Steve said, "What?" like he didn't know where I was coming from.

"I'm telling you there is something about him and you have got to be very careful with this man. His mouth is extremely big." The fact was, and is, that I talk a lot but I listen a lot, too. You let a person talk enough they'll show you just how full of shit they are. Ziggy bragged about taking a limousine and a few of the girls and a floorman to South Carolina to see the New York Knicks. Ziggy's "girls" were all known for prostitution. They were the girls everyone knew to stay away from: Niko, Desire, Jamie, Ashley, Chelsea and, of course, Frederique.

In February of 1998, Dennis Rodman walked into the club. Nobody knew that I had known him from my Milwaukee days for at least eleven years. The night that he came in, every-body was making a big hoopla. Clear a path! They were getting rooms ready for him so he could go straight up there and no-body would bother him. That's the way they did big celebrities.

I told Steve, "Mr. Kaplan, I really want to be in that room. I know Dennis Rodman."

"Sorry, Diva," he said brushing me off. "But I think Ziggy already has people picked out for that."

I persisted. "No, you don't understand. I know him personally."

Steve was interested.

When Dennis arrived, his crew had all gone up to their room and Ziggy had brought some girls to put on a show for Dennis but no one wanted to.

Steve went upstairs. Outside of the room, he motioned for Ziggy.

Out of earshot, Steve said, "Listen, Ziggy, Diva knows Rodman. Put her in the room."

"Well," Ziggy hemmed and hawed. "I don't know if I want her in here, if I can trust her."

"What do you mean, trust her?"

"I don't know if I can trust her."

Steve gave him the look, the one that says: Shut up. This is my club. Go get her.

They brought me in the room and I went and sat between Dennis's legs and said in my sexiest voice, "What's up Denny?" His hair was like a rainbow—yellow, green, red and black and his long lanky legs came up high from the low sofa as if he were in a small sports car with his knees pressed up against the dashboard.

He looked up and it was so dark in there he couldn't see me. Ziggy opened the door so the light would shine on my face.

Immediately I was recognized. "What are you doing here, Jackie?"

"I work here!" I said like an old friend and we hugged each other.

"Sit down! Sit down!" he said, patting the sofa, and then waved off Steve and Ziggy. "I know this girl, it's all good."

We started chatting and Dennis said, "I didn't know you danced."

Ziggy interrupted the reunion. "I want the girls to put on a little show for him. Diva, do you think you could arrange that?"

I said, "What do you mean arrange that? I know a few girls around here who are freaks and just love shit like that and want nothing more than to meet Dennis Rodman." I told Ziggy go round up Marra, who was bisexual—she and I used to flirt with each other all the time—also, Frederique and Angelique.

Meanwhile, I kicked the original set of girls out, "All right, ladies. You have to go."

Mara and Frederique and Angelique arrived in short order.

They closed the door and that was when I realized just how much power I had around the club. I looked at all three of them and said, "Take off your clothes and do each other. Mara, you come and do me." And they just jumped! It was scary. In my mind, I was thinking, "They're just doing it because Dennis is here."

Dennis watched, impressed. "Look at you, in control."

I got an adrenaline rush to tell another girl to do something and she does it, just because you have Dennis Rodman in the room. Steve walked out but Ziggy continued standing there. He told a floor manager to go get a flashlight and he shined it on us.

I said, "What are you doing?! Turn that thing off!"

"I want Dennis to see everything that's going on between you girls," Ziggy snickered.

I was pissed off. "Girls, stop right now. Everybody just quit. Turn that fucking thing off!"

"You don't tell me what to do. I can have you fired," Ziggy shot back.

"Can you now? I don't think so. Why don't you go get Steve and ask him?" I got real cocky.

Dennis defused the situation. "Sit down next to me and don't move," he said. "Ladies," he continued to the other girls, handing them $200 each, "thank you, I appreciate it, but I'm getting ready to go in a few minutes."

They were miffed, took their tips and left. No $1,000 sex show tonight.

"Are you going to come over to the hotel and party with us?" Dennis asked me.

"I don't know, Dennis. We're not allowed to leave the club with customers ...."

"But I'm your friend!" he insisted.

"You're still a customer in the building and I can't leave with you."

Still, I thought I'd try. When Steve came back in the room. I asked, "Can I go home?"

"Home to what?"

"I want to go home."

"You want to go with Dennis, don't you? No, you can't leave."

Dennis got ready to go and said his good-byes and left without me.

I must have been sulking because finally Steve said, "If you want I'll take you over there. Where's he staying?"

"He's at the Ritz-Carlton downtown."

I called Dennis and told him I was on the way. He said, "Bring somebody else with you."

There was this waitress, Melanie Smith, who was cute and real sexy. She was also madly in love with Dennis

Rodman. She heard that I was downstairs and caught up to me, saying, "I hear you're getting ready to go."

"What are you talking about?" I played like I didn't know.

"I would do anything to meet Dennis Rodman."

I smiled, "You wanna go with me?"

She got dressed and we went out the side door and got into the truck with Steve and Ziggy.

At the hotel we walked into a lavish room with a spread of champagne and alcohol. There were at least 15 people there, partying their butts off in this huge two-bedroom suite with French doors. I introduced Dennis to Melanie and he adored her immediately. He had a thing for itty-bitty women, hence, Carmen Electra.

The three of us were in one of the bedrooms alone. The music was playing. Dennis leaned into me and asked if Melanie would sleep with him.

"Yeah, she will," I said without hesitation.

"Are you sure?"

"Yeah," I said and then turned to her. "Melanie, want to sleep with Dennis?"

So they started kissing and got naked and Dennis said, "Get in here, girl."

"I'm not sleeping with you! We've been friends too long," I said.

"Well, at least get with her," Dennis nodded to Melanie.

Dennis Rodman is a buck crazy freak. He just likes wild uncontrolled sex. He likes two girls on each other, on him. Wild freaky sex. You can tell what type of man he is just by the way he carries himself. He likes to be in control.

We were getting ready to go back to the club and Dennis and Melanie came out. "You gonna come back, Diva?"

"Yeah, I'll come back after work and hang with you."

"Cool cool cool."

We were leaving and I was walking with Steve, with Ziggy and Melanie a little ahead of us. "I'm telling you I don't trust Ziggy," I repeated my earlier warning. "I don't like that guy and you probably shouldn't have brought him with us. Someday he could use this against us."

In any case, I learned something valuable that night: Girls would listen to me. It got to the point that if there was a good customer in the building, I knew which girls to call to go in that room. I knew what was wanted and who would give it.

Dennis Rodman got what we girls liked to call the Royal Treatment but he wasn't the only one. In short, the Royal Treatment meant that when you got a movie star in the Gold Club, you would pay attention to what they wanted and keep your mouth quiet about it.

What celebrities wanted didn't always follow the rules of management. Sure it's a strip club but even in a place with booze and naked women, there are still things that you are not supposed to do. I'd heard that Steve knew everything that was going on in the club. It made me laugh. "No, Steve didn't know," I thought to myself. "Because I did things Steve didn't know."

You weren't supposed to touch. Period. You were not supposed to be drugged.

You could sit in somebody's lap but you had to have underwear and clothes on. You weren't supposed to sit on a guy's lap naked. We would though, all the time in the Gold Rooms, sit butt naked on customers' laps, chatting away.

* * *

Celebrities are so used to getting what they want because of who they are. People just fall at their feet—even the minor celebrities—celebrities not as big as a Tom Cruise or a Brad Pitt. They operate like normal rules don't apply to them because they've got money and even more than money, they've got fame. They're right.

Robin Leach, for example. He was one of the lesser celebrities who came through the doors of the Gold Club. One night, I was downstairs on the main floor and someone ran up to me out of breath, saying, "Diva, go on up to Gold Room 7!"

Gold Room 7 was the room reserved for the hot shots: the King of Sweden, Madonna.

"When I walked in, I saw Robin Leach.

I sat down with him and had a glass of champagne. Ten or fifteen minutes later, he said, "My dear, I'll give you $5,000 if you do something freaky."

"It's tempting," I said as congenially as I could. "But I have a better girl for you. Let me go get her."

I didn't want to do it so I went downstairs and found Frederique to keep Mr. Leach company. I wondered how this would play on "Lifestyles of the Rich and Famous."

I didn't have to tell Frederique what Leach had offered me. I knew she would do anything for the right amount of money, and sometimes not for the right amount of money.

She went in and I believe Leach offered her the same deal because later when we passed downstairs, she pulled me aside. "That man is a frigging freak!" she said. "Some people are so gross."

There were the big shot celebrities, the b-side celebrities, and the minor celebrities. Jermaine Dupri of SO SO DEF was a big crab-leg eating, harem groping regular. Ryan Cameron, a local DJ with his own FM morning show, came in and ate Gold Club Sundays off my breasts.

KC and JoJo, the R&B singers, came in. Both of them looked like geek monsters because they appeared to be high. Their teeth were sliding together, sweat running down their faces and, the dead giveaway—wearing sunglasses at night. I wouldn't talk to them the way they were. I just sat on the couch and listened. I loved their music. They sang the most beautiful, romantic songs in R&B. It was sad to see them just wasting away.

Jerry Springer was another freak. When he came in, he was out on the main floor grabbing titties and booties. I passed by his Gold Room and saw his legs spread wide apart with a girl straddled over each thigh, his hands on their Asses. It got comical after a while.

I know why girls give so much of themselves to the stars and, well, to anyone with a bankroll. I was there. It was I. It's an inner conversation. You start thinking about how bad your man is treating you at home and you start thinking, this guy is awfully nice. He's cute too! You're drunk and hormones are raging. By the time you get home you're so tired you don't feel like making love to anybody if you have a husband or a boyfriend. You might not have had sex in two-three months so, some big shot starts coming onto you and you're thinking, Hmmm? Alright, I'll just let him touch it.

Dan Ackroyd and Jim Belushi came in and enjoyed the fruits of the infamous Gold Room 7 with the door that closes.

I heard Jim Belushi was really rowdy and was getting the Royal Treatment from the group of girls who were in there: Infinity, Angel, and her sister Denise. They were part of a group of girls who tried to act like they never did anything wrong, that they just danced for their money, when everybody knew the truth. Having been in Gold Rooms with them, I had seen some of the things that they would do: getting fingered, getting their boobs sucked on.

Rule of thumb: If you want to continue enjoying a celebrity's work, don't meet them in person. They are almost never the same people—the one on the screen and the one that walks down the street.

Dan Ackroyd, for instance, had a beautiful blonde named Infinity. Word had it that he fingered her and she did not deny it. I spoke to him when he was coming out of the room because I loved his movies. I walked up and said, "Hi, Mr. Ackroyd. I'm Diva. I just wanted to stop and say hi. I don't want to crowd you."

He was a real shit, like speaking was beyond him. He made me feel small and insignificant, like I was worth less than a book of free matches.

The small feeling immediately turned to anger and then to indignation. "You know I like you as an actor," I said as I began to turn away. Then I threw out these last words, just something for him to think about, "But your attitude sucks and I may write a book one day."

I wish all the celebrities could have been just a little bit more like Heavy D. He came in with his friend, Joe Torrey, the actor and comedian, and when I walked over to introduce myself and gush, "I love your music and I love you!" He said, "Thank you," like he meant it and hugged me tight, like a big cuddly teddy bear. The way he portrayed himself on video was exactly the type of man I met. I went around telling everybody, "Heavy D's upstairs!"

Chapter Six

As a little girl, watching my mother, I was learning a lot, fast. For one, men cheated and there was nothing you could do about it. Men beat the shit out of you and there was nothing you could do about it. Basically, in my mind, it seemed that it was a man's world and my place, as a female, was second.

Not far into second grade, the teacher called my mother in for a conference. The teacher was nervous because I had announced promptly at 10:30 every morning I would need a glass of water to regulate my birth control pills. My mother chalked it up to my penchant for storytelling, lying.

Dad was gone so much that he would make promises to come see us, just like a weekend parent. Since it was Dad, he just about never showed up. Me and Jimmy would get dressed and sit outside on the curb waiting for him. My Mom hated that look on our faces when he didn't show up again.

One day when Dad didn't materialize, we went to see the little boy next door who had a pool table. The room was full of boys between the ages of 12 and 16—big boys—all kids me and Jimmy saw every day in the neighborhood—kids we hung out with.

We were shooting pool, the balls clacking against each other, dropping thunk into the pockets. I don't remember what started it, what I did to start it, but the big boys were saying what a sexy little girl I was. They'd look at me and Jimmy, then whisper to each other and roared with laughter.

With no warning, two of them grabbed Jimmy and held him while the others started beating the hell out of him, punching him, hitting his tender 8-year-old stomach, blows finding his eyes and nose and mouth with precision.

There was an unused bedroom off of the recreation room and they grabbed me at the same time and held me down on the naked mattress, pulling my clothes off as they continued hitting Jimmy. Off came my tennis shoes, my bellbottom blue jeans and sweatshirt. The neighbor kid, Paul, was the first to have a go at me. There was a bare light bulb shining down on us, in addition to the late afternoon fall light slanting through the basement windows.

The two biggest boys sat my brother in a chair and made him watch as each of the six took a turn on his seven-year-old little sister.

They were all laughing, making jokes, egging each other on. Get her, man! Get her! She likes it!

I just cried.

My brother was yelling, "Get off my sister! Leave her alone! You're going to get it!"

And I screamed and cried until one of them put his hand over my mouth and told me to shut up or otherwise he'd beat the crap out of me, too. The pain—I can't describe it.

After a while Jimmy just put his head down, and shut his eyes.

I had met the worst of human nature out of the starting gate. Nothing after that—in all the things that followed—would ever hurt as bad.

When I got home, I had blood in my underwear. I told

Mom what happened. She just said, "You watch too much TV." Then when I showed her my blood-stained underwear, she misunderstood the way she needed to at the time, "Oh God, you're starting your period!" That's how far gone my Mom was. Reality didn't exist for her. She stayed numb to keep from feeling anything. As for Jimmy, he totally blocked it out. In his mind, the rape never happened. Why didn't I tell my Dad? You figure it out.

Every summer from the time I was seven until I was fourteen, we went to visit my great-grandmother whose house was by the airport in Shreveport, Louisiana. Everyone called her Miss Kitten. For six weeks we had the time of our lives. There was Aunt Mattie, my great-grandmother's daughter who lived up the street with cousin Leslie. There was Uncle Pumpkin and Uncle Leroy and we'd go for rides in back of Uncle Junebug's truck. My great-grandmother had eleven kids by midwife.

She looked like a Cherokee Indian and had long straight black hair, which she parted down the middle and wore in braids with beads. Her features may have been Indian but she was only half—the other half was French. Grandpa Ben, my great-grandfather, was Chickasaw, Irish and Jamaican.

They lived in one of those old Southern clapboards. You could crawl right underneath that house. On the back porch was a roller washer with a wringer. The furniture was from when my great-grandparents first got married but still looked like the day after it came home Cock's, the originators of the Cock's Sucker Suit (later the Sears Sucker Suit). It was also hot as hell because they didn't have air conditioning. We about burnt up.

In my great-grandparent's backyard, grew a watermelon patch and so we had seed spitting and eating contests.

They also kept chickens. I learned the three best ways to kill them. First of all, once you catch the chicken, you hold him down by his back and feathers and reach around his neck and twist it around your hand, pull and snap. Then you let go and the chicken runs around until he dies. Secondly, you can just chop off the head with an ax. Thirdly, hit the chicken in the head with a bat.

They let the chickens run free, and at night, they'd come up on the back porch. You could only see their eyes shining green like demons.

When I was seven, I saw flying roaches for the first time. One came flying at me and I screamed and ran for Miss Kitten.

"Baby, what is it?"

"It's a big old bug with wings! Kill it!"

"Oh those are just cockroaches, girl. Go to bed." I was so terrified.

I had my first experience in a Southern Baptist Church there, too. Men and women were falling out on the floor and it really worried me because I didn't know about the Holy Ghost back then. I asked, "Grandpa, are they dead?"

"No, baby," he reassured me. "They got the Holy Ghost in them. They're happy right now." I thought they were crazy.

Chapter
Seven

Conventions in the City of Atlanta make up a good-size chunk of the city's annual revenue. For the adult entertainment industry, and stripping in particular, girls could count on about $2,000 to $7,000 in extra cash from each round of conventioneers. This was especially true in 1997 through 1999 when Atlanta hosted the Chicken Pluckers, SuperCom, The Super Show, Microsoft, Sony, and the famed Southern Baptist convention.

The Chicken Pluckers rated high. They came in January bringing with them all the biggest names in hens, roasters and fryers: Perdue, Tyson and Golden Chicken. They were the chicken farmers of the world, the guys that raised the birds that get eaten every day from the grocery store to KFC. They were beer drinkers who wore overalls and cowboy hats, ready to kick back and have a good time.

The most interesting of all of the Chicken Pluckers was Frank Perdue, the head of Perdue. He not only looked like a chicken on the commercials but was equally so up close in person. The Perdue guys took over Gold Room 8 & 9. They had umpteen girls running in and out. The girls were laughing because everybody kept calling Frank the Chicken King. I danced for a couple of guys and we all ordered Lemon Drop shots and Blue Motherfuckers. The only complaint: chicken pluckers get very touchy and you have to kung fu fight to get them off of you. The Super Show was also in January. They were the guys who sold all the athletic apparel and products in the world: Nike, Reebok, Fila. They were straight business-men but on a billion dollar level—much more corporate than most of our customers. Nintendo and Sega also appeared at the Super Show. One of the guys I spent time with just wanted to hear about my life. I went downstairs and got some pictures from my locker and he was genuinely interested. He acted like he was really proud of me for handling my life, taking care of my kids. He gave me $2,500 for a three-hour visit in a Gold Room with champagne, shrimp and crab leg platters. Four days after they left, he sent a Nintendo 64 back to the Gold Club for my three daughters.

In February came SuperCom, the computer convention that hosts all of the geeks you'd ever want to know. They were very polite to the ladies in the room but they were discussing business—we could have what we wanted. Every so often, two would pair up and talk more business, then come back, we'd dance and they'd get back to their work.

In March, the Microsoft Convention came. Girls used to love them because these guys had millions of dollars and would come in and pamper us. If they liked you, you were guaranteed a Gold Room and no less than $2,000. Some of them were a little touchy and some expected more for what they were paying. It was up to the girl as to how much she was willing to put up with that night. If you weren't in the mood for a guy to grope all over you, you put up with it because it's a little hard to tell a guy to stop when you're making $5,000.

In April or May came Sony, with the Japanese, and their American counterparts. The Japanese didn't typically speak English so they brought an interpreter along, usually a woman with a briefcase full of money. The idea was to befriend the interpreter, get girls over there to dance for the guys, explain to the girls it's by the dance and if you're nice, the lady will let you stay and tip you really well, that's being a hundred bucks for two dances.

I like to get into the interpreter's good graces, bringing girls over, making sure everyone is being taking care of. I figure my job was hostess for the hostess. Even if a girl could convince one of the guys to go to a room, they still had to go through the interpreter. If she was in a bad mood, it was no go.

For some reason, I could relate to women who came to the strip club. I could make the women relax and not feel intimidated by all the beautiful women in there. I would put myself in their shoes and relate. Say she's a little overweight or just not that pretty and she's with this man she loves. Immediately, I introduce myself to the woman and even talk about the other dancers, pointing out their flaws. I get the girl up and dancing with me so she is relaxed. Then the guy is comfortable. He sees his girl with me and thinks maybe if he wants to get a dance or something the girlfriend won't mind.

But the interpreters were for the most part American women who worked for these big corporations and it was their job to show these guys a good time at any cost. One group of ten Japanese men came in with their interpreter who was a white lady with reddish brown hair. She pulled me aside, "I don't care how much it costs. These guys have to have a good time tonight. We're signing a multi-million contract tomorrow." I got them a Gold Room and helped pick out the girls they wanted.

At the end of the night, the interpreter thanked me profusely. They had had a wonderful time. She said the head guy came to her and said the deal was done. She ordered me a $1,000 in Gold Bucks and the other girls got $600 each.

In May, 1998 I also met August Busch IV. Mr. Busch may be best known for giving the green light to the hugely successful Anheuser-Busch frog campaign. Later the frogs were then dumped for a pair of lizards and a ferret who hated the frogs.

I knew him as Auggie, about 34 years old, an attractive millionaire.

The Gold Club had a contract with Budweiser and Auggie used to talk to Steve about their account. They were really good friends. One night, around May of 1998, he asked me to come back to his hotel room. "All right, no harm done," I reasoned. We went to his hotel and the whole place looked like a lavish New York apartment. He had a ten-chair dining room table! What Auggie wanted was for me to dress him up, to put nighties and heels and lipstick and makeup on him and tie his tie around his neck and drag him around the room and command him to do things. My shoes fit him because I wear a nine-and-a-half. He put on my dancer thong and a burgundy chiffon short gown that dropped to a V in the back, ending in three sweet bows. You could see right through it.

He wanted me to treat him like a dog. He said, "Treat me like a bitch! Push me around!" I was kicking him with my feet in his butt and then made him kiss my feet.

I thought it was humorous. This big corporate man, a billionaire from the Busch family that everybody thinks is a hard ass in the business world, putting on my lingerie and makeup and lipstick and high heel shoes, crawling around kissing my feet! It was a power rush for me. I got Auggie Busch kissing my feet and I'm talking shit to him, kicking him.

I made him call me Mistress Diva and then I said, "You have to beg me to talk to you this way."

"Mistress Diva, please command me to do something," he begged. He was crazy. I'm thinking, He's sick. Then I got into it. Well, hey, this is fun! I'm making him crawl around the floor and dragging him by the tie.

"Hurry up, you're moving too slow, you fucking piece of shit! You fucking little bitch, kiss my feet!"

"May I please kiss your feet, Mistress Diva?"

When we were finished, he begged me again. But this time it was, "Please don't tell anybody about this."

"And?" I said coldly. "I didn't sign no damn contracts with you, buddy. I'm telling."

He gave me $2600 for thirty minutes and no sex. He didn't even want me to spend the night. He probably masturbated when I left.

When I told Steve what happened he almost died. "You are lying to me!" he said incredulously.

"I am so serious, Steve." I was falling out laughing.

"No way."

"Yes, he did.

Like I said, Auggie was good looking, but as a rule, a man is not cute dressed in women's clothes unless he's shaved his mustache and he's a drag queen.

There were two cross-dressing sessions. The second time, Auggie just wanted to try my clothes on and see what they looked like. He pranced around in front of the mirror in my stripper clothes and high-heel shoes and lipstick and that was about it, a quiet night for him.

The money Auggie gave me helped pay for my boob job that same month, May of 1998. I had thought about getting my boobs done for years. In Milwaukee, I couldn't afford it. But now I had the $5000 I needed and I immediately found a good plastic surgeon and expanded my bust line from a modest size A to an ample D cup.

Not only did I enhance my self-esteem and earning power, I decided I wanted a home for my kids to come home to. A girl at work, Wooyan, told me her boyfriend was a broker and they invited me out to look at a house at Trotter's Ridge about thirty minutes outside of the city. It was in a quiet neighborhood at the bottom of a cul de sac. No traffic. All the houses were big and beautiful with tons of kids.

When I walked in I knew I was home. The kitchen sold

me. I could see myself cooking Thanksgiving and Christmas dinners. I could see garlands wrapped around the stair rail with lights, the Halloween spider webs.

I walked out on the deck that wrapped around the back of the house, the sky so black, and the stars so bright. Peaceful. Crickets. There was a wooden swing set in the backyard. I said, "I want this house. This is it."

When I was a kid, I never would have guessed that I would have the resources to buy a house with four bedrooms and three and a half baths.

On May 14th, I gave them my down payment of $10,000, signed the paperwork, and Wooyan's boyfriend handed me my keys.

I did a double take. "These are my keys, aren't they?"

He nodded. "These are your keys and this is your house."

The next two months I spent every free minute shopping and decorating. Since Bethany was the youngest, I decided to give her her own room. Everything for Bethany was done in Barbie. I went over the top. There were Barbie borders midway up the wall, Barbie sheets, comforter, pillow shams, dust ruffle and throw pillows. Giant poster of Barbie for the head of the bed. Barbie flowers around the room. I found a My Size Barbie and stood it in the corner next to the Barbie stove and refrigerator set. I bought a Barbie dollhouse and extra Barbies and Kens with a Corvette for them to drive.

Brittany and Breanna were the oldest and didn't want to be separated. I turned their room into a Winnie the Pooh fantasy. I bought twin beds with red headboards and blue and white reversible comforters; one side was dark blue with clouds and the other side had Winnie, Tigger and the whole gang. I repeated with themed throw pillows and wall borders, and then I bought stuffed animals and puppets for the bed. I filled the closet with Winnie the Pooh overalls and T-shirts, shoes and clothes. The bathroom that all three shared was split down the middle: half Winnie and half Barbie. And it matched.

In the beginning of June of 1998 Steve Kaplan came to me and said, "We're going to Vegas. You have been doing exceptionally well with your champagne sales and I'm very proud of you and I think you deserve a vacation."

"You're kidding!" A Vegas trip. Hard work does pay off.

"We're leaving in two weeks. Why don't you get together a few girls who can go with you?"

I picked Melanie Smith because she was one of the top five waitresses in the club. Frederique and Dina went. Big Arthur, the floorman, was one of the top people who sold memberships and champagne and Gold Rooms. I chose the hard-working people who worked six nights a week. That was my basis for picking who went on the trip.

I told them, "We're going to Vegas and Steve's paying for everything, but everything is under my control. I'm choosing the people who are going, and I know you've been working really hard and you deserve this trip with me."

Two weeks later, on cue, we all got in a limousine and went to the airport, headed for Vegas, and had the time of our lives.

We stayed at the Mirage because Steve knew the hotel manager and got good room rates there.

The way Steve handled logistics was a recipe for jealousy. As on this first trip, my room was the only one allowed to order room service, order in-room movies, make long distance phone calls because the charges were guaranteed with Steve's credit card. If anyone else wanted to call long distance, they had to come to my room or Steve's room and ask to use his phone. I had free rein.

Steve made a few rules to start us off. Number one: Nobody is allowed in your hotel room. If you meet somebody there, that's your business. Sit by the pool with them; get to know them but no company in your room. Number two:

Everybody is to meet down in the lobby at 7:30 to go to dinner. During the day you can do whatever you want.

Usually everybody was with me because if they wanted to order drinks from the cafe and get lunch—if you wanted all expenses taken care of—I had to put it on my room and sign for it. We all wanted to be together anyway because we didn't know anybody in Vegas.

So at 7:30 we all met for supper. On the way, I told Steve to fire Jeff Johnson. He dialed the number, told him he was fired, and that was that—for the moment. Dina and Frederique gave each other a look. Disgusted. They didn't understand how I had gotten so close to Steve, what was so special about me, what was different.

Steve took us to the most expensive restaurants, to the Palm and Caesar's Palace. There was a restaurant inside the Mirage that was wonderful as well.

It was complete relaxation. All day we spent tanning at the pool or in the spa downstairs, getting massages, manicures and pedicures. He said do whatever you like. I got to go shopping, separately, by myself.

We'd go back to the room at about six to give everybody time to get their showers, get their clothes on. We had to dress really nice, to the hilt. We'd go to dinner and then Steve would either set up tickets like for Legends, a show of copycat stars— Elvis, the Four Tops, the Temptations—or we'd go to the movies. One night after dinner Steve felt like gambling. We went into the casino and he handed everybody a couple hundred dollars and said, "Have fun."

I won $800 with a dollar coin, popped it in a machine and the coins spilled out like cornmeal from a sack. Arthur won $1,000 at craps. Steve said, "Don't spend that money, Arthur. Give it to Larry and let him invest it for you." Larry Gleit, the Gold Club accountant, did as Steve asked and invested Arthur's money. It wasn't a fortune but a lot of good things came from it. Arthur established credit and was able to buy a car. He got a bank account, invested some money. He was really proud to start saving money and get stuff together. He did really well. He deserved to do well. He was just a big country boy.

That trip, I learned another favorite Vegas pastime—shopping.

"Everybody get in the van. Let's go!" Steve says. He's one of these people when he says let's go, you go or he'll leave you. You don't have time to pick up your compact from the counter. I can't stand going out to dinner with him. When he's done eating, he wants to get up and go. He doesn't care if you have a plateful of food. Everything is: Let's go! Let's go! He's a typical fast-paced nonstop New Yorker. Sometimes I would grab him and say, "Stop! Slow down for a minute. I'm not rushing tonight." The rest of them, if they were to tell him to slow down and stop, he'd look at them like they were fucking crazy. But he listened to me for some reason. Maybe because when I got these feelings about certain people I would come to him and say, "This situation doesn't feel right to me and you should second guess it." A lot of times I would be right. So he would come to me and ask how I felt about this or that. I'd tell him, and most times he did just the opposite of what I told him. Then when it was the way I told him it would be, he'd say, "You know I hate that you're always right."

This particular Let's go wasn't dinner. We were all jumping in the van for my first shopping spree. Steve knew his way around Vegas like it was New York. He loved it like a kid loves Disney World. We walked in Niketown and I thought, what the hell are we doing here, and he said, "Pick out whatever you want."

I found this one little cute jogging suit I wanted and he said, "Did you not understand the words that just came out of my mouth? Would you please pick you out ... get some shoes!

Here. You need a baseball cap." He started picking up stuff and giving it to me. "Didn't I just say pick out whatever you want?"

I said, "Steve, I don't feel right." I didn't feel he needed to do that. To me it was enough that he was paying all these expenses, dinners, ordering $800 bottles of wine at dinner. To me, that was extravagant, coming from where I did. This was all new.

"What's wrong?"

"You shouldn't have to do this," I said.

"I'm not doing this because I have to. I don't owe you anything. I'm doing it because I want to. I like to see people smile."

While I was shopping for myself I found this pair of jogging pants and T-shirt that I thought would be adorable on him and put it up on the counter. We got back to the room and got out everybody's stuff and I went and laid it on his bed. We walked in and he said, "Whose shit is this on my bed?" Steve cussed constantly. Fuck, for him, isn't punctuation, its every other word.

I said, "It's yours. I picked it out at the store." You would never know Steve Kaplan had any money. He always wore jogging pants with one leg pulled up, raggly tennis shoes and a big old wrinkled T-shirt with something spilled down the front of it. He had a mess of little curls sticking from under his baseball cap.

That afternoon, me and Ziggy, Steve and Melanie, went over to the Hard Rock Resort and Casino to hang out by the pool.

Ziggy knew a lot of people in the basketball world because of his Brooklyn USA kid's basketball program. So while we're there, he calls up his old buddy, Billy Baino, the head coach for University of Nevada Las Vegas and tells him where we are, to come over.

Steve and Ziggy were getting massages when Billy Bano arrived. The conversation starts and Frederique and Dina join us.

Me and Billy walked off together, talking about the things we had in common, movies, basketball, food.

Later on that evening Billy and I went off and did our own thing. I think because we were so attracted to each other we attacked each other. This was an extremely attractive guy. He'd just gotten back from Tahiti or Hawaii and his tan was just perfect. He had these shells around his neck. The passionate kissing, the way he caressed my body, I knew he wanted me. In the bedroom by ourselves, we were kissing and squeezing and holding. We had a great sexual experience. I was moaning so loud he shushed me, "Keep it down!"

"I know, I can't help it," I uttered the words as I climaxed. Then he pushed me onto the bed, put a condom on and got on top and started fucking me with a good eight and a half inches of dick, my legs wrapped around his back taking it all in. His face was buried into the side of my neck. From the bed, we moved to the shower. Billy got up and picked me up with my legs around his waist, carried me into the bathroom, turned on the shower and I bent over with my hands by the faucet by the edge of the tub and he started making love to me again. Then we both came and I turned around, we started kissing. We finished by washing each other.

When I got back I went to Steve's room to tell him what had happened. We talked about some graphic shit. He didn't know I slept with Bill, he had no idea, I said, "I fucked him."

"You fucked him?"

"Yes, I fucked him."

"No way!"

"Yeah, I did," I said pleased with myself. I could talk openly. There was nothing I couldn't tell Steve Kaplan, nothing was too personal.

The next night Steve didn't feel like going out so we sat up in his room and laid on the bed, talking openly about our lives. He said, "I want to know more about you."

I began telling him about my marriage, how my ex used to beat me. He was angry. He had no tolerance for people like that. It made him sick. "I can't believe you went through that," he said pensively.

That night he told me how he felt about me. "I wish my Dad was still alive to meet you. You don't know how he would take to you. You're like a sister and daughter all in one. I wish you were my biological daughter. You are a caring, loving person, very loyal and I don't trust many people," he confided.

That took me aback. It was hard to believe that someone cared for me so deeply. My real father was like a distant shadow. We never talked, hugged. I barely knew him. My thoughts must have showed.

"If I have to stand on the rooftops and shout I love Diva that's what I'll do," he continued. "You're my everything. There's nothing I wouldn't do for you." That was how he and I established how close we really were.

Immediately when we returned to Atlanta we had a big club meeting and Steve embarrassed the hell out of me. He made me sit up on stage with the management. Everybody in the club was looking at me, like this fucking bitch, who does she think she is?

Steve stood up in front and introduced himself to all the people who were new and then he introduced me. "This is Diva. She is the epitome of the hard-working individuals I want to see in my club. She works six nights a week. She is here from seven in the evening until four in the morning, faithfully. And she sells a shitload of champagne. Nobody, I mean nobody, can do anything to her. She cannot be fired. She cannot be disciplined. Nothing."

Rose, the housemom, Norbie, and Ziggy put this big dry-erase board up, edged in sparkling Christmas lights. It read: "Sixty bottles sold by Diva. Congratulations, Champagne Diva." I had sold 60 bottles of champagne in that one month when the average girl was selling 12-13, so that was a big thing.

Steve continued. "I'm hearing a lot of girls bitch and complain. The housemom hears you bitches and, yes, I'm talking to every last one of you. Because you are bitches if you are gonna complain that we're advertising that Diva sold sixty bottles of champagne. You should be damn happy for her. Proud of her. She's making money and she's making money for this club and that's going to keep this club moving. All of you should be more like her." He paused. "And I love this girl more than anything. This is my girl."

After that, everyone called me Champagne Diva.

Selling champagne meant drinking a hell of a lot of it. Drinking every night, all night, there were several times at work I got really drunk and blacked out and then didn't remember what happened the next day. The other girls were more than happy to fill me in on what I did.

One night we were in this room with these guys, they were telling me, and I asked, "How much did we get paid?" They said, "I think we got like $800 apiece." It really bothered me. You have a hangover the next day. You know you can't even remember the night before. I used to get that fucked up to where I couldn't remember the night before.

But that happened a lot. I'd hear, "You let that guy finger you." I'd freak out on that shit because I'm supposed to be in control. I'm not supposed to let things like that happen. I have no doubt I sucked a couple of dicks that I don't remember. I just don't remember and I wish I could, because then I could say, it was this person's dick or that person's dick. I'd drink myself so over the top, I'd be in the back passed out on the floor, sleeping back there for like four or five hours. The night would be over; I'd wake up wondering what the hell happened.

While stripping is a business, it's also a way of life and as such, it has its emotional toll. Sixty percent of the 300 girls who worked at the Gold Club would say they were bisexual. To me, it was a fad. Girls would start working there and in a few months, suddenly they like girls. They were only doing it because other people were doing it. To be truly bisexual I believe is something within you that you've had all your life. Not something that comes out of the blue one day. That's more like bi-curious. People like that will fool around with other women but would never get a girlfriend and be seen out in public with her holding hands.

Anyway, the other 40% of the Gold Club girls were a mixture: some were married; we had a few straight lesbians. Some of them didn't like men or women. They just blocked out everything that they did.

Soleil was one of the straight lesbians. She'd be climbing all over guys, let them finger her. She was there for the money and did not care. But if her girlfriend knew what she was doing, she'd have been in trouble. I used to ask her all the time, "How could you be lesbian and be dancing for these men?" "Fuck them. I just want the money." That was her pat answer.

Not that there is a difference between being lesbian, straight or bi, when you're dancing. It's all in how you do it. You're either business-minded or you're not. Some of the girls were there just to get the money.

No matter how much money you could make if you had the stomach for it, there were a few girls who couldn't hack it. They became overwhelmed. It was emotional for them. They couldn't understand how they got there, why they were doing it and eventually they would quit. It was too much. One girl like that who was a friend of mine, Arial, committed suicide, took a gun and blew her brains out. She didn't leave a note.

The girls who could hack it would do just about anything if they were in the mood. My girls, the Sluts, were Frederique, Angelique, Dina, Amanda, Megan, Cory and quite a few others. A girl named Suzanne had a guy in his mid-forties in a Gold Room and they called me as I was walking past. I came in the room and Suzanne asked me to dance for them. She said, "Diva, I'm about to do something, just don't tell on me." I figured she knew the guy, that he was a regular customer. All of a sudden she unzips his pants and opens them. She didn't even pull them down. She kept her dress on and sat on top of him. No condom or nothing. She started having intercourse right in front of me.

I said, "What are you doing?"

She said, "I'm drunk and I'm horny as fuck."

I couldn't argue with that. "Well, all right, knock yourself out."

While she was sitting on top of him, fucking him, she threw up. I held a champagne bucket in front of her. She's still fucking this guy, and throwing up in a bucket.

Most of the customers who came to the Gold Club came in for conversation, for a little attention, then the other ten percent were looking for a little action. Usually these were the guys who weren't having sex with their wives. They say the wife is too busy, or doesn't find her husband attractive anymore. They start drinking and they get this thought that since this is a strip club their mind flips—no, it's a whorehouse. They forget they're in an adult entertainment establishment and so they offer money for sex.

A big hint that you were dealing with one of these guys was the tan line from where their weddings rings used to be before they tucked them away. I used to call them out on it. One incident I saw a guy take his ring off and stick it in his pocket. I passed by and he asked me to sit down and ordered me a drink. I said, "Oh, by the way, we prefer it if you keep your wedding ring on."

He said, "What?"

"I saw you slip your ring off. That's so tacky. You know what that says to me? That says that you're not proud to be married to your wife. You think that somebody is going to judge you for being in here and being married?"

Of course, I did judge the married ones who were doing something wrong. I'd be thinking, "If I was your wife you'd be out the door so fast it'd make your head spin."

Again, its only business but it bothers you. It makes you wonder. If they can do this here maybe my man is doing it someplace else. The opportunity is out there. It's whether the person you're with will take advantage of the situation. It is trust.

With Elliott, I understood his not trusting me because I was an entertainer. At the same time, it was a double standard. He had no room to not trust me when I knew what he was doing. I had the password to his voice mail and I listened to the women leaving him messages, different cities, different girls. It was standard for him to lie to me about all the other women he was doing.

But really, in strip clubs, to the credit of most guys, it's not even about sex. The average man at a strip club is not thinking about sex when he hits the front door. He's thinking, "I won't get any nagging, bitching, or whining about the day's events. I'll get somebody who'll drink, listen, and laugh," which is a relaxing thing for a man. So it's about him in a little fantasy. Say his wife is 400 pounds. He loves her to death but at the strip club you get a woman who is 5'10", 126 pounds, gorgeous and she can have an intelligent conversation with you, laugh at your jokes and make you feel special. That's why men come into strip clubs. They need that attention.

We were, in a way, like nude psychiatrists. One sad guy came in and told me his wife was battling breast cancer and he was miserable because he couldn't do anything for her. He apologized for even coming in, like it was a betrayal or something. "I'm there for her. I go to all the treatments with her. This is the one night I spend anytime out." It was the only time he'd leave her for a couple hours to come in, get a Gold Room, drink champagne and sit and talk. It was killing him.

Then there were the guys who defied logic. One strange fish was this guy called Preacher Man. He was an old white guy, gray hair, kind of scraggly looking, kind of dusty. He used to wear the same tired-ass suit, gray pinstripe. The floormen let him in for free he'd been coming in so long. He drank beer, Budweiser. He'd come up to the front of the stage while you were dancing, hand you a dollar, and tell you, "You need to get Jesus! You need to get saved! You are all sinners. I don't know what you're doing up there, but maybe this dollar will save your life." Okay, Preacher Man. He was in there almost every night.

It was funny because at the same time he was yelling at you, saying, "You'll be going to hell if you don't change your ways," he'd be in there watching you take your clothes off.

I'd ignore him, for the most part, then after a while, I said, "Preacher Man, sit down." I'd talk to him any old kind of way. Shut the fuck up, I don't want to hear your ass. He'd look up, okay and he'd sit down. He was sort of pitiful because he didn't seem to have anything better to do.

Most guys that came into the Gold Club knew their place. We had one guy who used to sit in the back toward the dressing room, wearing jogging pants, and he used to beat his dick through his pants as the girls came out. He'd stop them and ask, "Will you dance for me?" All the girls knew who he was and said, "Hell no!" But one night he asked a new girl to dance for him. She didn't know, poor girl, and he told her to sit on his lap first before she danced, to talk. She sat down and he started rubbing himself and she started screaming, jumped up, and ran in the dressing room, crying, "He's out there touching himself!" We all calmed her down and told her to stay away from him. They finally kicked him out and told him to stay out.

For six months, every two weeks like clockwork, I had a guy named Tim come in, bringing with him an expensive foot fetish. He would pay me $1,000 to sit and let him rub my feet for an hour. That's all he wanted to do—rub my feet. We didn't talk. He never asked for anyone else. I thought, if this is what he wants, all right. I'd be sitting there and girls would walk over and ask what I was up to. "Nothing, I'm getting my feet massaged," I'd say, sipping my drink. "I can't talk to you right now. I'll talk to you when I'm done." I never knew where he was from. He said, "Don't ask me any questions. Just sit and relax." And then one day, he just stopped coming.

In between the jack offs, the feet rubbers and the preachers, were the honest to goodness celebrities. I'd pass Evander Holyfield on the stairs on the way to a Gold Room. It was hi and bye. "You're a great fighter," I said like I'd stepped out of the pages of People Magazine where I resided on a daily basis. Evander answered, "And you're a beautiful woman," as people rushed him up the steps.

I got to speak to Keanu Reeves who was with Pauly Shore from MTV. Pauly Shore is a bit of an asshole. He's got a smart mouth and he's very cocky, not the fun-loving humorous guy you see on TV. I was telling Keanu what a fine actor I thought he was. He was very shy, timid almost. To see him in his movies, he's strong and powerful, but in person he's withdrawn and kind of quiet.

Pauly Shore, interrupted me in a huff, "Can't you see we're in the middle of business right now?"

"Nice to meet you too, Mr. Shore!" I said, ignoring him all the way around the block. He gave me a look like nobody pops off to him.

Pauly Shore had two girls he knew at the club, one of whom had posed for Playboy a few years back. Keanu came back a few more times and got Gold Rooms, a couple of girls to dance and a few sitting around like decorations, but he just sat on the end of the couch by the door like he was bored. He wasn't drinking and I don't think that he really cared to be there.

Boyz II Men came in all together one night. Then a couple of them would come sporadically by themselves. They just wanted me and this other girl to dance together. They sat and ate crab legs and chilled out.

My personal stories, however, were child's play compared to the stories Frederique racked up by the hour. I think it was because she was used to guys using her, cheating on her and treating her bad. She was used to being abused emotionally. Every guy that she dated was like that and she just couldn't break the pattern.

In some ways, a lot of the shit she did was like her way of getting gratification or some type of love, but sexually. Either that or she was a nymphomaniac.

She behaved like an exhibitionist. I'd see her masturbating in front of guys she'd never seen before.

One night we were in a room with Dikembe Mutombo, a basketball player for the Atlanta Hawks at that time. He was a little uneasy about what was going on at first because he knew Elliott and Henry. He told me to sit down on the couch because he had a couple guys with him and he told the guys not to even think about coming near me because he knew me.

Frederique came in and didn't say a word. She just unzipped Motombo's pants and exposed his penis because everybody wanted to see just how big it really was. We had heard stories about it and when we saw it, it was scary. I don't know how his wife sleeps with him.

His penis was at least twelve inches and you could not get your hand all the way around it. Frederique not only sucked his dick but she put it all the way down her throat. From this physical feat we gave her the name, Jaws. She swallowed when he came and laughed, saying, "Got my protein fill for the day!" She finished and he gave her some cash, then she bragged about it around the club about how big his dick was.

Chapter Eight

Later, the same year of the rape, my mother would leave again, taking only baby Marquita with her to Canada. Through tears, she told us, "I have to do this because your father's going to kill me if I don't." Me and Jimmy just said, "Go. Get your stuff before he gets back." We knew the threat of death was real.

In the meantime, Dad was seeing a lady named Jeannie White, who would later become the stepmother who raised me from the time I was nine until I was twenty. But before my father took us, or rather before my mother gave us up for good, our parents made one last attempt to "save" their marriage. By then, Dad was staying with Miss Jeannie so my mother got a new boyfriend, which made Dad oddly jealous.

He came over and suddenly it was "I love you and I want to be a family" and my mother gave him another chance. He moved back in but it wasn't long before Mom found out that he was still seeing Jeannie and they got into a huge fight. She took this picture that my uncle down South had painted of one of our ancestors, the Cherokee chief, and smashed it over his head. Then she grabbed a lamp and hit him in the face with it. He was chasing her through the house. Jimmy couldn't take it any more. He ran into the kitchen and grabbed a butcher knife to stab our father. He said, "If you put one more hand on my mother I'm gonna kill you!" My father backhanded him and knocked him halfway across the room. Then Dad stopped fighting and left the house. That was the end. No more dramatic or violent than their life together had ever been. Maybe it came with a nine-year warning and then maybe it also came out of nowhere.

Dad retreated to Jeannie.

Mom beat us with belts and extension cords in the past but when I turned eight, she had this gray board about two feet long and a half a foot wide. Every time you got a whipping she'd write your name on it. That last year with our mother, we lived in an old house in the downstairs apartment. Our land-lady was an 86-year-old woman who lived upstairs.

The landlady's name was Anna and her only daughter and her son-in-law had both drowned in the bathtub a year apart. She was very lonely and I'd go visit her because, I guess, maybe I was lonely, too. She would call me Girlie. Before long, she asked my mother if I could come stay upstairs and help see after her. So with the situation downstairs, I gladly moved upstairs and she gave me her daughter's room, which was just the way she left it. My mother loved the idea. She said it would be a wonderful opportunity for me to realize where I could be one day. That one day, I'd need somebody, too.

I loved living with Anna. The furniture was all ancient and her dead daughter's bed looked French—white with gold trim. The comforter on the bed was chiffon and had a rose pattern—pinks and greens and whites. So soft. It was like Anna dusted it with a scent, not lavender, but I haven't smelled it since. On that bed, I had my first bisexual experience with a little girl named Angel. That was the point I realized I loved women. But growing up, you couldn't tell anybody that. Not back in those days.

But most of my time was spent between school and Anna. In the living room, she had a candle that burned in front of her daughter's and son-in-law's pictures constantly. I had to keep those candles lit at all times. I would catch the city bus to go to Walgreen's to pick up her prescriptions. She always gave me extra money for Pixie Stix. I would buy a bag of Pixie Stix and eat them all on the way back, except for one, which I saved for her. She'd pour it on her old tongue and smack the sourness with relish, complaining at the same time, "How do you kids eat this garbage?" I couldn't find anything wrong with her.

We used to sit in the kitchen. It was Anna's favorite spot. There was a table with silver legs and trim, and yellow seating, and an old porcelain sink. The fairy tale ended one day when Anna had a heart attack in the kitchen while my mother was visiting. My mother took her in her arms and I tried to dial 911 but Anna kicked the phone out of my hands. It was like she wanted to go and didn't want us to stop her. My mother got her into her bedroom. Inside, there was a giant dark wooden dresser with the big legs on the bottom, and brass handles. Next to it was a high sleigh bed with knitted coverlets. Mom managed to get Anna next to the bed and then got down on the floor with her and was holding her while I tried again and succeeded at calling for help.

The paramedics came and immediately began trying to revive her while I stood outside into the front living room peeking through the door. I stood in front of her big old stereo set with the TV. On top were Anna's family pictures and the burning candle. The second she died, the candle went out. It was like a wind came out of nowhere and the candle blew out.

That very morning Anna had given me her daughter's bedspread. I took it downstairs and made my bed with it while they took her body away. Later that night, as I was falling asleep, my door cracked open about an inch and I felt cold air and the covers peeled back from my chest and I felt a warmth on my forehead. My mother always said Anna had come to kiss me goodbye.

Anna left the house to my mother but we didn't know that until much later. Come to find out Anna's son hid the will so he could get the property. By the time they found it, it was too late. They had already turned over the property to him. My mother never gave it a second thought, saying it obviously wasn't meant to happen. In this life, you get the things you need. Somehow, you always get the things you need.

Chapter Nine

I decorated and cleaned until the new house sparkled. Elliott came home from France. When I picked him up from the airport he thought I was joking when I said I had bought a house. The limo pulled up and he believed me. "That's like a mini mansion!" he said.

"No, it's not," I was pleased with his reaction. "It's just a regular house." The day he arrived was the day the bedroom set was delivered to complete all of my work. It felt like home.

Two days later, on Brittany's birthday, July 29, 1998, Joe drove the kids down while Elliott flew to Wisconsin to see his family. I bought a cake to celebrate the homecoming. They pulled up in the driveway and all I heard was Mooom! as the children came running into the house. They hugged me tight.

"Let me take you to your rooms," I said, releasing the little arms from around my neck. Bethany ran upstairs to her room and cried, "Oh my goodness! Look at all this Barbie stuff!" The girls went in their room and began screaming and yelling, "This is really our house?"

"This is really our house," I said, feeling content and complete after being separated from my children for eight months.

Joe said, "Jackie, this is really nice." He meant it.

They weren't tired so we took the kids over to Stone Mountain, the largest piece of granite sticking out of the ground in the world. We hiked all the way to the top, rode the old-timey train that skirts the bottom, took a boat ride and then came home tired, in time to make dinner and sing Happy Birthday.

The girls wanted me to light the fireplace in the middle of summer. I cranked up the AC and lit some Duraflame logs. We all curled up on the floor together, watching TV and talking. I could see in their young faces how happy they were that this was their house.

The next morning I made a big breakfast and suggested we go take a ride to see the city or catch a movie. They just wanted to stay home and play in their yard.

It was good to hear the sound of my children again. That night, coming back from the grocery store, I got out of the car and looked around: "This is my house," I thought with gratitude. "But best of all, my kids are home." I was so overwhelmed that tears were streaming down my cheeks as I stood in the driveway looking through the windows. I could see the kids in the kitchen. It was what I had always dreamed of. All I needed was a husband to complete the scenario.

That first night we didn't go to bed until three in the morning. Joe stayed in the spare bedroom downstairs for a month, until he could get on his feet and start his own new life in Atlanta.

Then Elliott went back overseas and it was just me and the kids.

We were always moving when I was a kid, never had a house to call our own. A lot of friends from back home down-talked my decision to move South. They said, "She's never going to make it." The day that I moved in I thought, "I did make it. I'm doing it."

I enjoyed the quiet time after work until the kids woke up in the mornings. I took extra pleasure in making a home, cooking breakfast, ironing clothes, doing their hair.

Getting them out the door to school. With Joe in town, I no longer needed an overnight babysitter. He picked the girls up after dinner and brought them back, still asleep, in the early hours on his way to work.

My girls always got good grades, and did their homework when they walked in the door. I alternated between Joe and the children's aunt and cousin for the evening routine. Both places provided a good environment and made the girls feel at home.

Living the way we did, my kids were very strong. With the short nights for sleep they still maintained their grades and were very helpful around the house. They matured quickly, being the children of a single mom.

Elliott was around the children a lot and so were my two girlfriends, Amanda Pappas and Mulan. They were the only ones that visited my house while working at the Gold Club. They were the only two girlfriends who were around my kids. It was hard to juggle a relationship and work with having the kids anyway. A lot of the times I'd have somebody but not have them at the same time. Like with Lacey and Megan, our relationships, including our sex lives, took place at work. If we wanted to do something on the weekend, that was cool because the kids were at their Dad's.

As far as girlfriends and boyfriends went, the children were a strong influence. There was no way I was going to bring anybody around my kids if they weren't permanent. I thought Elliott was permanent but things didn't work out.

As for my bisexuality, the girls were too young to understand and they've only ever seen me hugging. My children never saw me in my work clothes either. If they ever decide they want to understand fully what Mom did, I'll take them and show them when they get 17-18 years old. Other than knowing that I was a dancer and took my clothes off to pay the bills, the children are really too young to comprehend.

My spring that year, was marked by Malcolm Jamal Warner who was good friends with one of the dancers. As we were sitting around talking, I noticed he had a tongue ring. I said, "Let me see. Stick it out."

At first he was shy. But when he finally stuck it out, I saw he had a big diamond in the middle of his tongue wrapped in gold.

I said, "That is so cool. I want to get one of those but I'm scared."

"It doesn't hurt," Malcolm said. "What are you, chicken? Okay, I tell you what: tomorrow I'll come pick you up and personally take you to get one."

Nobody calls me a chicken and I was more than happy to take a dare. "No, you don't have to do that. I'm going to go get one and I want you to come here tomorrow night so you can see it."

The next day, I was in the chair at the piercing shop ready to back out. First, you have to hold Listerine in your mouth for three minutes to kill all the bacteria. Your mouth is packed with cotton. Then, the piercer takes tongs that have holes in the bottom and top. They clip it around your tongue and put a rubber band around it to hold it real tight. He takes a hollow tip needle and sticks it through your tongue. Take the ball and barbell part and sticks it up thru the needle, pulls it out. There's minimal bleeding. While he was doing it, I almost had an orgasm. It gave me such an adrenaline rush through my body that I almost came.

Malcolm Jamal Warner did keep his promise and returned the next night.

"Wow. You're great. I didn't think you were going to go through with it."

It was just a dare. He called me a chicken. Silly as it may

seem, I was quite pleased with myself. I had joined the ranks of the body-pierced like Nurse Cindy who had her clit done. She would take her glasses and hang them by the ring in her clit and let them dangle back and forth. Guys loved that.

Things were trudging along at the club through the hot Atlanta August and it was time for the Brooklyn USA Fundraiser, a celebrity golf outing that Ziggy was involved in. Steve must have donated in the neighborhood of $250,000 over the course of the couple of years that he was the so-called CEO of the Gold Club. At least that's what he used to tell everybody.

We all pitched in and recruited people to come in. I got Dennis Rodman, Dale Davis, Dominique Wilkins, Spud Webb, Mookie Blalock and Dikembe Mutumbo to sponsor the event.

It was exciting getting ready, and then all of the celebrities gathered for the kickoff at the Hyatt Regency in Buckhead for a black-tie auction with thank-yous for everyone who contributed. Everybody was there. Dale Davis, Carl Malone, Drew Barry, Charles Oakley, Spud Webb, Larry Johnson, John Starks, Kevin Willis, Jack Haley and Stephon Marbury. The vice president of First Union Bank, a regular, showed up as well as Lou Saab who owns a big Saab car dealership. Lou and Steve did a lot of business together and he sold most of the girls in the club their cars.

There were boxing gloves autographed by Evander Holyfield and baseballs signed by Andruw and Chipper Jones among an array of celebrity-marked items.

The auction was followed by dinner and cocktails and a huge party. Little did I know the Feds were at the party videotaping everything going on. They must have been disappointed to see through their lenses that we were presenting

Steve with an award just for being who he was. Me, Tyler, and some others got together, bought and planned it.

When we presented it, Steve was overwhelmed. Ziggy made a grand speech, about how much he loved him and what he did for him and how he will never leave Steve's side. It was heartfelt but unfortunately, the speech didn't mean shit.

I told Steve that night, "I really don't trust this guy." I didn't have any proof. It was just a gut instinct, one that kept coming back like ipecac.

Steve said, "Diva, lay off Ziggy. He's a good guy. C'mon, give him a chance."

The morning of the Brooklyn USA event, Monday, August 16, everybody got ready quickly and on the busses waiting outside of the club. The celebrities were paired up with dancers—two dancers each.

The golf course was the Covington Plantation Golf Club. There were eighteen teams of five with almost 200 caddies and volunteers.

At first everything was festive and fine. Teeing up and the usual psychological banter on the golf course. Then one of the dancers got caught having sex in the bushes with a customer. A couple of girls with Dennis Rodman whipped off their tops.

They were getting drunk out there. People's houses overlooked the course and before you could yell "fore!," the head guy of the golf course came stomping across the perfect green, mad as hell, and kicked us out. I was hung over from going out with Dale Davis the night before and so stayed on the sidelines in dark shades, watching it all happen.

When it was all over everyone retired to the Gold Club

where we had the Skit of the Year contest. We performed seven of our best skits and asked a couple of celebrities and a couple of customers to judge them. Thriller won. There was a dancer Nicky who could do Michael Jackson dead-on without a hitch. It was a great show.

That night Dennis got on the microphone in the DJ booth and started out with $5,000 as a donation to Brooklyn USA. Somebody downstairs yelled out, "I'll donate a thousand." They had this bidding war going on. It was crazy. They were throwing out money to this charity. Dennis Rodman jumps on the mike again and says, "$25,000! Who can top that in this building right now?"

Everybody started applauding and they were screaming and yelling. I was standing in the DJ booth with Dennis. No other dancer was allowed near him or in the room unless I said so.

Steve got on the mike and said, "Dennis Rodman's the man!" The crowd erupted a second time, louder. I was walking past Gold Room 5 on the way back from checking on my and Dennis's room and I saw Terrell Davis having oral sex performed on him. Just like it was no big deal.

I grabbed a floorman and said, "Here, stand right here."

He says, "Why?"

"Just stay here because Terrell Davis is in this room and we don't want anybody just walking in and out of there." The floorman had his back to the room so he didn't even know what I was talking about. All the Gold Rooms, 1-5, were bright with neon light.

I couldn't believe what I was seeing, this chick is down on her knees just going at it. Three minutes at it and she's still going, and now his friend, Charles, is getting a blow job. They're both getting their dicks sucked sitting next to each other. The floorman never turned around. I think he knew but he just didn't want to see.

The club was packed with 1500 people in the building. It was hard for the girls to get to the stage for their skits. I was looking for Dennis but couldn't find him. I found him in room 10. I see Arthur standing in front of the door and I walked in to find Dennis sitting up on the back of the chair with his feet on the cushion.

So I say, "What's up?" Gold Room 10 is right next to 8 & 9 and the walls are dark smoked glass.

Dennis said, "I ordered some food. Are you hungry?"

All of a sudden, Holly, our waitress, walks in with this giant platter of hot wings. We didn't have hot wings at the Gold Club. Dennis ordered them from across the street, along with breaded mushrooms and beer-battered shrimp.

We ate some and then Dennis got antsy. It's time to walk around again. So he grabs my hand to come with him because he will not let me out of his sight—that will not happen, it does not exist. So we're walking over near the DJ booth and Dennis grabs me and sits me up on the bar. Angelique was sitting next to him.

He says, "I dare you to have sex with her, right here on the bar."

I said, "She can't do that. There's people here. Are you crazy?!"

"I'll give you $300," Dennis said to Angelique.

She said, "No. Four hundred."

Dennis hands her $1,000 in Gold Bucks, a dare.

Angelique grabbed me. I was pushing her away from me, yelling, "Dennis, I'm going to kick your ass!"

"Okay, Angelique, stop." Then he gave her the $1,000 just because she would do it.

We continued walking around and met the makeup artist, Christian, who dresses in drag. His nickname is Strawberry. Dennis has a thing for drag queens. He loves them.

Strawberry walks up and says, "You're not going to introduce me to your friend Diva?"

Dennis turned around and says, "Whassup?! I like this one!"

Christian is very dramatic and says coyly, "What's up, Mr. Rodman? I would love to know what your rod is like ..."

"Oh you couldn't handle my rod, Strawberries and Cream."

There was a bottle of champagne unopened on the bar. Dennis asked the bartender whose it was. The bartender gave it to him and Dennis said, "Diva, pop the bottle!"

Dennis announced on the microphone, "Diva's gonna make the champagne flow!" Everybody upstairs stopped and looked towards me sitting on the bar. So I do the whole thing, making the bottle cum and pop the bottle. Dennis takes the bottle, shakes it up, and holds it over the rail, spraying everybody downstairs.

Then Dennis grabs a stack of Gold Bucks—about $500—and tosses them over the rail.

"Dennis, you are on fire!"

Meanwhile, Chuck, the regular over in the Viper Lounge, orders a double jereboam that's about two feet around. He says, "Diva, I want you to pop the bottle."

"I don't know if I can do a jereboam," I said. But then I found I could and opened that double jereboam with my mouth that night. Dennis flipped. He says, "Look at my girl go."

They got on the mike, Dee-va! Dee-va! The party was rocking upstairs. Then we took the bottle and had this contest to see how many gulps you could take before you put the bottle down. Chuck grabbed the bottle, turned it up, did five gulps. A couple of the girls tried it but they could only do three-four gulps.

Being a professional alcoholic, I held the bottle for 12 gulps. They were counting over the mike one, two, three, four ....

I put the bottle down and I picked it back up and put one more big gulp in my mouth and piss-sprayed it everywhere.

Chuck yells, "Order me ten thousand in Gold Bucks right now!"

The Gold Bucks girl comes over, and asks, "Chuck, are you serious?"

"Get the fucking money!" That's the way he talks. When he tells you something he shouldn't have to say it twice. You go get it. You don't question him.

She comes back half an hour later with the ten thousand. Chuck handed me ten Gs, right there. I'm standing there with a stack of GBs a half a foot high because they used to be printed on cards. It wasn't until later they were printed on sheets of paper in ten dollar increments. I had them put it in the safe downstairs.

Chuck says, "I need five thousand more dollars!" He and Dennis are competing, throwing money over the rail.

They must have thrown at least $12,000 in Gold Bucks to the girls downstairs.

We had a lot of couples that used to come in to the Gold Club, too. Every night you'd find a few of them.

I had couples who were regulars. My favorites were Deanna and Blanton, and Skip and Mina. They liked the atmosphere. They could relax, drink and hang out, see beautyful women dance. They liked that atmosphere as opposed to a nightclub. You're left alone and not bombarded like in a squished up club where you're packed in and have to yell to talk to each other.

Skip and Mina first came in in 1998 and we got Gold Room 7. They came in during the day. Back then you could close the door in Gold Room 7 and wouldn't get in trouble. After a while they had to stop that because there was too much going on with the door closed. So we went in and ordered champagne. I think they were celebrating something that afternoon.

We got really drunk and were in the room from three until seven or eight. I was wearing this cute Austin Powers-type dress, short with psychedelic colors. She spilled champagne all over the front of her outfit so I gave her my dress to wear out of the club. She says, "Try on my outfit to see how it looks on you." She was wearing a short black skirt with matching top.

So I did, then took it off and sat naked the whole time. They were kissing on each other. Four hours later, everybody was drunk and they were all over each other. At one point, they forgot I was in the room with them. She straddled his lap and they were getting ready to have sex until she looked over at me. She looks at Skip and says, "We are still in the Gold Club." They gave me $1,200 in Gold Bucks.

We swapped phone numbers and kept in touch. They used to come in and we'd get Gold Room 6 if it was available. Me and Mina were kind of like two peas in a pod which leads me to believe she's bisexual, doesn't want Skip to know, but rather to just think she's bi-curious. We got into the habit of swapping clothes every time they came in. She loved dancer clothing and trying on my shoes. We would dance and she'd say, "I'm the stripper tonight."

Another couple that used to see me all the time was Batman and Robin from Alabama. They used to come in to see me every once in a while and we'd do coke together. I didn't really care for it but I would get high because I also smoked weed back then. I would always go back to their hotel room after work and they'd come see me at work because they wanted me to make some money. They drove all the way from

Alabama for my 30th birthday party. Recently I got a card from them saying they'd had their first baby. So nice of them.

Both couples loved a trick I used to do with my butt, which happens to be an ambidextrous butt. I could make my butt do like a roll, clap, bounce up and down, and move from side to side.

It's steady income, guys you can count on, that you know certain nights of the week they're coming to see you and each time it's the same amount of money. You want as many regulars as you can handle.

There were about four or five couples that made my regulars list. And then I had 40-50 guy regulars throughout the year, I saw an average of 10-20 a week. Some nights they'd bump heads and I'd entertain three at once.

There are two categories of regulars. There are the ones who think if they keep trying, they're going to take you out of the strip club and you'll be their wife and love you forever. Then there is the regular regular. This is a person who keeps coming to the same establishment and has invested their time and energy and trust in you. They don't want to develop that friendship with anybody else. They like you: who you are, what you stand for, how you look, how you come across. I catered to my regulars and tried to make them feel like, "You're all I want tonight. I don't want to talk to anybody else."

There's also a comfort level and some laziness involved. They get stuck in the grind. They've been coming to see the same girl for four months, so why switch? A regular is almost like dating somebody. You know what night of the week they're coming in, what time. You expect to see them, enjoy seeing them, not just for the money but you enjoy seeing that person. And you know you're going to make your money so you don't have to work that hard that night.

About 70% of the regulars were married. Since the girl-friend or wife is lacking somewhere, that's where I come in. Strip clubs are like therapists for men.

Over the four years I spent at the Gold Club, I developed roughly 200 relationships. You look at it like anything else: this could be my cousin, or good friend who's having these problems. That's how you don't let it consume you.

I had a customer die in 2001. His name was Steve and he was my regular for three years. He was very understanding. If I wasn't available Frederique or Angelique or others would dance for him for me. Otherwise he'd stand at the booth with Steve the DJ, and talk all night.

When you come into the stripping industry, at first it's exciting because you're in the limelight. You think, cool, I'm making money. I'm drinking. I can be sexy. It's like a fantasy land. It separates your regular life from this nightlife of eroticism.

From that point, there are only two routes to take. Be business-minded and make your money or you get caught up, as I mentioned before. The way you get caught up is with the drugs and drinking and losing yourself in stripping. Those are the only two roads you can take. You forget who the hell you are. You can't distinguish between being a dancer and dealing with outside life. You take your dancing home to your boy-friend or your husband and you start to treat other people in your life as if they were potential customers. That's how you get caught up and it's sad because it happens a lot.

It happened to me. When I first started making money at the Gold Club, I looked at my boyfriend and what I expected from him. This logic was: I'm sleeping with you and I'm being your girlfriend and you need to be taking care of me. It was a fucked-up way to look at things. A relationship is a partnership.

You get caught up you feel like everybody owes you something even if you're just sitting and talking with somebody. Say you got a regular customer, he's in town and he wants to take you out to dinner. He has to pay you to go to dinner. My customers could not take me out to dinner unless they were paying my babysitting fees and giving me at least five to six hundred dollars for my time.

I'd go out with customers outside of the club at least once a week. Sometimes two dinners in one evening. I'd meet one at five until about 7:30 and then say, "I gotta go to work," and go meet another one.

If they don't pay, you blow them off. Not surprisingly, it's a good way to lose friends. One night a customer of mine came into town and he wanted to go out to dinner and dancing. I was getting ready to say, "Well, it's going to cost you," and then I caught myself. Dinner for me to go out with a customer could cost him about $500 because I expect to go to Chop's, Bone's or Pricci's and I expect champagne and a really nice time which gets costly.

I gave customers my real name and home number as a rule so they could get in touch and let me know they were coming in town. I'd go out with them but I always took my own ride and met them. There are rules to that particular game.

You drive your own car. You always bring a credit card and extra cash with you because you never know what's going to happen. He could get pissed off in the middle of dinner and walk out. You always have to have a back-up plan. You never meet customers anyplace like a hotel or anyplace where you're alone. And if you are going to go to a hotel room, you take a friend with you so he can't try anything.

My boyfriend, Elliott, ironically, was the first person to say something about the change in my personality. He said, "You're making money and doing things and I'm tolerating customers who call our house. I'm putting up with all this shit but you have completely lost yourself and I can't deal with you anymore."

"You know what?" he continued. "I don't like what you've become. You can't distinguish between Diva and real life." He broke up with me and left.

At first, I got angry and couldn't understand. I thought, I'm a good woman. I make a lot of fucking money and I do a lot of good things for him. In fact, in some aspects, I felt used. I used to wire him money whenever he needed it. When he came home in the summertime every day we were doing something, going to the movies, miniature golfing, bowling— and I was paying for all that. At the time I didn't pay attention to it.

When we moved into our apartment together in 1998, we went to the furniture store and I paid for the loveseat and then he picked out the dining room set and I paid for it, too. Then, my dumbass turned around and handed him $500—my half for the dinette set.

I didn't even think about it I was so used to paying for myself and doing for myself that even with Elliott, I had to pay. Eventually, I had to acknowledge that he was taking advantage of it—my need to feel independent, that I take care of myself. It was his way of getting what he needed.

It was a stereotypical stripper technique for feeling in control. You might think a girl would look for someone in her outside life, a permanent sugar daddy. After a while she gets so independent because she's making so much money, the girl doesn't want anybody in her life like that. She wants somebody underneath her that she can take care of. If she had a man with oodles of money, she wouldn't have her independence.

Some nights I would make three or four thousand dollars and I would give him a thousand. "Here," I'd say like I was handing him a tip.

"What's this for?"

"Just because I made $4,000 tonight sitting on my ass getting fucked-up drunk."

Of course, he put it in his bank account. It didn't bother him that much. He left and then, like any player, he came back.

Whatever. I remained lost for about two years. People owed Diva. My time was money and that's the way I looked at it. Because in the Gold Club, your time is money. You don't have time to bullshit around. You've got bills.

It was maintenance, upkeep, the way to keep regulars, to go out with them which is not to say sleep with them. I'd keep them company for a little bit and it made them want to see me even more. It was almost like selling cars. I considered myself to be a Bentley but I had to sell that Bentley. Once it was sold, I had to do the upkeep, an oil change. Take it to the shop. That's how I looked at customers outside the Gold Club.

I wasn't doing anything new. Eighty percent of all strippers in America go out to eat with a customer. It's part of the business and it makes it hard to be in a relationship because your profession hangs over you like a dark shadow.

The worst words I endured along those lines were from Elliott during a fight. He said, "I don't know what I ever saw in you anyway. You're nothing but a stripping whore." It cut through me like a knife. I thought, I wasn't a stripping whore when I was giving you a thousand dollars. I wasn't a stripping whore when I was out buying clothes for you, taking you on trips but because we're fighting and you're upset, now I'm a whore.

On the flip side, to some guys stripping is the most erotic thing a woman could do. It turned Elliott on to know I was dancing sexy for some other guy. And he liked to have threesomes with me and another woman. On that front, Elliott contradicted himself. The fact was, he loved to watch me dance but was jealous at the same time. Once he left a voice mail message: "I've been trying to call you for two days! If you could get the dicks out of your mouth long enough maybe you could answer your phone!"

It made me mad. How could he throw it in my face like that?

So Elliott took the money, left and came back like any player. It was all about the game. And game recognizes game. If you play the game right, you come out okay.

A player is a guy that can have more than one woman at one time and reap the benefits from all of them.

Maybe every man fancies himself a player, wants to feel big and invincible. And there is no other ritual so male, so disgusting in my opinion, as the bachelor party. At the Gold Club, we had a whole routine for bachelor parties like they were birthdays.

When a bachelor party came in, they were greeted by the floorman and told about their options. For $150, a group got a bottle of champagne and the bachelor went up on the main stage to be totally humiliated by four to five dancers. That bought a Gold Club baseball cap and T-shirt.

The bachelor was set up on stage in a chair and they announced when he was getting married, his fiancée's name, then the DJ ripped him to shreds. For one hairy guy, the DJ said, "We heard about your fiancée! Her legs are as hairy as yours!"

The girls would come running down the stairs at the bachelor, taking their tops off. They'd take his shirt off, put the Gold Club T-shirt on him, tie it in a knot in the back, and then bunch up his shirt to look like he had boobies. They took off his belt and one would take a high heel shoe, poke a hole in the guy's underwear, rip the rubber off his underwear, and give him a serious wedgie. They tied his belt around his neck. Made him do push-ups. The music playing was "White Wedding" by Billy Idol. The DJ continued making jokes: Put some muscle into it, you weakling! They lined the groom's group up in front of the stage so they were hooting and hollering. It was entertainment and fifteen minutes of fame for the bachelor.

One night a guy named Todd pulled his pants down and didn't have any underwear on. His friends said, "Pull them up! Pull them up!" The DJ jabbed, "That is the smallest penis I've ever seen in my life." Todd got on the pole that went up the railing of the steps and tried to hump it.

These guys were typically so young and inebriated, they were grabby and obnoxious. One night I danced for a bachelor whose best man was sitting next to him. I leaned over and had my bottoms off, making my butt jiggle. The guy stuck his finger in my pussy. I was so pissed. I turned around and I clocked that guy so hard that people turned and looked. Arthur came over and kicked him out.

Nothing to do with bachelor parties, but everything to do with assholes, I sat with this guy who claimed to be the CEO of IBM. He was very attractive, salt and pepper hair, early forties with a wedding band on. Right off the bat he ordered me a bottle of champagne. He seemed nice at first. He wanted to get a Gold Room. I'm sitting there next to him and asked, "Do you want me to dance?" and he said, "I want you to sit there and shut your fucking mouth. I'm paying you $200 an hour to be in this room and you'll do what I say." He went through this whole spiel about how he hated women and how we were the root of all evil in the world. He said he wished that women had never been created and that he could kill every woman in America.

I tried to leave and he grabbed me by the arm and pushed

me back down in the seat. Okay, I thought, I got one for this fucker. I waited for the floorman because they pass by all the time to check on you. Big Arthur was a 6'5", 400-pound dark black guy. He came past the door, I said, "Arthur I need you right now in this room," and I told him what this guy was doing. This guy flipped the switch so quick. "I don't know what she's talking about. I asked her to dance and she started swearing at me." Arthur knew me better than that. He looked at the man and said, "You need to pay her right now." That was it.

When I walked downstairs, I saw Bliss on the main stage. She could take one leg and put it straight up in the air without wobbling and then put her hands on the floor. Guys used to love to watch her dance and I did, too, especially after spending twenty minutes with a potential mass murderer. Bliss was in the middle of her dancing pearls act. She was wiggling her hips and rotating the pearls all down her body, maneuvering her arms through them. She looked like Faye Dunaway, nearly six feet tall, with an hourglass figure and long dishwater blonde hair. She was making her butt bounce and the pearls went up and down. Then she took her arms and stuck them through the pearls so that they just hung on her nipples. Very artistic.

Jeff Johnson was bad as a floorman but when he became an assistant manager, he got worse. Jeff seemed to have lost his mind. He thought he was calling the shots in the club. Jeff was so busy trying to flirt with the new girls that he didn't pay enough attention to his job. I used to complain to Steve that half the time I'd find him in the back hallway with some girl trying to get her phone number. Anytime he wanted me reprimanded he'd get Norbie or somebody else to deal with me because he knew I'd cuss him out. I was Steve's girl.

One night, Jeff hit a floorman named Felix who was

black, tall, and had a soft, sweet demeanor, not violent at all. Felix had a daughter he took care of. Jeff hit him so hard he almost punched the eyeball out of the socket and put him in the hospital for a week. Steve tried to help by paying Felix's hospital bills to get him back on his feet financially. Felix's eyeball shrunk and the blood vessel around it turned permanently red.

Jeff would get fired and rehired like all the other fuck-ups in the club but then by the time he hit Felix, he got fired for good.

Chapter Ten

My mother's whole philosophy about life is: Fuck it. So what if I did it? It's over. No big deal. That's how she looks at life. Fuck it. If it's something you can't change, that's too bad. If you don't have the money to pay a bill, fuck it. They can hunt you down but you can't get blood from a turnip. That's my Mom. She's a great woman.

Maybe my childhood was just a litany of violent scenes. And maybe you wonder how anyone could live that way, how anyone could let such things happen. Is it true that people make their own environments? Or do environments, in some way, make their own people?

After Anna died Mom got a job in a nightclub downtown that her boyfriend owned. Me and Jimmy took care of our two little sisters—by now there was not only Marquita, but Mom had had Tina as well—the fruit of her relationship with Rock. During one of their make-ups Dad decided that Mom could have Tina and he'd adopt her as his own, give her his last name and all that. She was just a year younger than Marquita. Including the brothers and sisters who went up for adoption, there were nine of us spawned by my father and mother, along with a broad range of second string players: Rock, Jeannie, Sue Dagey, a lady named Edna, a third wife named Sandra. And those are just the ones I know about.

So until my Dad took us from our home at Linda's one night while Mom was at work, there was only Jimmy, me, Marquita and Tina. When he did come under the false pretenses of a "visit" and take us, our mother didn't fight it. She didn't have it in her anymore. She told my father she'd done all she could to raise us and now it was his turn. If he thought he'd make her miserable or start another fight by taking her kids, he was sadly mistaken. And then when we went to live with Jeannie, we got another step-sibling, Matthew. On my dad's third marriage with a lady named Sandra, there was Heather. To add to the confusion, Dad and Jeannie got together and had Juanita.

It's hard to believe but the truth is, my father didn't grow up in an abusive home. My grandmother, Ann Hardy, who we called Grandma Ann, and my father's stepfather, Ernest Hardy, raised their daughters to become school teachers and bank manager types and they raised their sons to become wife beaters, drug dealers and felons.

Both my Dad and my uncle were psychos. Both of them. And of course Grandma Ann couldn't see anything wrong with either of her sons. She protected them like they were saints.

Grandma Ann was the built-in babysitter. When one parent or the other parent runs off or there's a fight or someone goes to jail, there's Grandma Ann with open arms. She helped raise practically all the kids in the family. You got kids, you take them to Grandma Ann's.

It's still hard to know what happened to her sons. My uncle, for instance, is an interesting case, all on his own. He's a mess. He did nine years in prison for having his friend kidnap his wife. He wanted to talk to her but her family wouldn't let him. They were split up. So instead of taking the wife someplace to talk, his friends went into the house, raped her pregnant sister, tied up the family, and set the Christmas tree on fire. Nice way to start the holidays if you ask me.

My uncle comes out of prison like the outside world is a vacation and then immediately does something else to get back in: drug-dealing, not paying child support for the four children he fathered.

In contrast, there was my father's sister, Barbara Young, who worked at Miller Brewing Company for fifteen years. Her kids had the best of everything. Me and my brother were so jealous when we were growing up cause they had all the latest stuff and we would catch their hand-me-downs.

Even raised good like they were, Barbara's son, Clarence, got into crack and he was always strung out and hooked. He stole a car to get more and the cops caught him in an alley and shot him to death. They said he was reaching for a gun but he didn't have one—it was just a wallet. And Clarence was really a good kid—just a little on the damned side, I guess.

My mother always says that it was just me and Jimmy who were so badly effected by our childhood. Me in my abusive relationships, playing out my mother's role, and Jimmy in his, playing out my father's role.

Jimmy started smoking weed when he was thirteen. Maybe because he resented our father so much for taking us away from our Mom. The fact that my Dad beat all the women in his life—my brother did the same thing. When he finally got a girlfriend, Chrissy, they knocked out three kids together. But right in the beginning of that relationship he started beating on her. He managed to turn this wonderful, sweet, young, intelligent girl into this stark, raving, ghetto maniac. Every time she said something he didn't like, he hit her in the mouth—total control. Jimmy went to jail so many times I couldn't count them: traffic stuff, domestic violence. The last thing he was in for was taking Chrissy out to an abandoned field, beating the shit out of her and leaving her for dead. The mother of his children. He did three years in prison.

Even with that, I have to hand it to Jimmy. He is the only male in our family who's managed to change. Something happened in those three years, having his freedom snatched like that. Now he's a completely different man. The word that comes to mind is rehabilitated. He holds a good job, pays child support and is dating my best friend.

My teenage years? In short, I just wanted someone to notice me. I wanted to feel like someone knew I existed. I wanted a closeness with my parents that I just didn't have. It was always like something was missing.

I started high school at Divine Savior, an all-girl Catholic school. I was on the scholarship program for underprivileged kids on welfare. I got the idea of a private school from a friend of mine who lived two houses down. It was her uniform that hooked me. I used to get teased a lot though because I was poor and I couldn't take it. So, you talk about me I'm going to kick your ass. That's how you deal when you're from the ghetto.

While the Catholic girl school was short-lived, being on welfare wasn't, which was a good thing since I had a lot of extracurricular activities. Welfare paid for the free lunch program, all my school books and uniforms.

I switched to public school and worked on being the most popular girl in the hallways. I was homecoming queen all four years and prom queen my senior year. I wrestled, though I got kicked off the team because they said it was too much physical contact. I played football my freshman year. I was the first girl to play football. I was a cheerleader. I was in drama club. I was on human resources and student council. Considering my poor grades, I was very active.

My parents never came to see any of it.

In drama club we did Grease and West Side Story. I was in the show choir, too, which was great because we danced and sang. We put on a show when they redid the War Memorial. It was on the news and in the newspaper. I was constantly involved in something, thinking I could get my parents' attention, but they just didn't care. It was no big deal. Even my graduation ceremony was a wash. Nobody came.

Chapter Eleven

A girl who is fascinated by all the money, stars, glitter and glitz, and excitement is considered to be turned out by the industry, she will do just about anything to be involved. Usually, a woman like me takes a young girl like Amanda Pappas, who is 19 years old.

The young girl is old enough to have her own mind and she's going to do what she wants to do. But when a woman on my level takes her and shows her another side of life—somebody who's never been in a limousine—they're going to want to see more. I said it's no big deal. This is how I live life. I'm around millionaires and movie stars every day.

In the case of Amanda Pappas, she was not bisexual. She was normally with men but she was bi-curious. Knowing that in the back of my mind, I thought it's okay. This girl is bi-curious so go in and fuck the shit out of her and then she's sprung. Nobody has ever made her feel this way. It's very similar to what happens between a woman with a man.

If you have a man who is fucking you right, you will give him your car keys, your house keys and your bank book. You will give this man practically anything he wants because he is making you orgasm on a regular basis. It's the same thing woman to woman.

A lot of the times, girls who came to the club were subjected to things they had never seen before. The first time you see two women dancing, not touching each other, just a silhouette, just acting like a lesbian sex show—that is deep for a girl that hasn't been around it. When they see that, their minds become curious. And if they come to you and you see that curiosity and you are in that frame of mind of control, which I was, you take them and mold them to what you want them to be. That's how you turn somebody out. It's not peer pressure.

I wanted the girls I turned out to be strong women. Girls came to me whining and complaining that they couldn't make any money and that they didn't feel pretty. I took them and showed them how to put make-up on, the proper clothes to wear, how to walk, talk, act and carry themselves. That was the first step in selling them because I had just transformed them into a new person.

After that, the girls get a whole new attitude about themselves. Even outside the club. I'd see them outside the club and they would be acting differently, dressing differently and acting more grown up, more like a lady than a silly twenty-year-old girl.

The sexual part of it fell into play because they were in an atmosphere of women 10-11 hours a day and drinking. When people start drinking their sexual side has a tendency to come out. A girl is drinking and watching girls up on stage and they are dancing very sexy and she can't help it. The girl's mind starts to work.

After a while, when they get to my level, they're like me. It sounds cold, these girls get turned out, but then it gets to the point where you've seen one, you've seen them all. I couldn't shut it off. It becomes second nature to remold somebody into your own image.

I met Amanda Pappas at the Cobalt Lounge the Sunday after the Brooklyn USA Golf Tournament. She worked as a shooter girl selling shots. I was with Dale Davis. I saw her and thought she was pretty. I talked to her for a few minutes. Dale gave me enough money to buy her whole tray of drinks. She was feeding everybody the drinks. I had her sitting on my lap and I asked if she wanted to leave.

Amanda was only 19 at the time and she had never been around any stars before. I didn't know these things until later on that night when we were talking. I went to Brian Arlt, that night's manager, and said, "I just bought Amanda's tray of drinks; can she leave?"

He said, "Sure, go ahead."

Amanda got ready and we were leaving. Dale had the limousine parked out front. He said, "You guys get in the limo. I'm going to say goodbye to the guys."

We were getting in the limo and she said, "I've never been in a limousine before."

"Well, just enjoy and have a good time," I said. There was champagne in the car and Dale got in the car and we were all talking.

Amanda went down on Dale and me in the car, so I knew she was kind of loose right then and there. Either that or drunk as hell or star struck. Or all of the above.

I invited Amanda to come over to the Gold Club the next night.

It was the Skit of the Year contest, the Monday night of the Brooklyn USA Golf Tournament. I invited her up to the club to watch the show. She walked around with me and I introduced her to everybody. All night long, just to make her feel comfortable, I introduced her as my girlfriend.

She was fascinated by my life. "Oh my God, it's Dennis Rodman!" she squealed seeing Dennis. She was star struck.

I introduced them and he tried to reach for her dress but I slapped his hand and said, "No!"

"What?!"

"She doesn't dance here, that's what."

"Fine," I said. "You get a permit and you can work." I gave her a job. I hired her. The next day she said, "What does this mean for you and me?"

"I don't know. What do you want it to mean?"

"I would love to be your girlfriend."

I said, "We can date and see how it goes from there."

The second trip to Las Vegas came in September for the Adult Entertainment Awards. I was dating Lacy, a tall dark-haired girl, and a girl named Meagan.

Steve, Larry, and Ziggy left the day before we did. We got there the next night. On the flight out, the man next to us was the owner of the Men's Club in North Carolina. At the convention we met the club owner from Solid Gold and several others.

Me and the girls were getting fucked-up on the plane because I couldn't fly without drinking. I was just nervous. Next thing I knew we were sitting on these guys' laps and they were saying they wanted to take us out to dinner when we arrived.

There were a few prudish people on the flight who were complaining about us, wishing we would shut up. Meagan went nuts. "We're having a good time and we're on vacation, we're going to Vegas and all those who don't like it can kiss our asses!"

The stewardess just said, "I'm sorry I can't serve you any more. Besides I don't know what else you would want to drink because we are out of vodka on the plane now since you have emptied our vodka cabinet."

We weren't exactly sorry. We went, "Yeah!" We got off the plane, staggering to Steve and the crew who were waiting for us. Steve ran up and gave me a big hug. "You guys got drunk, didn't you?"

Everybody who had anything to do with adult entertainment was there: Playboy, all the production companies, lighting companies, club owners, dancers and everyone.

There's not really any crossover between stripping and porn though all the porn stars were there. Both strippers and porn girls make about the same amount. The majority of the girls in the porn industry are exhibitionists and nymphomaniacs. They simply enjoy having sex all the time with different people. I made it a point to ask the girls at the convention why they did what they did. The answers was always, "Because I love having sex and I like having unadulterated sex with different people. It's exciting."

The convention hosted all of the businesses that create and manufacture stripper clothing so we looked at what they had that was new and upcoming. We saw girls in little Daisy Dukes—shorts that ride up your butt—and bikini tops. They didn't play that at the Gold Club. It was very elegant. They had all these neon colors and spandex, cheesy clothes, too, like cowboy outfits and nurses' uniforms for character dancers. A lot of the exhibition space was taken up for feature dancers, the ones who travel nationwide and do big exclusive shows at major nightclubs.

At the awards, The Gold Club was acknowledged as The Club of the Year. They said if they could give an award for the club that grossed more than any club in the nation and the classiest club, it would have to be the Gold Club. Me, Dina, Meagan and Lacy went up to accept, dressed in the nines. The Gold Club grossed $20 million a year.

* * *

The next big event on the calendar was the Miss Gold Club contest. One of the girls had dropped out and there was an opening, so I told Steve I'd do it. The preparations for Miss Gold Club began in September in time for the show which was slated for November 18th, 1998. Rehearsal schedules were set up for the girls on the main stage. The contestants were working with the housemom to find their props.

The theme that year was "Studio 54." They constructed an elaborate disco setting with the roller-skating girls. It was the last Miss Gold Club competition that would be held.

I reigned as Miss Gold Club for the last three years the club was in business because there wasn't another show to pass it off to anybody else.

The Miss Gold Club competition was the biggest event of the year. It was on the Internet. People could go on line to *The Atlanta Journal-Constitution* to the Concerns section and find letters from people writing in, asking when Miss Gold Club was coming up. We would go out and promote it like nobody's business, handing out professional invitations with raised lettering and hand calligraphy.

We also sent the invitations to thousands of companies on our mailing list. We hand stuffed the envelopes in the dressing room. The promotion crew included everyone in the club: entertainers, dancers, bartenders, waitresses, floormen and managers. Two months in advance of the event, we blanketed the city—the Georgia Dome, hotels, and every address in Buckhead—inviting people to our big party. November became not only the month of Thanksgiving but also the elite black-tie Miss Gold Club competition where anybody who was anybody made an appearance, from Dennis Rodman to Ted Turner.

Not only did the girls compete but there was a pre-show. In front of the building the red carpet was rolled out and the spotlights criss-crossed the sky. It was the closest Buckhead, Georgia would ever come to a Hollywood affair.

The building was decorated with black and gold balloons—the Gold Club colors—ice sculptures and big trays of food. For the 1997 Miss Gold Cub competition there was an Olympic Swan that covered a six-foot long table. No expenses were held back. Ten thousand jumbo shrimp, meatballs, and a champagne fountain spouting all night long. The Gold Rooms were all booked in advance.

There were a few girls who worked that night to entertain the people in the rooms but for the most part, everybody was in evening gowns, looking their best. You would swear you were at the Oscars.

Leading up to Miss Gold Club, was a full dress rehearsal two days before. Each girl did her entire show, as it would appear the night of the event, for Steve. Steve looked at all the props, paints, explosions, and assessed how safe the show was. Eight girls performed for six to seven minutes.

The day before the show, a Sunday, the club was closed but thick with chaos. Everybody scrambling, last minute preparations, chairs being set up on the main floor. Every last piece of furniture in the club was moved out back behind the building and covered with plastic.

I came up with a Batman skit from the original movie Batman and paid almost $900 to have a real Batman costume made. My body had to be dipped in this rubberizes material to make the breastplate. There was a Batman symbol in the middle of the belt, thigh pads and cape. My girlfriend, Amanda Pappas, played Catwoman, and I had the Joker, along with a whole entourage of characters from the movie.

The idea was to re-create the birthday celebration scene from the movie. We came in on a giant cake, throwing money out to the crowd. I threw out $200 in $1 bills and the other three threw money and candy. The extra characters went on stage and did a choreographed dance before my grand entrance when the DJ says, "And where's Batman?" Explosions went off and I came through the crowd with my cape open, running up to the stage. We did the museum scene from the movie. I had Catwoman at a little table. The Joker comes out with his big long gun and he shoots at us and I throw my cape around her. Next, me and Catwoman take fluorescent paints: purple, orange, green and yellow, and paint each other like a lesbian show.

Tatiana did this white wedding theme. She started out with Prince's "Purple Rain" and then she went into Billy Idol's "White Wedding" and danced in this big champagne glass. She poured water on herself and the audience was spellbound. She had to have two guys on either side to make sure she didn't rock and fall out.

I took second place but got the crown at the end of the 1998 because the winner, Tyler, retired. The winner of Miss Gold Club received the crown, a trip to Vegas, a thousand dollars and a TV. Once a girl became Miss Gold Club she became the representative of the Gold Club and had to carry herself accordingly. I ate it up. When I was in the building I was acknowledged as Miss Gold Club rather than my stage name. If I went on the stage, which was very seldom in 1998, the DJ would announce me as, "Miss Gold Club Diva."

If I walked in the front door and came down the ramp that the DJ watches to keep up on who's who, he would say, "Miss Gold Club!" Miss Gold Club's picture goes in Creative Loafing, a local hip rag, and in Jezebel Magazine which appeals to the twenty-something crowd with money.

As Miss Gold Club, I had to go out promoting. We'd go to restaurants and I'd sit and talk with guys. They'd ask, "What do you do at the club?"

I was only too happy to answer. "I'm an entertainer. I'm

Miss Gold Club. The top girl in the club." It put me on a pedestal, above all the others.

The day of the event, I got to the club about four o'clock with my crew. All the backdrops and props were lined up in order of appearance in the back hall.

The guests started arriving. The red carpet is lined with red velvet roping draped over brass stands.

The night of Miss Gold Club 1998 the fire marshal shut us down early because there were too many people in the building. As the staff was trying to get everyone out of the building, Dale Davis showed up. Me and Amanda were getting ready to leave with him and his group when Ziggy comes flying out of the front door. "Get the fuck back in the building!" he ordered me.

I turned around and looked at him. "I'm leaving. Are you kidding me?"

"You heard what the fuck I said!" He was cussing me out in front of all these people and Dale was standing right there.

Dale was getting pissed off because he didn't want to get involved in a confrontation. Amanda ran back inside the building, me following. I went and got her, and said, "Hold on ... on second thought, fuck him!"

I went over to Steve and said, "Dale's outside. I'm leaving. I'm tired. I've been doing Miss Gold Club for two months. Now that it's over, I'm going out to party."

He said, "Go. Goodbye." I came back out front and Ziggy started in on me, yelling, cussing, and calling me a bitch. "If you get in that car, you're fired, you fucking whore! Why don't you go work at the Gentlemen's Club where you belong?!"

I pushed Amanda in the car. Dale's brother, KD, was driving.

I looked at Ziggy through the window and said, "Fuck you! I'm out."

He said, "You're fired!"

"We'll see about that tomorrow."

Our group went to Chili Peppers and then back to Dale's house. Amanda and his best friend had sex so I was pissed at her. Then me and Dale got into an argument because of the whole scene in front of the club. It was his contention that I should have avoided the scene and met him later.

The next day I called Steve and met him at the club. I complained, telling him the whole scenario. Steve made Ziggy apologize to me in front of the whole management staff. Ziggy liked having control over everybody and hated that he couldn't control me.

One day Norbie was sent to New Jersey to open up at a club called the Gold Mine. Ziggy was jealous of Norbie, because he had known Steve for 15 years. Norbie had worked for Steve his whole life. Ziggy and Norbie's relationship was horrible. Part of it may have been that Ziggy wanted to be "Steve Kaplan The Millionaire." Ziggy wanted to be Steve so bad.

Ziggy pulled me aside in the club parking lot and says, "Tell Steve how you have to tip Norbie out at night." It was almost as if Ziggy was wired and had a questionnaire to get me to give him information about Norbie.

"I don't have to tip Norbie out; and no, he doesn't come to me and ask for money. What kind of shit is that? Yes, I have customers I know that will tip Norbie and let him know that you run a great place here and have customers say thank you, but that's it."

Ziggy was trying to make Norbie look like this horrible person. He said, "Tell Steve how Norbie let you have sex in the Gold Rooms."

"I've never had sex in a Gold Room. What the fuck is wrong with you?" I couldn't figure it out. He was trying to get me to say "yes" to this in front of Steve so that Steve would react.

Steve stood there looking at me like, what the fuck? I think Ziggy had talked to him prior because Ziggy kept saying, "Tell him, Diva, tell him."

"Tell him what?! I'm not telling him nothing cause it's not true. What are you trying to do? You are so fucked up." I turned to Steve. "You need to bring Norbie back here right now to run the club." People were taking advantage of the fact that Norbie was gone. Norbie was the law in the club. When he was in town, shit ran right. Girls were being disciplined. When Norbie left, things went a little nuts and that club was out of control. All over a period of a few months.

Norbie was on punishment. That's why he was sent to open the Gold Mine, because New Jersey is fucking cold.

I repeated myself. "You need to bring Norbie back. This is fucking shit. Let's go for a walk."

I took Steve's arm and Ziggy went inside. "Ziggy is always saying bad things about Norbie. I don't like him, don't trust him and I think he's setting you up."

"He wouldn't do that!" Steve defended him.

"Steve, stop trusting people. Can't you see what's going on? This guy is brutally talking about Norbie. Yeah, Norbie is an ass sometimes and he yells and screams and he's got a bad temper but for the most part he's a good guy and he's like a brother to me."

No matter what I said, I couldn't get through to Steve about Ziggy.

We took a group of girls, some floormen, waitresses, and the housemom, Rose, and we went to NJ at the end of October for the grand opening of the Gold Mine which was our sister club.

We promoted our butts off twelve hours a day on the streets of New York, passing out invitations to the grand opening. We brought down our own dancers and waitresses to show the New Jersey girls how to run a club and make money. These girls didn't know what the hell they were doing.

We got to the hotel late at night. Amanda went with me. Everybody was up at seven o'clock and dressed and downstairs at the vans by eight o'clock. Steve knew the owner of a family diner and we all ate there every morning and then went to the club. Norbie was waiting for us, standing outside. The Gold Mine was in Hoboken, strategically set close to Giants Stadium.

I was so happy. "Norbie!" I yelled as I ran and wrapped my legs around him. "Norbie! I miss you!"

"I miss you too, Diva," he said.

I didn't waste any time. "You have to come with me. We need to go for a walk." So I told him what Ziggy did. That motherfucker. "You've never tried to bribe me. What the fuck is wrong with him?"

"Norbie, I don't trust this guy. I think he's up to something."

Me and Norbie decided to go to Steve. We told him our fears.

"Norbie, I trust you and Jackie and I know you're not going to lie and cover up something if you're scheming like this," he finally said.

"Thank you. It's good you believe in us because it's not true. What the fuck is up with Ziggy? You need to get rid of him."

Steve fired Ziggy a lot. Ziggy went down on his own. If he got pissed because Steve didn't take his side in a matter, he would leave for a few weeks or a couple months and come back. One time it was because a waitress complained that Ziggy said she had to sleep with him to get a job at the Gold Club. Steve suspended him for that so Ziggy went back to New York and did his basketball thing with Brooklyn USA, which he continued to do the entire time he was still working for Steve. There was a squabble between him and Norbie about running the club. Steve took Norbie's side in the matter. Ziggy was gone for another three months. Everybody was so happy. Steve announced it at the meeting. "Ziggy's out of here." A few months later Ziggy was back.

In any case, we had about 25 people who went out in New York and New Jersey and promoted and handed out invitations to the opening of the club. We were on Wall Street and at the World Trade Center, everywhere. We had groups in rented vans that went out in every area of town. We had walkie-talkies to keep in contact with each group to find out where they were so we didn't cross over territory.

The Gold Mine passes were printed like wedding invitations. We handed out tens of thousands of them.

We covered all of Manhattan, the Bronx and Brooklyn. Every night after we finished promoting, Steve planned a field trip to thank everybody. One field trip was to Chinatown to Steve's favorite Chinese restaurant. They all knew him well.

We went to the top of the Empire State Building and got a private tour when it was closed because Steve was a big businessman in New York. We went out one night to a club called the Tunnel and to the famous Scores strip club.

Me and Rose were in charge of teaching the New Jersey girls the skit concept. We decided we would take costumes and music from some of our skits. On opening night, we were going to do two skits. It wasn't the Las Vegas Revues because the Gold Mine was a lot smaller than the Gold Club, including the stage.

136

We did S&M, my favorite, and Country for which you wear a stars and stripes bikini, cowboy hat and boots. The place was jam-packed. It used to be a five-star restaurant so it still had chandeliers and a ballroom. When you walked in the front there was etched glass, mahogany and cherry wood. The main floor area had a fireplace.

In New Jersey, however, lesbian sex shows and oral sex were against the law. You do that shit and you're going to jail. Every state is different. In New Jersey, you can't have two girls dancing next to each other unless you are putting on a choreographed show. That was our loophole and where our skits fell in. We could do the skits but we had to be very careful how we presented them. Georgia is the only state in the country that allows nude dancing and alcohol in the same establishment. Too bad for New Jersey.

In the end, the Gold Mine didn't make it.

Michael Mitzen of Tallahassee, FL and his business partner Keith Rackly, came in in August of 1998. His bill came up to $6,500. At the time to pay the bill he pitched a bitch saying, "I don't owe this much!" He only wanted to pay $2,500. Mitzen and his buddy had a great time with us girls and decided after it was over he didn't want to pay the bill.

The bill wasn't outrageous for the Gold Club. Three or four of us girls were in a Gold Room for a couple hours and then the room itself was $250 an hour. Each girl was negotiated up front for an hourly rate of $400 per girl. We had champagne and food, the basic scenario. When he saw the bill Mitzen realized he had spent too much money.

Mitzen complained loudly to management. They resolved calmly and matter-of-factly, "I'm sorry, sir, but you've been thumbprinted, you signed a paper saying you understood the cost of each item. How all of a sudden do you think you owe this much? You think our services are free?"

Mitzen call our corporate offices in New York and they handled it by taking several thousand dollars off his bill.

There was nothing to do but work out some sort of agreement to get the money. The credit card company wouldn't stand for losing money so the Gold Club had to pay the balance.

That happened a couple of times a week. With thousands of guys coming through that building, somebody was bound to complain. They'd get too drunk and if they started to sober up before they left and realize how much they spent, they'd be like, "Oh shit!"

The majority would realize what they'd done the next day when they looked at their receipts. It was the same story over and over. "I didn't charge all that." Even when they were confronted with the truth the fact that we had fingerprints, a copy of their driver's license and credit card, that they'd signed five documents before they left including a sheet that said they agreed to pay a 20% surcharge to order Gold Bucks, including the charges for the Gold Room—these guys would still swear up and down they were being cheated in some way.

Even going into a Gold Room, the Gold Room VIP manager had a form for customers to sign saying which girls were coming into the room and that the customer was okay for them to be there including their hourly rate. The guy would have to sign it before anyone started drinking. Management was always very thorough with documentation in the event there was a question.

There was this one guy who ran up a tab of $15,000. He stayed too long and too late. He knew he was in trouble for spending the money right off the bat and he was late getting home. His wife was in the driveway when he got home, maybe that's one reason he disputed the bill.

She was standing there when her husband got out of the limousine, drunk as a skunk. There's a little plate that says Gold Club on the front and the wife is blazing.

If a customer was too drunk to drive, management either got the limo ready or called a taxi. If customers were too intoxicated they wouldn't put them in cabs because they didn't trust the fact a customer was out there by himself after leaving our establishment. The cab driver could rob a customer and then it would become the fault of the Gold Club. There were also a couple companies the Gold Club used to drive our patrons home and make a little money. They would pay Steve a certain amount a week to be able to drive our customers home because they would make tips off the guys.

Steve Kaplan had no idea what he was getting into when he bought the Gold Club in 1995. He grew up in Brooklyn and struggled and worked hard. He started out with a shoeshine shop and built an empire from there. He opened club after club, like Club Boca in Florida. He had a roller-skating rink. Now he owns practically every store in Penn Station: drug stores, a Smoothie King, Ranch One Chicken, Rose's One Pizza.

It was his brother Ronnie's idea to buy the Gold Club. He came down to Georgia and met the Kirkendolls who wanted to sell it. The Kirkendolls also went up to New York to look at Steve's businesses. Ronnie thought it was a good idea. When Steve came down to Atlanta, he didn't even know where it was. He thought it was on the West Coast. When they showed him on the map, he thought he was in California.

They showed him the club and he said, "No. I don't know anything about running strip clubs." Next, Ziggy came down and they decided it was easy. You got a bunch of girls that pay you money to dance in your club and you're making money on it. That's what he thought . He was blind-sided.

There's a lot more to strip clubs than meets the eye. It was a business that had to be built and it took a couple of years before Steve was able to get the Gold Club running in such a way as to maximize profit. It took a lot of people brainstorming together to find ways to make it work.

It came to be known as "The Formula." The first ingredient was promotion.

In New York and Florida, Steve reasoned, when you want somebody to come into your establishment, you hand out complimentary passes. That was the concept he brought with him down to Georgia that brought people in.

The next ingredient in "The Formula" was stepping up customer service. He hired more bouncers, who he called floormen, and more waitresses. It was Steve Kaplan's intent to provide constant service to the customers.

And more girls. Unlike John Kirkendoll, Steve didn't look at race or beauty or size. If a girl was nice, he hired her. John Kirkendoll didn't want black women in his club—just blonde, big-boobed, drop-dead gorgeous women.

Not Steve Kaplan. He said, "Any color girl can work in my club." He started firing people hired under John Kirkendoll and got his own staff. He brought in his own philosophies about how a business should be run and it worked for him. He started from not knowing his ass from a hole in the ground in the strip industry to running a multimillion dollar enterprise.

Steve made an agreement with the Kirkendolls to buy the club in 1995. Everything seemed to be going smoothly in the transaction when Steve got a call from his brother, saying, "They won't let me in the Gold Club."

"What do you mean?"

"They won't let me in."

Steve came down and was greeted by armed guards who not only would not let his brother across the threshold but wouldn't let Steve enter the building either. Steve busted through and demanded to know what the fuck was going on. Then he got a lawyer and they went to federal court.

It turned out that the armed guards belonged to the Kirkendolls. They decided they were unhappy with the deal, they didn't want to sell and tried to take it by force. Steve hired a lawyer, called the police, and went to court. When the judge heard the story he said, no way. You guys already started this. It's done. In the meantime the Federal government took over and had former FBI guys run it until Steve was finished with court, about a month or so. The judge at the Russell Federal Building granted Steve the club and made the Kirkendolls get out. Steve ended up giving them a nice pay off.

Through the course of the dispute, Steve was very upset. His attitude was: Do these people think they're going to bully me out of my own club with guns and guys? I'm not afraid of that. Steve worked within the system.

With Steve Kaplan at the helm, the image of the Gold Club evolved into what it was when it closed. Not just dumb blondes for insurance salesmen but a place of glamour and high style. A place where men could enjoy royal treatment.

Chapter Twelve

Through my teenage years living with my Dad, some of the old stuff still went on. Dad still beat Jeannie and went out on her like he did my mother. We were still poor as dirt. Jeannie anesthetized on wine and gin, uppers and downers, just like my mother. But, to be fair, there was some stability from Jeannie's family. They acted like what I imagine to be a real family—big celebrations on the holidays—no fighting—and so even though me and Jimmy missed our Mom, in a way, we adjusted.

I took out a lot of those frustrations, like missing Mom, on Jeannie and was a real bitch, the classic case of the evil stepdaughter. That first year of high school, I beat her up. The fight started because I had just had surgery on my nose and was really sick and she slapped me because I used a cup for my chili. All of the bowls were dirty and I was too tired and dizzy to wash one out. I just whaled on her.

I threw her down a flight of steps. I jumped on her. Just whaled on her. To this day I feel horrible for doing it, but at the time I was like, you have lost your mind hitting me. My grandmother came downstairs, it took her, my brother and both my sisters to pull me off of Jeannie.

When I was sixteen, I was dating Joe and got pregnant. The only person I could go to was my Mom. I told her and Mom said, "Don't worry. I'm going to help you."

We snuck into a clinic and I had an abortion. My father found out because he found the birth control pills and was mad as hell. Joe dumped me right after the abortion and started sleeping with my best friend. I couldn't handle any of it, the loss and betrayal, and so I tried to kill myself. One Sunday morning when I was supposed to be up getting ready for church, I emptied the medicine cabinet. Just like my Mom, my stepmom had her doses of downers or uppers every day because she had to take her mind off my Dad driving her crazy. I took over 475 pills and then got on the phone calling everyone, saying my good-byes. It was my little sister, Wanita, who found me.

In the hospital, while I'm lying in intensive care, my Dad is screaming, "Why did you do this stupid shit?! What are you, fucking crazy?!"

I was in the child/adolescent treatment center for thirty days because I didn't want to go home. When I got out, I went back to school. Word had gotten around that I tried to kill myself and it was really hard to deal with because everyone was taking shots at me.

With no boyfriend, I started babysitting for my stepmom's sister, Becky, who was paying me really well. I had always babysat around the neighborhood to buy the clothes I wanted to keep up with my friends, but Becky paid me so much that every time I'd come home, my Dad would take my babysitting money.

It got so frustrating that I didn't want to go babysit because I knew he was gonna take my money. The last time I babysat it was for a weekend and Becky gave me $100 to watch three kids. I told her on the way home, "Becky, Dad's going to take my money when I get home." I started crying.

"As hard as you work, he takes your money like that? That's terrible," she said.

So we made an agreement in the car that I would say I accidentally left my money at her house and I would get it the next weekend when I went to babysit.

My Dad called her and asked her and she said I was telling the truth. Well, that whole lying thing kicked her up in her ass and she called back and said it wasn't true, that I had the money.

My Dad beat the shit out of me. Physically punched me. My nose was bruised. I had a black eye. He grabbed me by my throat and slammed me up against the wall, yelling, "Give me the money!"

"I'm not going to give you anything!" I yelled back through the tightness in my throat. "Fuck you! You're nothing but a drunk and I hate you!"

He just kept beating the crap out of me until my sisters were screaming and crying so much that he jumped off me.

Chapter Thirteen

Towards the end of 1998, I started noticing people in the rearview mirror, over my shoulder, and I felt like I was being followed. In 1999, when we got raided, I knew I wasn't crazy. I started recognizing the FBI agents. I didn't care too much and went on with my life. I was having a good time. I wasn't doing anything wrong. So I copped an attitude: Fuck all of them. You can watch me all day long.

Nine days before Christmas a courier carrying a gun showed up at my door. I signed for the package and opened it up. The note said: Merry Christmas! Hope all your days will be bright. I won't be back to Atlanta for a long time but I hope the kids have a wonderful Christmas. John. Then there was something else written at the bottom. P.S. Thank you for sending my husband home and saving my marriage. The note was signed by John's wife.

The gift was a seven-carat emerald-cut diamond ring that appraised for $52,000.

I never met John's wife. He was just a regular who came in every couple of months. John used to come in and see me, tipping $3,000 like clockwork. I never had to take my clothes off. He liked for me to dress as if we were going out to dinner, not in my work clothes. I would wear a cocktail dress or suit if he let me know he was coming to town. We would go upstairs to Gold Room 6. The last night he came, he gave me an extra

$3,500 for my kids, a thousand for each and $500 for me, and told me to be expecting something in the mail.

In Gold Room 6 John poured out his troubles. "I travel so much and my wife gets so irritated. By the time I get home there's so much to do that I've missed out on that I'm constantly busy. My wife's so mad at me, I think she's having an affair."

I told him, "The next time you go home, why don't you just surprise her? Take the week off. You own the corporation. Leave everybody at work to do the work for you. Take your wife and go someplace quiet." He did. The last time I talked to John, I found out his wife picked the ring out for me. Her Christmas present was a little bigger: a 12-carat diamond ring with matching necklace costing $425,000.

Another Christmas customer who came in two weeks before Christmas day was this guy who came from England but it might as well have been out of nowhere. He had a long, horsy face and was in his late 40s with an upper-class accent and an extended vocabulary. The things he said, the way he said them. He had a very distinct smile. It was like a ray of light.

Me and my friend Sundae were working and something told me to go over and talk to him.

The guy tells us he likes dancers but he doesn't want us to take our clothes off. He didn't think it was necessary. "Dance with your clothes on," he said. "It leaves something to the imagination."

After we talked a while, we decided to go up and get a room. He was in town for three days. The first night he gave us $2,000 apiece. The second night he came in he told us to dress nice in regular clothing. He gave us $3,000 apiece. The last night I surprised him. I got him a dozen roses and a card to say thank you.

That last night he gave us each $5,000. He asked if I believed in guardian angels. I looked at him, "Of course I do. Why, are you mine?"

He just smiled at me and then started crying and leaned his head on my shoulder. "Oh, Jackie, you've had so much sorrow in your life and I've tried to be there and I hope this helps you."

It freaked me out. "Huh? You are my guardian angel, aren't you?"

Sundae walked back in the room and he sat up and cleared his head and started smiling again. He said, "You've always been that caring person," as if he knew me all my life. I asked him for his phone number and he said no. I asked for his last name and again, he said no. All he told me was his name was Ian.

Before I could utter out of my mouth, he knew how many kids I had. "How are your three daughters?"

"How'd you know I have three daughters?"

"I can just tell."

Every time he came in, this weird sensation came over me. The Gold Bucks girl was trying to pressure us to order a tip for ourselves from him but something told me no. "He's already given us ten thousand apiece. Don't you think that's enough?" I asked the other girl.

Ian overheard our conversation. When I came and sat back down with him, he said, "That's a very smart move on your part."

"What is?"

"What you and that girl were just talking about. You know when enough is enough, don't you? You're finally learning your lesson?" He was talking to me as if he was trying to tell me, All right, you've done enough in this industry and it's time to stop. "I hope you take this money and do something with it," he finished.

I guess it was the stripper equivalent of fruit baskets. I'd get packages at work, and cards with money. One guy named Ralph from San Diego called when he got home and asked what sizes my kids wore. I thought he was trying to figure how tall they were next to me. He bought them four outfits apiece and a huge box of Barbie dolls.

Then there was Steve who always did for my girls like for his own grandkids.

As a result, their Christmases are ridiculous. In 2000, I spent $5,000 in addition to all of the other gifts that kept pouring in. Every year something new comes out—digital robot doggies or Dancing Debbie. Airplane Barbie. So much crap every year.

Michael Jordan came in and was taken straight upstairs to Gold Room 7. The floormen were standing outside, guarding the room, in addition to the fact that he had his own personal security—two big black bodyguards in black T-shirts with black military style pants and boots. The VIP managers went to hand-select two girls and the girls went in the room. Michael had a couple little friends with him and got a few girls for them, as well. Michael's main girl was Yvette.

She was happy to volunteer. What went on in their Gold Room—Michael was feeling on her chest and she was sitting on his lap and they were kissing. It was really dark in a Gold Room so if other people were doing stuff, unless you were right up on them, you never knew.

Yvette wound up going back to Michael's hotel room that night. He paid her $5000. She told me that they slept together but wouldn't go into the details. I could just imagine.

I know Michael a little bit. When Michael gets drunk, he gets very cocky and arrogant. He thinks he can have any woman he wants. That's how he is. During the Super Bowl, when it was in Atlanta, he had a private party in the White Room of the Cobalt Lounge, which was managed by BA and

Boyd, the Gold Club's head promoters. That meant, I was VIP, A-list Atlanta wherever I went.

In any case, I walked in the Cobalt Lounge and I was standing at the bar right next to Michael. I didn't say anything to him because I could tell he was drunk.

He thumped me on the shoulder. "You don't speak to people now, huh?" he slurred.

"What's up, sweetheart?" I gave him a hug and said, "You are fucked up, I know." Before I knew it, he unzipped my pants and put his hand inside, reaching for my crotch. I yanked his hand out, "What the hell are you doing?"

"Girl, relax!"

"Michael, this is me. You are not going to disrespect me up in this bar."

"You're right. You're right ... let me get a hold of myself."

Then he just started randomly walking around the club grabbing asses, tits. I told his bodyguard, "You better get him out of here. He is a lawsuit waiting to happen."

Michael looked at me, like he was just out of control. So his bodyguard said, "Mike, it's time to go."

He got ready to leave and he turns around and says, "Well, I guess all you fucking football players can have the chicks now cause I'm leaving."

Needless to say, Michael Jordan is a married man. They all are. That doesn't stop the show. Eighty percent of athlete's wives, businessmen, musicians, actors, dignitaries, senators, their husbands cheat.

In addition to the Sluts and the Vultures, there was a whole other breed of dancer we called the 69 Girls. The name didn't come from the sex position but from the fact that these girls are athlete groupies and are only looking for guys 6'9"and over.

Like Larry Johnson of the New York Knicks. We were in a Gold Room one night and there was this girl named JC who let him finger her and whatnot.

That same night we were talking about how he got this little white girl pregnant and his wife found out and she was threatening to leave him. That's why he was having such a hard time in the season of '98. I was yelling at him, "Larry, you should have used your fucking head! If you're going to cheat, cheat the right way and use a fucking condom!"

He excused himself. "It broke."

"Your fault."

The 69 girls are after ball players and these girls are good. They know how to pull a condom off while they are having sex and he never knows the thing is gone. Just so they can try and get pregnant, just so they can get money. For some girls it's a way of life.

In January, 1999 we started getting ready to go to Miami for the Super Bowl. Steve says, "Depending on whether the Falcons go, we're going to the Super Bowl."

The Falcons won, so the party was on. Steve and I got together and took thirty people to Miami. Dancers, floormen, managers, and a couple of good customers. We took Lou Saab, the car dealership owner. I knew Dennis Rodman was supposed to be there and we were going to hook up.

The first night we got there we checked into the hotel and everybody settled in. We got up the next day and hung out by the pool with Steve. At night he drove back up to Boca Raton to be with his wife and kids.

The rest of us used our nights to indulge in partying. The first night we all got together and went to an Italian restaurant and Dennis met us. First words out of his mouth were, "Where's Diva?" Steve and Ziggy were standing in front of me and they stepped aside and there I was. "That's my girl. Clear a path! Let my girl through!"

Dennis pulled me in like I was Cinderella, hugging and kissing me. The papparazzi were outside the window clicking. They had their video camera going, filming the week Dennis Rodman was in Miami for the Super Bowl.

One of the girls got up on the table in the restaurant and went topless. The manager says, "She's got to put her top on!"

The topless girl wobbled the table and all of the glasses fell and broke. So as not to offend the diners, we finished dinner, got in the limousines and went to the Solid Gold Strip Club.

Dennis ordered $2,000 in their funny money and gave me and Frederique each $1,000 for dances or whatever. Instead of ordering drinks he orders bottles of alcohol and you serve yourself. He likes it that way, it's easier.

Steve and I were talking. I met this girl who was so beautiful. I had her dance for me and she sat down and draped her legs across my lap. I gave her $400 and said, "Stay here."

A little later Dennis decided he wanted me and the housemom Rose up on the stage at Solid Gold. He goes to the manager and says, "Clear the stage. I want these two up there."

Me and Rose were pretty drunk so she was game. Rose is a flashy woman anyway. To be her age, close to fifty, she's in pretty good shape. She has big hips and a short waist. She wore stiletto heels and tight leather pants, a child at heart.

We got up on the stage and she pulled her top off and then she takes my top off and we were dancing and the crowd went nuts, along with Dennis and Steve who were cheering.

Steve says, "Can you believe this guy? He had them clear the stage! I want power like that."

"Steve, you don't want what he has," I said, shaking my finger.

"You're right, I'm too quiet for that," he conceded.

Dennis was ready to go because he was hosting a party at Club Liquid. We get there and I've never been so bombarded in my life. I had girls' panties hitting me in my face. Girls were throwing them at Dennis! With room keys attached. Girls were coming up to me, touching my arm, "You're with Dennis!"

Dennis was holding me, pushing me through the crowd into the club, just to get in and away from the people. We go to the VIP area. I got up and started dancing to the music. Cher was playing in the next room and I got to meet her. She was a phenomenal lady.

We were sitting there holding hands when Jennifer Lopez walks past and is standing by me. Someone introduced us. I said politely, "How do you do? Nice to meet you, Jennifer."

She looked down at me and then spoke to the girl with her, "Who is that and why is she holding Dennis's hand?"

Carmen Electra was on her way into the club, his wife at the time. She walked up and stood between his legs. He was still holding my hand on his lap. She said, "Who is this?"

Dennis was cool. "Carmen, this is Diva. Diva, this is Carmen. Carmen, this is the girl I was telling you about from Atlanta."

"Oh hi, nice to meet you," she started, kind of cocky. "Why are you holding her hand like that?"

Dennis put a stop to that line of questioning. "Shut the fuck up," he said simply.

So we started drinking and when Dennis wants you to drink what he wants you to drink, you're going to drink it or you're going to wear it. He was doing shots of Jaeger. I hate Jaegermeister. He was adamant that this was his bottle and this was my bottle. I drank the whole thing. He drank about three that night.

We left Club Liquid with Carmen but when we got outside, me and Carmen and her brother James got separated from Dennis because the crowd was pushing to get to Dennis and pushed us back at the same time.

Dennis yelled, "Meet me at the Living Room!" Then the people started running after me and Carmen. We were hauling ass on seven-inch heels. We kicked off our shoes and James put Carmen on his back because she's so tiny.

Finally, we got to the Living Room, got inside, and me and Carmen were chitchatting. Dennis walked over and took Carmen to talk to her in private. I could tell they were arguing. And then I heard him loudly say, "Get the fuck out of the club. Take your things and get the fuck out. Go. I don't want to be with you tonight."

Carmen Electra used to be a dancer a long time ago. Then she got her job with MTV. When she was about to lose her job with MTV the publicity came out about her and Dennis getting married and that saved her. Later they divorced but at the time, Dennis told me he was really upset because she was doing a lot of Ecstasy.

In any case, at the Living Room, Carmen and her friend left. I walked over to Dennis and he put his arms around me and kissed me on the cheek. "Why did you make her leave?"

"I don't feel like dealing with that shit tonight. She is jealous and I'm not up for that. I want to have some fucking fun."

"All right," I shrugged. "I ain't complaining."

We left the Living Room and went over to Bash where we ran into some friends from the Gold Club on the trip. I ran into Tyson Beckford and as we were standing there talking, he was looking Heather over. Heather was easy. She fucked so many people she would wake up next to people not knowing their names or where they came from.

Tyson Beckford asked me, point blank, "What's up with her?"

"Oh, you can hit that tonight," I said matter-of-factly.

"Seriously?"

"Yeah, you could fuck her easy."

"All right, introduce me."

So I introduced them and of course she went back to his hotel and fucked him.

Me and Dennis, some drag queen, and a girl from New York that he had dated previously, went to a condo, Eric Clapton's place, that Dennis was renting for the week.

Early the next morning, I got a cab and went over to the hotel where I took a hot bath and got ready for the day. Me and a couple of the girls went shopping, wandering around.

That evening, I met back up with Dennis and hung out with him and his crowd all night. We got a stretch Benz limousine and the Gold Club limo was with us, too.

The cast was me, Dennis, Ziggy, Lacy, Frederique, Bridget the waitress and the talkative ex-girlfriend from New York.

We're riding out on the town for the night, and Frederique and Lacy got on the floor and started doing a lesbian show in front of Rodman. This smell came through the car when they got naked and started getting it on. Dennis rolled down the window, and demanded to know, "Who the fuck smells like that! Somebody's got some rotten ass pussy up in this car! Oh my god, this is nasty."

He grabbed both of them between the legs and smelled them. It was Frederique. "Your fucking pussy stinks! Put on your fucking clothes and don't you ever take them off in front of me again!"

There was dead silence in the car. Dennis said, "You know, Diva, when we leave Velvet, I don't want her with us. She ain't getting in this car." He stopped the car, and said, "Frederique, get out of my car."

He put her out and she got into the Gold Club limo.

She was so embarrassed that I think she was happy to get out of the car. Later we wound up losing everybody from the Gold Club. It was just me, Carmen's brother James, Rodman's sister Debra, and Floyd, his flunky.

We're riding around and Dennis got hungry so we stopped at a pizza joint. When we stepped out of the car there were four guys standing there. I was the first out of the car. Those four guys grabbed me and tried to pull me away. Debra is almost his height. I screamed and she turned around and snatched two of the hoods.

She said, "I dare either one of you to step up. Please, so I can beat the shit out of you." She put her arm around me and walked me into the pizza place. She told Dennis what happened and he said, "Fuck that. From now on you get out ahead of me and I'm getting out right behind you."

We got our pizza and got back in. I sighed and he asked, "Are you all right?"

"I'm just overwhelmed. I didn't realize how hectic your life really is when you're out and about. It gets on my nerves."

"I get tired of being chased, too," he agreed. He paused a moment in thought before adding. "But isn't this fun, to know that people are yelling for you?"

At that point, actually, Dennis and Madonna were all over the tabloids. I asked him, "How was it?"

He said, "She's incredible."

He was saying how Madonna made an impact on his life. She taught him to be him. Be who you are, stop trying to hide and be something that you're not. She brought out a lot of who he is today and he owes that to her.

That night we ditched the limo and decided to walk through town, back to the condo to the beach out-front.

The sound of the ocean, the moon in the sky. We looked at each other as if we could read each other's minds. Without saying a word, me and Dennis stripped butt naked and jumped in the water. We saw the papparazzi coming up the beach and we quickly got out and ran for the building. Trying to wrap towels around ourselves, we finally made it inside, got on the elevator and Dennis said, "I can just see the headlines: Dennis and a Strange Woman Skinny Dipping—Where's Carmen?"

The next day Rose and I went down to the beach for a swim. After a while, I left Rose in the water swimming, and ran back up to the pool bar to get more drinks. By the time I came back, Rose is out in the water crying, diving under the water. I said, "What in the hell are you doing?"

She was hit in the face by a wave which knocked her false teeth out into the water. So we were all out there trying to find Rose's teeth.

She got back upstairs to the room and called her husband to look for her extra set of teeth but he couldn't find them so she was toothless. The same night we went to Solid Gold and word got back to Steve and Ziggy that Rose had lost her teeth in the water.

Steve came up and said, "Smile for me, Rose." She said, "No." She was upset and crying. Our friend Mike brought her a bottle of vodka that she was drinking straight out of the bottle. Finally, I sat down with her and said, "Rose, you know what? Shit happens. Just hold your lips together tonight and try not to laugh out loud." We sat there for a minute and she calmed down and could see the humor in it. She started to loosen up and she got clean that night.

Rose looked like a million bucks walking out of the hotel room. You'd never know she was missing her front teeth. We all got piled up in the limousine and went to dinner at Ruth's Chris Steakhouse in Fort Lauderdale.

There's about 25 of us. Steve says, "Everybody order the oysters tonight. You might find Rose's teeth! Actually, everybody order the seafood because we might find Rose's teeth."

The waitress came and we asked what was the catch of the day. Rose was sitting in the corner laughing. Ziggy called the Gold Club and told the DJ to announce over the PA system that Rose had lost her teeth in the ocean. We were sitting next to the cell phone and could hear the DJ saying, "Attention! Attention! I have an announcement to make! You know the group is down there for the Super Bowl, and Rose the housemom has lost her teeth in the ocean. They got a search party out there. The Coast Guard is out there trying to find Rose's teeth. They're at Ruth's Chris right now. They ordered the catch of the day to see if they can find Rose's teeth!"

Later on that night we met up with Dennis and we were getting ready to go out and party for the night. Steve told Dennis about Rose's teeth. Dennis says, "Smile for me, Rose."

She smiles and her teeth are missing and he says, "Baby, you are still beautiful and look at that body." He made her feel good. He said, "You don't need teeth. And besides, they get in the way sometimes, don't they?"

Rose looked at him and fell out laughing. After that, she was drinking and smiling. She didn't care any more.

By six in the morning, with Dennis passed out, I wasn't feeling good. I had caught pneumonia from jumping in the ocean. It was finally the day of the Super Bowl and I had to fly back to Atlanta. I got home, went to the doctor and got medication. I was pissed I had to give up my seat at the Super Bowl. Watching it on TV was just not the same.

Everybody came back from Super Bowl.

There was a guy named Greg Herring who had been coming in the club for a short time and spending a ton of money. They started catering to this guy. Jeff Johnson was his personal assistant. One night Greg came in, got there at five and stayed all night. Jeff Johnson had this group of girls, Jaycee, Joyce, the Gold Bucks girl Paula, Passion, and Frederique. All of these girls were having oral sex and sex with this guy right in the Gold Room. Greg Herring's visits went on for two weeks, three to four nights a week. He dropped 30-40-50 thousand every night he was in.

One night Greg Herring was in there and we were closed. I was talking to Mitchell Lafleur, a friend of Steve's and owner of Prestige Limousine in Atlanta. He used to come in and buy champagne and dances and spend pretty good money. Next thing I know, Greg pops a bottle of champagne and squirts it into my face, my eyes were stinging. He poured it all over my $300 dress and ruined it.

I jumped up and started cussing at him and Greg Herring pushed me. Jeff Johnson ran and picked me up by my waist, snatched me out of the Viper Lounge, and took me out into the back hall. Jeff punched me in my leg and tried to knock me down the back steps.

I tripped a couple of steps but I grabbed the rail and saved myself.

"You don't fucking talk to him like that. He was playing with you!" he yelled. He was protecting Greg Herring. I just looked at him, "Fuck you! You're in big trouble. You don't put your fucking hands on me!" I went downstairs to call the police but Norbie wouldn't let me.

Norbie said, "No, let Steve handle it."

I took it to Steve who suspended Jeff Johnson temporarily but he was allowed to come back to work because Greg Herring was spending so much money. Norbie took up for Jeff, "Let him come back to work. He'll stay away."

I said, "I don't believe this shit." I was pissed.

A couple nights later, Greg Herring showed up at the front door of the club and paged Norbie and Jeff outside. He did not want to come in the club, he said, because he didn't want to hang out with me around. Norbie told Greg Herring I wouldn't bother the big baby and he was happy and came inside. They kissed his ass as usual and played some of his music.

On Greg Herring's birthday he took Norbie, a bunch of dancers and Paula the Gold Bucks girl, out to dinner. Then they all came back to Gold Club to celebrate. Greg ordered the big triple jereboams of champagne. That night he called every employee in the Gold Club to the front stage to get a glass of champagne out of that bottle to celebrate his birthday. He especially called me to the stage. He wanted Diva on stage.

Naturally, I didn't want to go up there although I did. Greg was being magnanimous, "Can't we squash this? Can't we be friends? I would love for you to celebrate with me."

I thought maybe he was so drunk he didn't mean it but I agreed anyway.

He said "I want you to go up to Gold Room 7."

So I went up there and was waiting for everyone when Jeff Johnson came in the room and sat down next to me. I scooted over, ignoring him. He says, "Diva, I'm really sorry for what happened the other night. I didn't mean to do that. I was drunk too. I was drinking shots of tequila."

I said, "Whatever, I gotta work with you ..." and it was like his cue to grab my hair and push my face down in his lap. He had his dick out. He had already raped one of the waitresses and was pending going to court on that. I had heard he had raped some other girl in the club one night. He was disgusting, a nasty, lying piece of shit. He slammed me face down in his lap and I started screaming and ran into the back hall and was sitting on the steps shaking and crying.

This time when I went to call the police, I was able to go through with it.

Norbie caught wind of it and took me into the office. They called the police back and said it was a false call.

"What did you call the police up here for?" Norbie wanted to know.

"Jeff shoved my face in his lap and his dick was out. He's disgusting and I'm freaked out and that's why. I want him arrested."

"Diva, we don't need this type of stuff going on. We don't need the police here right now."

Rumors had been going around the Feds had been in and we might be under investigation. "We don't need that right now," he repeated.

Little did his dumb ass know, but Jeff Johnson was working with the FBI. Not only did he not let me call the police but Jeff Johnson got away with that. When he testified against the Gold Club, the Feds dropped his rape charge.

Jeff Johnson allowed the girls to do whatever Herring wanted them to do. If it was sex, it was okay. He was even having sex with girls at work because Greg Herring was paying these girls a lot of money. At one point he had given Frederique $8,000 and Joyce $8,000. That night they had a problem with his charge card and these girls couldn't tip out. They went through this process where Steve fronted him the money until he could clear his accounts, switch money from one to another. His wife died and left him a nice nest egg. He was out blowing money because he was very depressed about losing his wife and wasn't himself.

Chapter Fourteen

At sixteen and half years of age, I moved out from Dad and back in with my Mom. Thank God. I was so happy I was old enough that I didn't have to go back. The only thing that worried me was that I was leaving my sisters in that hell.

I got my first job making pizzas up the street from my Mom's place and we split the rent. I was Little Miss Independent. I was so excited I got my first job. Back in the old neighborhood, I ran into my old friend, Debbie Lightheart. We started hanging out again all the time and soon decided to become roommates and moved to the east side of Milwaukee.

I turned seventeen and got a fake ID and a cocktail waitress job at a nightclub called Club Maryland, where I would spend the next six months up until my 18th birthday.

Jeffrey Dahmer was one of our best customers. He was the nicest guy. You would never know that he was eating people. Ernest Miller, a guy that I went to middle school with, was one of the victims. Jeffrey ate my friend. All they found were his bones in the refrigerator.

He was gay so all of his victims were men. He would drug them, have sex with them, then kill and eat them. He would dip their bones into acid and formaldehyde. They found drums of formaldehyde in his apartment, a freezer full of skulls and bones. There was even an ass in the refrigerator.

Every time he came in, it was just the usual: Hello. How are you? I'm Jeffrey. I'm Jackie. I'm going to be your server. Never really anything spectacular. He told me where he worked at Ambrosia Chocolate but other than that, he was a really quiet guy who preferred to sit back with his screwdriver and just watch people. Oh, and he was a good tipper, too—about three dollars per drink.

Chapter Fifteen

Sex is a lethal weapon. I have known situations where women have bankrupted men because the men were addicted to having sex with them. It is a male weakness.

I tried to improve upon a situation that was almost perfect with little tricks. One of my favorites was to stand and put a deep arch in my back and have another girl pour champagne down the valley it made. The arch of my back is so deep it's like a crevice and the champagne didn't run over the sides but straight down the middle and into the guy's mouth. I'd have a guy put his mouth right to the top of the crack of my butt and I'd feed him champagne.

I also have a double jointed tongue so if I was in a Gold Room and there was a lull in the party, a girl would say, "Diva, show the guy the trick with your tongue and see if he can do it." I would take my tongue and stick it out sideways and make it go back and forth. It's also a trick that's good for sex. Needless to say, my ex-girlfriends all loved it.

One girl could take a beer bottle and put it between her tits and shake them back and forth without the bottle falling. She could squeeze her boobs together and take the bottle and put it in her mouth and blow on it like it was a dick between her titties.

Frederique could sit on the couch and put her legs up behind her head butt naked.

There was this girl, Charley, who everybody used to swear was formerly a man. We'd heard rumors from close friends of her and her husband's that she had a sex change operation years ago. Charley was built like a man, had an Adam's apple, and then her butt and legs and the crease in her crotch were all male. Well, Charley had this thing where she showed guys her clit which looked like her dick got chopped off.

She was one of the persistent people who wouldn't give up until they get a dance out of you. Finally one guy said, "Okay, just go ahead and dance and get it over with."

I was sitting two guys down, and when she showed him her clit he said, "Awww man!"

She looked at him and said, "Fuck you," and ran back to the dressing room crying.

I walked back there to check to see if she was okay because I felt bad for her, even though she and I didn't get along. I said, "Are you all right?"

"What the fuck do you care?" she sobbed. "You think I'm a man anyway."

"Bitch, don't get smart. I came back here to check on you." And I walked out of the dressing room.

But still, that was fucked up of that guy to do that to Charley. A lot of people heard it and his friends were laughing at her and pointing at her. I went and checked him. "You know what? You're a bit of an asshole. All you had to do was tell her you didn't want her to dance for you, she's not your type, tell her move around. Don't let her dance for you and then ridicule her like that while you and all your friends are pointing and laughing at her. What kind of fucking man are you anyway?"

"Fuck you, bitch, who do you think you are?"

"You want to know who I am? Hold on." I went and got the floor manager and told him the score and he told him they had to leave. I had to watch. Now that's who the fuck I am.

But, with men, most women can get them to do a lot of things for sex. The best way to use it, if you're smart, is to get a sugar daddy. I learned over a period of time working in the Gold Club. These are the men who take you shopping. You call them and tell them you need a thousand dollars and they send it to you. They are the ones who supply you with what you need.

The only reason they do it is in hopes of sleeping with you. Sugar daddies are typically middle-aged men, 55-60. That's the usual age of a sugar daddy because most younger men aren't that gullible. You promise the sugar daddies that you're going to sleep with them but you're just not ready yet. The longer you don't sleep with them the more you'll get.

Sex equals power and I'm living proof of that. You're a woman and what do men want more than anything? You've already got the right commodity due to nothing more than your birth.

Many men feel it's an accomplishment to lay as many women as possible. A sugar daddy meets a very strong independent woman yet she's so weak and so vulnerable. She makes him think that she's weak and vulnerable. As for me, I'd tell the guy some of my troubles. I'm a single mom who's got to take care of my kids but yet I'm beautiful. It makes it very hard for a man because he wants me and he'll do anything to get me. When he doesn't, there can be some serious repercussions behind that. I had stalkers. Guys freaking out, calling, blowing up over the phone. "Where the fuck are you? Look at all this shit I did for you!"

You have to be careful when you're playing that game.

To avoid the stalkers, you have to carefully choose your sugar daddies. The best ones are incredibly rich, older and single. If they're married that's all the better because there's no commitment. You don't have to worry about this man misbehaving because the words, "I'm going to tell your wife," are enough to choke him up ten times—especially if he's rich.

If he's rich and he's your sugar daddy and has a wife at home, nine times out of ten, he doesn't want his wife to know what he's doing at all. You threaten to tell that wife, you can get anything you want. Car, house, whatever you want. God forbid you sleep with him, then you can say, "I'm telling your wife you're sleeping with me." He's stupid. He's going to fall asleep in your presence and then the smartest thing you can do is get out his wallet and his driver's license and get his address. Look in his checkbook and get his phone number. Once you've got those two bits of information, you've got him. He's going to do whatever you say do.

Ironically, my most profitable sugar daddy wasn't married at all. He was about 55 and a millionaire. He basically gave me whatever I wanted whenever I wanted it. He gave me a copy of his credit card with a $2,000 a month spending limit. He took me shopping, out to dinner. The average shopping trip would run $3-4,000 shopping at The Gucci Shop, Lillie Rubin.

This relationship started in Milwaukee. It's in every woman to do this. Every woman has this gift. It's just if you're in the industry to use it or not. A lot of times, you don't want to place that title "sugar daddy" on what you're doing because that is so crass. I like to think of them as my "friends." Somebody that takes care of me.

I had at least five of those back home that I could call all at the same time. If I needed something, I just picked up the phone and called one of them. If I needed a couple hundred dollars or I needed to do something for the kids, whatever it was, they would give it to me. Birthdays came around, I'd get major gifts, diamonds, money, dinner. I always knew they were going to be there for me. There was one guy who took me Christmas shopping for my kids one year. I was just coming out of my divorce and started back dancing where I met him. He was the sweetest guy.

I never had sex with any of my friends. I just kept them company when they wanted company, talked on the phone, hung out together.

I kept sugar daddies on the side even through relationships. The whole time I was with Elliott—five years—I always had a sugar daddy.

Elliott knew. He didn't say anything but I could tell sometimes from his actions, the way he handled situations, he was not happy about it. He would blow up. It was one of the reasons he never trusted me. He thought I was fucking everything that moved. The truth is I didn't and I never had to. That is the glory of being a woman. You don't have to sleep with anybody to get what you want. Just be nice to them.

Men like trophies, a beautiful woman to put on a sexy outfit so he can parade her around. That's what most of these guys do. They take you shopping, Gucci shoes and a nice dress, nice handbag and they got you all dressed up. They get your hair done, your nails, your feet, and keep you looking good for when you go places with them.

There's another element that falls into play with sugar daddies. Some women cannot do what I did. You also have to know how to carry yourself in every atmosphere you're taken into. Over the years, I learned how to handle myself in the corporate world, with blue collar workers, on down to the trailer trash. I learned to maneuver myself through any given situation.

The night that I accompanied a friend of mine to the Black and White Ball, I knew how to mingle with the Governor and the Mayor and all these dignitaries and important people of Atlanta. Small talk, a little schmoozing here and there, I was adept. Not only was I in a beautiful evening gown looking like the Queen of Sheba, when I did something on that scale with somebody we always had to make a damn grand entrance. Me and my friend were always the last ones coming in.

Everybody's just staring. Here comes that grand entrance. Then you have to go talk to people and my friend is introducing me to people, clients, business associates. The key here is you absolutely have to know how to handle yourself. Some women are so strip-club oriented that they forget where they are and do something stupid and embarrass the guy they're with.

A stripper friend went to a black-tie affair and flashed her boobs. I said, "What the hell were you thinking?!"

"We got a little tipsy and I don't know what I was thinking," she lamented. "He won't ever talk to me again!"

Just like Sugar Daddies took pride in the women they kept, Norbie took pride in the celebrities he met like notches on his belt. Every time a celebrity came in he was up their ass like nobody's business. He didn't get anything out of it—just to meet people like Lawrence Fishburne, Wesley Snipes, or Keanu Reeves and shake their hand. You could look at him running after them, these mere mortals who happen to be in the limelight. DMX came in one night looking a little grungy. Norbie ran to his car to get some DMX CDs to play some of his music while he was standing in the club.

The night Karl Malone came in, Norbie was all over him. He was on the microphone, "Karl Malone's in the house. Hey, Karl Malone!" Whatever. We were in the Viper Lounge and I was sitting in Karl's lap. Just talking. He called a real pretty girl, a light skinned black girl named Myra, over. He had a couple other girls over there wrapped around him and dancing for him. I danced two songs and then Karl, Myra, his friend and another girl went to Gold Room 6. If I know Myra, something happened in that room. She was a big time groupie. She slept around a lot. I caught her doing things in the Gold Club quite a bit just with regular guys, so the sky was the limit as to what she'd do with Karl.

After a while, being Steve's girl, making the money I was, and running with the types of people I was, I abused my power to the ninth degree. I would throw it in people's faces: I cannot be fired. I would cuss people out in a heartbeat and know nothing was going to happen to me. It's an unbelievable feeling to know that you are untouchable. It's an over-whelming feeling.

I got to where I had the power to send girls home—hire, fire—do whatever I wanted in that club. If they did something wrong and I saw it, I'd say, "Get dressed and go home."

One night this girl was on the main floor rubbing this guy's crotch. I said, "Go in the dressing room, put your clothes on and go home."

And she knew not to question me. No one dared question my authority. If I told a girl or floorman to do something, they did it. If they didn't, nine times out of ten they were probably going to get fired or suspended for a while.

I caught a girl doing cocaine in the bathroom and fired her like that on the spot. It got to the point that I was calling Steve my dad. That was my dad.

Steve would introduce me to people, "This is my daughter." We were like two peas in a pod. He was the most giving man I ever met in my life. Girls would come to him crying because they were getting ready to lose their apartments, and the rent would be two months behind. Even though he knew what type of money they were making in the club, he would give it to them and never expect it back.

He saw something in me that I didn't even see myself and he took me very close to him and would not let that go.

One night Norbie came in and caught the tail end of a conversation I was having. He said, "You don't need to be in here talking about this. You need to be out on the floor making money."

I turned around and said, "First of all, you need to get out of my conversation. Nobody was talking to you and I didn't ask for your opinion. I will get out on the floor when I feel like it. Besides that, I have a guy in a Gold Room right now and he'll wait too. Who the fuck do you think you're talking to?"

"I'm fucking talking to you! I don't know who you think you are, Diva, but uh huh, that's it. Not tonight, Diva. You're going home."

"I'm going home? You and what army is gonna make me go home?"

"This is what I'm talking about—your fucking mouth. You walk around here like you're Queen Elizabeth."

"I am Queen Elizabeth, according to Steve, so if you want to send me home I suggest you get on the horn and call Steve and tell him you're sending his number one champagne-selling girl home tonight. Go ahead. Call him and tell him you're pulling me out of a Gold Room too!"

"Fuck you, you fucking big-mouthed bitch!" Norbie went off the deep end.

I said, "You know, it kind of sucks to be the general manager and not be the head motherfucker in charge." The housemom started laughing.

He turned to her, "What are you laughing at?"

"Nothing," Rose smirked. "But I think she just told you."

"Norbie, now get the fuck out of the dressing room and leave me alone," I said smugly.

Norbie went mumbling out. "I'm sick of this shit."

Me and Norbie continued to butt heads. He started in on me in the dressing room one night. I was drunk and forgot what we were arguing about but it went to a whole other level because I wasn't done speaking my mind. I was determined Norbie was going to hear it and I followed him up to the front desk.

The Gold Club was packed, dancers were going, men were everywhere: I got up in Norbie's face, "Motherfucker, don't you ever walk away from me. I was talking. You're going to fucking listen to what I have to say. And if you're not going to listen, maybe I need to call Steve and make you listen."

Everybody looked at Norbie like, are you going to take this from her?

"Fuck you! I'll kick your fucking ass," he shouted.

"Bring it on, Norbie. I'm not scared of your punk ass."

"You punk bitch!"

"What are you going to do? You can't send me home. You can't fire me—what are you going to do? You're going to take your scraggly ass on up them steps to the VIP and shut your fucking mouth, that's what you're going to do."

"You don't fucking talk to me like that."

"What are you going to do? You going to hit me, Norbie? Baby, go for it because then you're going to wind up in jail. Then you have to deal with Steve because you know he hates men who hit women." I was making him feel like a fucking child.

I went to Norbie later that night and said, "We can't be arguing like that in front of people. It's bad for business."

"You started it!"

"No, I didn't. Every time we get in an argument it's because you feel the need to put your nose in my business and I'm going to call you on it. Every time you do it I'm going to check you like that. Best thing to do to keep the peace is to stay the fuck out of my way. There's nothing you can do to stop me in this club. I do whatever the fuck I want. You don't like it? Oh, well, call Steve."

The power trip, once in place, lingered through 1998. I caught this girl, Shawna, in a Gold Room giving a guy a hand job. She was very pretty, about 5'10", pretty long brown hair, an exotic look like she was Serbian or Italian. I called her out of the room and said, "What are you doing? You can't be doing that."

It was an example of the double standards I had taken as mine. My girls could do whatever they fucking wanted to do—hand jobs, blow jobs, sex—but not other girls, I wasn't letting that shit go on. First, if a girl was going to get busted doing that shit, obviously she shouldn't have been doing it. If a girl was going to be slick about it and not get caught, hey, more power to her. If I could walk past a room and can flat out see a girl yanking some guy off, I was definitely going to call her out.

When I called Shawna out, she said, "Who the fuck do you think you are? You're an entertainer like the rest of us. You're not a manager."

"That's where you fucked up. I am an entertainer. And I could be a housemom. I could run the front door. I could just about do everything that needs to be done in this building. And yes, I am a manager right now and I'm sending you home so go down to the dressing room."

Dave Fast, the manager on duty, was passing us and Shawna caught him. "Dave, Diva's trying to send me home."

"What were you doing?" Dave asked dispassionately.

"Nothing."

"Bitch, I know you're not going to stand there and tell a bold-faced lie like that. What were you doing? Why am I sending you home for the night?"

Shawna rolled her pretty eyes back in her head like a 12-year-old hyped up on hormones.

I turned to Dave. "She's going home because she was in there beating this guy off in that Gold Room."

"Go get your clothes on," Dave said. "You're going home."

"Why the fuck does Diva get to send somebody home? Who the fuck does she think she is?"

"She just sent you home, didn't she? Go get your clothes on and I don't want to hear another word about it." Dave went in to the customers and explained. "Sorry, that's not permitted. I need to collect the money. Did you pay your girl already?"

They were all really bummed.

Chapter
Sixteen

The weirdest thing that ever happened in my life happened when I was working at Club Maryland in Milwaukee— weirder than Jeffrey Dahmer. Weird. I had the flu real bad but the week before me and Debbie had been playing with the Ouija Board and this boy from high school that died came through. He had gotten thrown out of a window at Madison High School. On the board he spelled out who he was, what happened to him, what school he went to. He remembered Debbie.

At first the ghost is real nice and then he started writing stuff on there like, "I'm going to come get you," and I was freaking out. We threw the Ouija Board in the garbage. It was out front the next day. Debbie said, "Okay, Jackie, this is not funny. It's a sick joke. Why did you take the board out of the garbage?"

"What?" I was freaked out. "I didn't take the board out of the garbage."

"You didn't?"

"No. Where is it?"

"Right here at the front door."

We broke it in half and put it in the garbage and then nothing else happened until three days later when I got really sick. I took a capful of Nyquil and got up underneath the covers and was shivering with a fever. That was Friday, I don't remember anything else until the following Sunday evening when I awoke.

My friend Jeff and his mom, Miss Parker, from the neighborhood, were sitting by my side with a Bible, praying over me. They strapped me to the bed with leather belts and I broke the belts. They wound up strapping three or four nylons around each arm and then tied them to the bed, my ankles tied up underneath the bed. They couldn't hold me down by themselves.

When I woke up I saw Jeff and his mother praying over me. What the hell? Miss Parker is known as the spiritual person who used to pray a lot for everybody. I'll always remember Jeff as the first boy I kissed. He's dead now. He was arrested and they claimed he hung himself with a sheet, though there are no sheets in the community jail cells in Milwaukee. Anyway, Jeff and Miss Parker are sitting there and tell me what I was doing. That I was talking like the devil. I had a hideous manly voice coming out of me, telling them I was going to kill them. They untied me and I looked down and saw scratches and bruises. I looked like I had been through hell.

Miss Parker said, "Jackie, you were possessed. But you were fighting him. You did not want him in there. You were fighting him and he was fighting you." She said the Ouija Board had caught me in a vulnerable state since I was sick and had taken the Nyquil which relaxed my body and gave it easy access to my soul.

I still question if it really happened. Did they beat the shit out of me and strap me to the bed to make me think something crazy?

Chapter Seventeen

Two months prior to getting raided, Ziggy pulled me aside and warned me the Feds had been watching the Gold Club for quite some time. "I didn't want to make you scared and have you quit because Steve loves you and you're good and you sell a lot of champagne but they have been watching you. They have pictures of you in Vegas."

The list went on. Ziggy was scared to death. "We're dealing with the Feds. You've got to remember everything you know about this club you have to keep to yourself." It was damn close to a threat. "I'm telling you right now if this place is raided or we get indicted, if you ever say anything to the Feds, you won't exist." There was no question it was a threat.

Ziggy explained that he didn't get involved in illegal activities. He said, he ran his business legitimately. "A lot of the stuff that happened in the club, I didn't know about." He finished piously, "I just hope that nobody gets in trouble. The FBI is watching, but if they do come to us, we just tell the truth. That's all you have to do."

I went to Steve but didn't tell him about the threat for a change. I didn't want him to go off. I did tell him that Ziggy pulled me aside to say the Feds had been watching us.

"Yes, it's true," Steve sighed. "They've been watching us for a while. For some reason they think I'm involved in organized crime. They've been watching me since 1988. Sweetheart, I'm not involved in that type of life. I don't get involved in wrongdoing."

That was all I needed to hear. I trusted Steve Kaplan implicitly.

In August of 1998, I went to work at a club for Mitchell LaFleur, the owner of Flasher's, for the Masters Golf Tournament in Augusta. LaFleur rented out his club and brought girls in from Atlanta to make extra money for four days. The Gold Club girls were Celine, Dawn and Sherry. Dawn filled a stereotype in our circles: she was a white girl who wanted to be black, messing around with black guys. She had a mixed child.

I waited for the activities to warm up before going down because although I'm a workaholic, I don't actually like to work. I had taken my Web TV with me so Elliott and I could stay in touch. He wasn't keen on me going to Augusta because he'd heard rumors that it was really scrungy dirty, like the girls prostituting themselves.

I told him, "You've just got to trust me on that. I'm not going down there to prostitute myself. I'm going to make extra money."

Me and the girls did the usual pampering and shopping during the day. My first night I made $2,500.

We were back at the house eating and talking. They asked how much I made and I told them. They had only made a few hundred each.

"Well, I got lucky," I said. I didn't want to rub it in their faces so I tried to change the subject but they went back to it and said, "You come down here the first night and make $2,500?"

"Like I said, I got lucky," I shrugged. "I got a room."

Mitchell was good friends with Steve. They were running

the business around the Masters like the Gold Club was run—renting rooms by the hour.

The next day as we were getting ready for work, Dawn asked if she could use my WebTV to e-mail someone. No problem. I set her up and she was sending e-mails back and forth for a while.

I had left earlier with one of the girls who needed to stop by the mall to pick up some body spray.

That first night, I wasn't at work twenty minutes when I met this guy who says, "The sky's the limit. I'm here to party and have a good time."

I said, "Well let's go downstairs and get a private room and we can get champagne. We'll have our own room and our own waitress." We picked up another girl along the way.

The Gold Rooms up there had just been finished and smelled like new paint and carpet. There was a small platform that came out of the floor with lights on it to dance on. They had little rooms inside the room where you could dance for your customer privately but since there was just the three of us, we didn't need to do all that. Each room also had its own jukebox so you could choose your own music besides, instead of being roped into what was being played downstairs.

Dawn was our waitress and made $800 that night. The guy said, "Tell her to serve the drinks and go." At first I thought, okay, we're getting naked. I hope he doesn't try to touch us or anything like that.

He didn't start groping though. He danced with us and then did his own strip-tease down to his boxer shorts. It was so funny. He was looking around at us and said, "I feel awkward dressed in only my boxers." He got dressed, but he gave me $2500 and the other girl $1500, Lisa $800 and the bartender $400. The guy was in his mid-thirties. He had brown hair and beautiful dark brown eyes, a buff body, and was fairly articulate. He said he was single, no kids. He lived in Boston. His platinum card was well oiled.

The other girl in the room was Spanish. Her skin was golden, long brown hair down to her butt and the prettiest lips I've ever seen on a woman. She had a Coke bottle figure and was wearing an iridescent long dress with strappy platform shoes that were iridescent to match the dress. The whole back was out with spaghetti straps over the shoulders. She had this really pretty choker on. It also was iridescent with little rhinestones hanging on it.

I had on a pink iridescent gown as well, very sheer, and little pink t-backs on underneath it with no bra. It was a spaghetti strap straight dress that split up the side to the hip. With my tan and the black lights in the room, it just glowed.

I met a guy named Rick the next night. He had a friend with him and some other girl that I didn't like. Sherry, one of the girls from the Gold Club who was dating Mitchell Lafleur a little, was on that night and I brought her in to take care of the friend. We left the club and went to this mansion they rented. Me and Sherry and Rick separated from the rest of the crowd and went upstairs by ourselves where we got a big bottle of champagne.

Rick wanted to know who we were, where we came from and where we grew up. When I told him I was from Milwaukee, he asked, "Have you ever heard of Funcoland?"

"Yeah, me and my brother used to shop there all the time."

"I own that line," he said, self-assured. "I started Funcoland."

He wanted to know if we had kids and we sat up until six o'clock in the morning telling him our life stories. By then we were drunk and everybody was tired. He said, "What do you guys want to do today?"

We shrugged.

"Do you want to go buy a car or go shopping? I know, I got it. I have a private jet, you can go anywhere you want. Where do you want to go?"

We were baffled.

In the house Rick rented, we went through the lady's drawers and found pajamas. Me and Sherry took a shower and put them on. They were very Bible belt conservative, flannel pajama pants and long-sleeved shirts. Rick found some of the husband's pajamas and put those on. We had a picnic/pajama party on the bed. Went downstairs to the fridge and got food to go with the champagne.

I kept wondering when this guy was gonna snap and be this wild man? We were nervous about it. We stayed up and he made the game plan. He said, "That's it. Hold on." He grabbed his cell phone and called his pilot and this is when we realized this guy is serious: he's got a jet. He said, "I want the plane fueled up and ready to go by one o'clock."

I called Mitchell who was still at the club counting the money and doing paperwork, and said, "Mitchell, we're going to fly on Rick's jet tomorrow to Atlanta and we need a limousine to pick us up on the other side."

He said, "What! Diva, what have you done? Tell me what airport you're flying into."

I told Mitchell "Peachtree Dekalb Airport" and he arranged for a limo to pick us up at ten o'clock in the morning.

The three of us had had about four hours of sleep. We showered and Rick said, "What are we going to do?" The third girl, April, joined us.

Me and Sherry still had on semi-stripper clothes, little miniskirts and high heel shoes. I said, "Is there any way we could stop at Dillard's and get some comfortable clothes to put on?" We could see it up the street from the limo.

We stopped at Dillard's and went upstairs to the junior department. Rick announced, "It's a yellow kind of day." We all picked out yellow and white outfits. All three of his girls had on matching handbags, shoes and outfits. We put our new outfits on in the dressing room and the salespeople were kissing our Asses. We were matching to the T.

We stopped at the package store where there was this big green blow-up frog on the wall. Rick told the sales guy he had to have it but the frog was for display only. "I'll give you a hundred bucks for it," Rick said, pulling out a roll.

The guy says, "Fine. Take the frog."

When we got back in the limo with the frog, the other girls cooed, "Is there nothing this man cannot have?"

"I can have whatever I want." We had bought a big keg bucket at the liquor store. We had ice and champagne, Bloody Mary makings, everything you would need to get plastered. We drank our way to the airport where we were treated like royalty, red carpet literally rolled out to the steps of his plane. I felt like Julia Roberts in Pretty Woman.

In Atlanta, we stopped by the Jaguar dealership. There was an X-J6 with a drop top, a $75,000 car right there on the salesroom floor. Rick threw his platinum card on the dashboard and said, "I want this car for her. She looks good in this car. She needs this car." He wanted me to drive off the lot with that car. It was a Friday evening and ten minutes to close and the salesman wouldn't make the deal. He was ready to go.

As a consolation Rick took us to Phipps's, the most expensive mall in the state of Georgia, and spent $25,000 on clothes for me. He spent $15,000 on Sherry and $10,000 on the other girl, April.

The other girls were frustrated because they didn't really make any money. That was the scene I walked into, weighted down with shopping bags and brand new clothes and handbags, all of which I unloaded on the couch.

I went to check my e-mail. Dawn had discarded four e-mails from Elliott. He was e-mailing me about something that had happened with his family and he was coming home. I wouldn't have ever known if I hadn't checked my discarded messages.

I snapped and started cussing her out. Dawn and Lisa were sitting there saying, "Fuck you! You think you're all that."

"I don't think I'm all that. You guys are just jealous because you didn't make any money on this trip like you thought you were going to make. I got lucky. I made over $6,000 and got $25,000 worth of clothes. A little while ago you were going through my clothes, talking about how cool they are. All of a sudden, after you see all this shit, you're angry because I had a good trip." Naturally, I cussed them out.

My fellow Masters dancers came into the Gold Club one night about two weeks later. Rumor had it that Dawn had been bragging about cussing me out in Augusta. A girl came to me in a Gold Room and said Dawn and Lisa were in the Viper Lounge. I told my customer I'd be right back and went downstairs where I found Norbie. "Either you kick them out of the building or I'm leaving," I said. "That's your choice. What's it going to be?" Norbie kicked them out. A few days later they came back wondering why they couldn't have their jobs back. I told Norbie, "Hire them back and I quit." It was one of the few times at the Gold Club that a firing actually stuck.

Meanwhile, Terry the housemom had started making tapes—recordings of conversations she had around the club. She came to me one day and said, "These girls around here really don't like you."

"What makes you say that?" I shouldn't have been surprised but I was.

"Because I talk to these girls all the time." They confided in Terry.

After a while, Terry decided she was going to start recording conversations to see how far they'd go talking about people. She would deliberately ask questions to bring out things. That's what she did with Lisa. She asked questions to open her up to get her to start talking.

"There you have it right there on tape," she said, showing me the cassettes. Basically, I thought I was "all that."

"How much do you have?" I asked, taken aback.

"I got a lot of tapes."

"You should get them transcribed onto paper. We could use those in court."

So she went to Steve, told him about the tapes that she was having transcribed.

He said, "Give them to my lawyer, not to me."

Almost every girl in the club was taped. They wouldn't be admissible in court but they would be useful in the questioning process. The defense used the knowledge of what they had gleaned to help with the case.

In March of 1999 the Gold Club was raided. I had pulled out of the parking lot three minutes before the Feds came. Greg Herring was in the building with girls in a Gold Room. The bartenders were closing out for the night. I looked in the rearview mirror and saw guys in black with big machine guns storming in the front door.

My first thought was, "The Gold Club is being robbed!" I didn't know if I should go back. I didn't know what to do. I had left my cell phone at home that day so I thought, "Don't go back. If they're being robbed, you don't want to go back."

I raced home to wait by the phone. Surely someone would call me. As I suspected, my phone was ringing like an alarm clock when I walked in.

The Gold Club was being raided. The FBI was there as well as the IRS and it was all over the morning news. I was up all night; and I couldn't sleep. I called Steve who told me that the Feds had raided the house in Dunwoody, the Gold Club and the office in New York, all at the same time that night.

The FBI and the IRS believed they would find a truck-load of drugs and weapons. They thought that Steve was drug dealing and part of the Mafia so he would have guns stored in the building somewhere. They went everywhere looking for stuff and were sorely disappointed when they came up empty-handed.

They arrested Charley, the dancer who couldn't keep her mouth shut. "How do I know you're the FBI?" she demanded as these guys had machine guns pointed at her head and were telling her to get down on the floor and raise her arms above her head. One of the other girls had an asthma attack. Luckily, Greg Herring, the only customer left, wasn't doing anything. They came in there like gangbusters.

The IRS seized all of the computers, the paperwork, receipts, everything. They filled up three U-haul trucks with boxes and paperwork.

The next morning at 5:15 the whole front of my house was shaking. Joe was sleeping in the downstairs guest room and went to answer the door. It was the FBI.

"Tell them I'm asleep," I groaned.

"I suggest you come down here," Joe insisted.

I got my robe on and came to the top of my stairwell. They were agent Simmons and agent Sewell, as I came to find out later. Sewell was a strawberry blonde redneck. Simmons was dorky, tall, skinny, dense.

"Are you Jacklyn Bush?"

"Why are you asking me that when you already know who I am?"

"We need to ask you a few questions."

"You need to talk to my lawyer cause I don't have anything to say to you people," I said with venom. "I know my rights. Besides, don't you have all the answers to the questions you need? You've been following me for two years."

From that moment on, they hated me because they knew they had an uphill battle with me.

We reopened the same night, even without the computers. We did every transaction by hand like in the old days. Steve brought out the old push button cash registers and never stopped making money. After the raid it was business as usual.

The first subpoenas came right after the raid. Everyone got one and Steve Kaplan had lawyers right on it. He hired Steve Sadow to pick the legal team. Then before you could say, "Fuck you" the subpoenas were snatched back.

A second round of subpoenas was delivered; this time they were more targeted though. Frederique went and testified before the grand jury and then came back and told Steve what she said.

By then, it was really weird at the Club, not knowing what was going to happen. Steve called a meeting where a lot of the girls cried, questioning the fate of the club. Norbie was sitting up on the stage with Jimmy Carillo, Larry Gleit, Patrick Doggrell, Roy Cicola—all the management.

Steve talked to us about the FBI and how they'd been after him for a long time. He felt the whole thing was his fault and that all the employees shouldn't have to suffer just because he had problems. He tried to reassure us that the Club wouldn't close, though I think he knew in his heart it was only a matter of time and pressure. No matter what happened, Steve was going to pay for everyone's legal fees, for the time it took for them to go down and testify, even pay for the shits who took the immunity deal and turned on him.

He ended the meeting with an announcement: Management had raised the $10 dance minimum to $20. For a brief moment, the girls went wild with the old enthusiasm. There was a reason to celebrate.

About a week later, just before Easter, I had planned to take my kids to Disney World. My stress was tangible. Word had come back that I was being investigated and that the Feds had pictures of me in Vegas and had been following me for a long time. "What the fuck are they following me for?" I asked myself over and over. I didn't do anything wrong.

Lyle from accounting rented a van with a TV and a VCR. Come to find out, my ex-husband had planned to take the girls to see his mother. So the kids went to Wisconsin with Joe. I didn't want to tag along—my family was asking too many questions.

The day before I left, Elliott called me and said he was coming in from Switzerland so we made plans for him to meet us there. Steve said, "Just tell him I said have a good time. It's on me." I protested to no avail.

Me and Lyle went to Disney World and spent two days together chilling. We picked Elliott up from the airport. And then Lyle got a phone call from Steve saying there was a problem with the investigation. Lyle had to get on a plane right then. So as Elliott was getting off one plane, we were putting Lyle on another back to Atlanta to help Steve pick out the lawyers.

May brought not only spring flowers but also the dreadful day when the bank came and foreclosed on my house. I had five days to move. That's when I found out my mortgage was only $1,400 a month and not the $2,500 a month I had been paying.

The broker, the boyfriend of the stripper who found the house for me, wasn't forwarding my payments along. They would pay the mortgage for a few months and then not pay it. I didn't have a leg to stand on and there was no way to go after the broker, who went by different aliases and was impossible to track down.

Elliott said we would just have to go get an apartment.

My girls, as usual, were resilient. On their last night in the house before they went to their Dad's, I said, "This is your last night in the house. When you come back we'll be in the apartment."

They were helping me clean. "We hate the bank," they cried. "We hate the broker, too!"

Losing the house was like losing a family member. Perhaps Breanna cried the most. I held her in her bedroom. Elliott and I both sat in there a long time explaining about the new apartment that had a pool and lots of her friends already living there.

After a while the girls all fell asleep and we turned off the lights. In my bedroom, Elliott held me all night. "I'm so sorry," I heard the words in my ear as I drifted off to sleep, release. "You worked so hard to get this house."

After that, we moved into the apartment, the Columns at Paxton Lane. It was right down the street.

Elliott went back to Europe and I found out that I might have to go in front of a grand jury. Hundreds of people—employees, customers, and celebrities—were being subpoenaed. No sooner was mine delivered than it was snatched back.

I had no idea what it meant. I was dumbfounded. I asked Steve, "What does it mean to be subpoenaed to the grand jury?"

"It means you have to go in. They're giving the employees immunity. That means you can tell everything that you did and you won't get in trouble for it as long as you don't lie. That's how they determine whether or not they're going to indict people."

"Okay, so when do I go?" I asked, feeling some relief.

"I got bad news. You're not."

"What are you talking about?"

"They will not grant you immunity. They don't want to grant you immunity."

Forty people had already been in front of the grand jury. I learned that testimony was being thrown around that I was Steve's girl, I was running a prostitution ring, working for him, and he's my pimp. People were testifying that I was laundering money for Steve, running a credit card fraud scheme.

All of these accusations were flying around and the FBI had predetermined that I was so close to Steve; they didn't want me to go in front of the grand jury. I could hear the silent threat: We're going to make you sweat.

They figured if they didn't grant me immunity, I'd get scared and wouldn't want to get indicted. Then, I'd work for them.

My take on the situation? You've got it fucked up. Steve hasn't done anything wrong and I'm not going to tell you something that isn't even remotely true to get myself off the hook. I'm not that type of person and I wasn't raised that way.

A couple of months down the road, they were still going through the grand jury testimony. It took a while to get testimony from all of the Gold Club employees and the credit card customers.

I got a phone call in the middle of the night from Elliott cussing me out. Janice Gordon, one of the US district attorneys (or whatever she is with the FBI) called him at three o'clock in the morning Switzerland time and woke him up: "Is this Elliott

Henderson?" she asked.

"Yes."

"Hi. This is Janice Gordon of the Federal Bureau of Investigation. Do you know a Jacklyn Bush?"

"Yes."

"What is her relationship to you?"

"She's my fiancée."

"Mr. Henderson, let me inform you about your fiancée. There are things back here that obviously you don't know are going on. Your fiancée is prostituting herself. She's sleeping with athletes, musicians, and movie stars. She's acting as a madam in the Gold Club for Steve Kaplan. Steve Kaplan is pimping her. She's laundering money." Janice Gordon went down this long dirty laundry list of things I was supposedly doing.

So by the time Elliott called me in Atlanta, naturally, he's freaking out. "What the fuck are you doing? What is this shit?"

"What?" I said, half asleep.

Then he told me what the FBI woman had said.

I said, "Elliott, it's not true. So not true."

But how do you hear the things you've probably suspected all along and deal with it? Elliott dealt with it the way the FBI gambled he would: he broke up with me. They figured they'd hit me where they knew it would hurt.

The FBI had my phone tapped for a couple of years leading up to the raid and had been listening to all our phone conversations. They knew how I felt about Elliott. When they couldn't frighten me by the indictment, they figured, okay, we'll get him to break up with her and she'll come to us.

No. You got me messed up.

After the stunt with Elliott didn't give them the desired

results, I guess they thought if they took my kids that would break me down.

Then the Department of Family and Children's Services, DFCS, came to my door. My ex-husband had just come over to pick up the kids because I had to go to work. The DFCS woman was white, bottle-blonde hair and heavy-set. They got a report that I had been indicted under the RICO Act on charges of prostitution and money laundering and she had come to find out if all this was true.

It was a kick in the face to even have DFCS come to my home. I wasn't a bad mother. The DFCS lady asked me in front of my daughter, "Are you a prostitute?"

Joe stepped between us. "Can we get the kids out of here before you start asking questions?" he said, taking control before I could even open my mouth.

I wanted to punch her in the face, I swear I did.

"Oh, I'm sorry," she said as if she'd no idea that she had stepped out of line or said anything that could be remotely damaging to a child.

After they were gone, the DFCS woman questioned me backwards and forwards. "Are you a prostitute?" she asked and then when the answer was no, she rephrased the question, "Have you prostituted yourself?" She looked around my house to see how I kept it and it was immaculate.

She said, "Well, I'm going to have to go through all this stuff and decide whether you're fit to keep your children. Somebody will be coming by periodically to check to see how you're maintaining."

* * *

I was irate. The FBI would do anything in their power to try to destroy my life and bring me down to the point where I would say enough, I'll cooperate with you.

They wanted me to go against Steve. I had no reason to. None. This man had done nothing but good to me and my kids. He gave me the opportunity to make a lot of frigging money. He took me on trips. He showed me a side of life that I never knew existed. I didn't know anyone could live that well and enjoy doing it at the same time.

I was steadfast. There was no way the Feds were going to make me work for them.

Other girls, like Wendy Whitfield, were threatened. Wendy was told they would take her kids away from her if she didn't testify in court.

She said, "No. I'm not doing it. You can kiss my ass." They sent her lawyer in and they didn't have grounds to take her kids and couldn't do it.

Strippers were, after all, an easy target for threats. About 70% of the girls had kids.

At first I thought I don't have to put up with this. When I was being threatened, I went to Steve Sadow, the lead attorney on the case, for advice. I didn't know what to do. We sat down with Larry Bronson and Steve Sadow who both explained the government couldn't just take your kids. "Don't let them fool you," Steve said. "They can threaten you all day long but they can't take your kids. So work it out with your ex-husband, let them go stay with him and do it like that. You could sue the hell out of them if they take your kids for any reason because you haven't done anything wrong. You're innocent until proven guilty in this country. If they're doing stuff like this, it's only because they want you to turn."

* * *

What I learned about the Federal Government was that they were ruthless individuals who would stop at nothing to disrupt my life. They will harass you to the point you will say or do anything they want you to. That's the way those guys work. They will tell you they can make your life a living hell and they can do it too. They are untouchable.

I got my target letter in August through the big law firm that Steve hired. Some letter. The first line reads: "This letter is to advise you that you are a target of a Federal Grand Jury Investigation in this District into RICO, RICO Conspiracy, ITAR-prostitution, wire fraud, Hobbs Act—police corruption, money laundering, harboring of fugitives, narcotics distribution, obstruction of justice—witness tampering, and other offenses, all of which constituted violations of the United States Code." The letter went on to "invite" me to "enter into negotiations" for a pre-indictment deal with the Feds, in essence. It was signed by Richard H. Deane, Jr, United States Attorney and Arthur W. Leach, Assistant U.S. Attorney. I would come to know and hate them both.

In September Jeff Johnson got his target letter. By now a bunch of people had them. The Feds were pulling in everyone down to the Federal Building, who had a grudge or gripe against Steve Kaplan, to tell lies behind closed doors.

Each of us had our own lawyer. We signed an agreement that said we knew we were all being represented by these lawyers and Steve was paying for everything through Steve Sadow: Larry Gleit, Ziggy, Lyle, me, Frederique, Norbie, Jeff, Patrick Doggrell, Russell Basile, Gregory Sage, Jimmy Carillo and Mike DiLeonardo. Steve also paid the legal fees for Lawrence Wooten, Reginald Burney, Aaron Maker and the cop, Jack Redlinger.

Later we found out that Ziggy had lied about me, like the dog he is, to the Grand Jury. He was two-faced from the start. And Jeff Johnson, he comes back to the grand jury a second time and starts talking about me and Frederique, just trying to save his own ass.

After my birthday, October 2, 1999, Steve lined up a lawyer for me to interview. His name was David Parrish but he talked to me like I was guilty already. I didn't like him or trust him. I said no.

The next lawyer Steve recommended was Bruce Harvey. I already knew who he was because I'd seen him on TV handling different high-profile trials. He rated in the top ten in the nation for criminal defense.

Bruce Harvey came up to the club to meet me. I had on a pink angora sweater with a black knee-length leather skirt, black tights and some dress shoes. I was in the dressing room when he arrived and Steve called me up to Gold Room 7. He had Charles, his private investigator, with him. Steve made brief introductions and left.

Bruce had heard a lot about me and when he met me, I looked nothing like he'd heard. He thought I'd look like a stripper, not motherly and conservative.

"Who are you?" he asked, as if somehow I'd cheated him, like Quasimodo without the hump.

"I'm Diva."

"You don't look like a stripper. Your boobs are a lot bigger than they told me they were."

It broke the ice. We sat and talked like two normal people, not a future convict and her overpaid lawyer. Bruce asked questions about the case, asked me to be frank, what it was I'd done wrong if anything. He approached me in that manner and let me know he was going to work hard for me. We ordered drinks: me a Gray Goose on the rocks with a splash of sour. Bruce had scotch.

"Are you comfortable with me and do you think I might be someone you'd want to represent you?"

"Yes, I'm comfortable and I'd be honored if you'd

represent me." I felt like he was someone who could protect me.

He gave me a great big hug. "I don't care what you did, Diva. My job is to defend you and give you the best representation possible." The meeting was over.

Around the second week in November Bruce warned me an indictment would be coming down. They wouldn't spend all this time and money without trying to nail somebody. He told me he would walk me through it, no matter what, and I wasn't going to get arrested. He would take care of it. I was on pins and needles, waiting.

At 8:00 a.m. on November 17th, my phone rang.

It was Bruce. "Today's the day."

"The day what?"

"You're being indicted." I had to be down at the Federal Building by 10:30 for my arraignment. It was no longer a threat. No longer talk.

I was sick.

It didn't really all sink in, what was transpiring. The news media was everywhere and I was in a whirlwind. Steve's whole thing was like a mantra: Just go in and tell the truth. If you did anything, so what? They can't do anything to you. Just tell the truth.

We got arraigned. The lawyers struck a deal that we could meet them at the jail instead of being arrested. It's a complicated process when you're being indicted. You get fingerprinted, photographed; sit for a while in a holding area. You go to this floor to this floor to this floor. Frederique was really upset that day. I smiled the whole time. I would not let these people see me this way. I wouldn't give them the satisfaction of knowing how upset I really was. Or that the question that kept rolling through my mind was pitiful: Why me? Why are you picking on me?

There were fifteen of us down there at different times and he bonded us all out. Thank God for Steve Kaplan. I couldn't have paid my ridiculous $50,000 bond. Steve's bond was $2 million. It never entered my mind that he wouldn't take care of me. He always had.

The next day, the story is on the front page of The *Atlanta Journal-Constitution* and there I am. Page one: Gold Club Linked to Mafia.

They listed all the charges: racketeering conspiracy, racketeering, prostitution, credit card fraud, money laundering, loan sharking, obstruction of justice, fraud involving Delta Air Lines, police corruption and harboring a fugitive. What I had to do with harboring a fugitive or Delta Air Lines had to do with this RICO shit which fucks everything up, I didn't know. Everybody had to all be in on it for it to be racketeering and racketeering conspiracy, so we all have to be charged with everything. My case wasn't involved in all of that.

I was quoted in the papers as saying, "I was the best. I was the top dancer in the Gold Club for the last three years." I told them whom I entertained. "Oh, professional athletes, movie stars. I've seen lots of people at the Gold Club. I'm not going to name names. They know who they are." As for the charges, I told them: "These are allegations they've got in the indictment which are totally false and I really have no comment on that. I can't speak further on that. It's false."

Bruce said it best right then, in the paper on November 18th, "The adult entertainment world is built on fantasy, and so is this indictment. We look forward to getting into the reality of the facts when we get into the courtroom."

I pleaded "not guilty," of course.

Even when Art Leach sent down a plea bargain in the beginning, I told Bruce Harvey, "Tell Art Leach to kiss my ass. We're going to trial." They wanted me to do five years in prison. He gave Art Leach my answer verbatim. Eventually we would be indicted three times, one superseding the other as they were rewritten and lengthened. They started out with 96 pages and ended up with 132. The offer of the plea bargain came after the third and final indictment.

Chapter Eighteen

George, the owner of Club Maryland in Milwaukee, also owned this place called the Airport Lounge, which everyone called the Bordello. A few months after I started there, my actual 18th birthday rolled around and a group of friends wanted to take me there to celebrate.

We walked in and there's a girl on stage with no top on! It's a strip club. The girl was so ugly. She was just prancing around. Then the music cut off just at the same time I opened my big mouth to say, "I could do a better job than that."

George happened to be there and came out of the back, looks at me and says, "I got a proposition for you. I'll give you $150 to go up there for three songs." Like that! I was half in the bag anyway but I said, "Okay! Give me a shot of tequila and I will!"

His girlfriend, Wendy, took me backstage to the dressing room to get me ready. You had to wear band-aids on your nipples back then to cover them. I had on this little cute dress and some T-back shoes. I also had on some cute underwear, thank God.

I was nervous as hell but drunk as hell, too and I'm thinking to myself, "So I'm fixing to get up here and show these people how to do this."

I made so much money guys were just throwing it. I had so much fun. It was like it was my own little arena and I had everybody at my disposal, an overpowering feeling for someone that young. Then I was looking at all this money lying on the floor, tens and twenties. Holy shit! I'd never seen that kind of money cocktail waitressing.

After I got off stage I threw all the money down in my purse, didn't even count it. George gave me my 150 bucks and asked if I wanted a permanent position there. I said yeah, drunk as I was.

The next morning I didn't remember. My girlfriend, Amanda, said "Get up! We gotta go shopping."

"For what?"

"You need to get some lingerie and stuff to work in," she informed me.

"Since when did they change the dress code at the Club Maryland?" I asked.

She told me what had happened during my drunken blackout and I slowly remembered my purse and looked inside. There were googobs of money in there. I had made $800 on three songs!

Good as the money was, my first reaction was, "But I can't do this!"

"I do it every night," said Amanda. "I work there." She was paying her way through law school and eventually passed the bar.

So I got dressed and we went shopping.

I went to work that night and had a couple shots to relax me. As the night went on, I had a couple more drinks and really got into it. I thought this ain't as bad as it seems. Not like I was taking off my underwear. Then I was making really good money, almost a grand a night.

Not that I saved any of the money. I traveled. One night, right by the airport, me and some of the girls got off of work and decided we wanted to go to New York City, drunk as hell. We bought airline tickets, took the redeye and woke up in a hotel but didn't know how we got there because we didn't even remember the flight.

I was also taking care of my sisters with my newfound wealth. My sisters had the best of everything and good clothes for school. I wanted to give them all the things I didn't have. I would give my stepmom money for dog food every now and then. I just loved her to death because by the time I was 18, I had gotten respect for her. She was like my Mom after she raised me.

My whole family knew I was stripping and they weren't very happy about it—especially Jeannie. She was disappointed in me. She thought I was dancing butt-naked in front of guys and probably being touched on and she didn't know that it was a very controlled atmosphere. She looked at me, like, "This is my daughter and I don't want my daughter doing that."

My Aunt Amy wouldn't allow me to come to her wedding. Everyone was afraid one of the guys would recognize me. I said, "You're afraid of that?! What are these guys doing at the strip club?!!"

I was really hurt. Jeannie's mother hated the whole thing, too. She said, "You're grown and I can't make your decision for you but I don't support it. You're better than that."

My mother was a different story. She said, "Don't just go up there and take off your clothes and pull your garter out for money. Get up there and show them that you can be an artist at what you're doing. You're not going to get up there and at each song take off some clothes. Be dramatic. You're a drama queen anyway, be dramatic, show people what you can do."

I was hurt and pissed off with everyone else, though. While nobody liked what I did, everybody was benefiting from it and I thought that made it okay. I was taking care of business.

At nineteen-and-a-half, I switched to another club called Ricky's On State which was the hottest strip club in

Milwaukee at the time. The money was flowing like the beer. I was making a shitload. You go to any strip club owner in town and the owner wanted me to come work at his club. I was up on stage 10-12 times a night and in between I was working the floor. And, I had a body from hell.

Chapter
Nineteen

By mid-August of 2000, I had finally made arrangements with Joe to take the kids before they started school. I was prepared for it. Me and the girls had prepared for it together, as a family. It took me a week to pack their stuff up. Then on a Sunday night, Joe came to get them.

I had bathed them one last time. Like triplets, all three had their hair tied back in neat little buns while it dried. They all had their pajamas on and robes and house shoes.

"Don't worry, Mommy, we understand," Brittany said, kissing me on the cheek with her tiny arms around my neck. The other two nodded in agreement.

"I'll try to make it as fast as possible, okay? Just bear with me until I can get everything situated."

They hugged our dog, Chanel. "Don't worry, poopy. We'll be back this weekend. Take care of Mommy." I marveled at their strength to be concerned for me when they had so much hurt themselves.

I stood back and inhaled my three precious daughters with my eyes.

Breanna was wearing her gray jogging pajamas, bear claw house shoes, a white robe with tiny print flowers, and her headphones. Brittany wore her favorite teddy bear gown, red and brown with red ribbons around the neck, Tweety Bird slippers, and a red robe with a lace trim collar. Prissy Bethany had on a two-piece pink satin nightie, with a white and pink robe that tied up with pink ribbons, and Barbie slippers. Bethany held Baby Dill, a near life-size Rugrat that Steve had bought for her. And because Steve bought it, it was her favorite toy.

I got really drunk that night. I kept thinking, I gotta get my kids back. I can't go to prison. I was sick with it. I drank almost a fifth of vodka. I was angry at the world, the government, at myself for working at the Gold Club. If I'd never worked there, I'd still have my kids and wouldn't have been indicted. I sat in a room by myself and drank until four o'clock in the morning. At one point I called Elliott and we talked for 30 minutes. He gave me the positives of why I did what I did—it was best for the kids. But as I started getting drunker and drunker, he became cruel. "If you hadn't turned out to be a stripping ass bitch, maybe you'd still have your kids and I don't want to hear you cry and moan about it."

That first week, the girls called, crying, wanting to come home almost every night. It was torture.

It seemed like everyone was against me. My family said if I had made better choices, this wouldn't be happening to me. "You did this to yourself," they said righteously.

The only family members who were supportive were my aunt Barbara—my father's sister—and my cousin, Kim. "You did what was right at the time. Their Dad is going to take care of them. They're in a good environment," they said, trying to ease some of the guilt and self-loathing.

My mother felt helpless that she couldn't even come down to be with me.

Word got out at work and a lot of the girls felt sorry for me. Most of them had kids and nobody wants to see anybody lose their kids. There were a few whose hate ran deep. They hated me for doing what the fuck I wanted to do with no consequences. "You don't deserve your kids. It's good they're living with their Dad. You're a fuck-up anyway." Most felt sorry about the kids but glad about the indictment. A lot of them said, "I hope she goes to jail. She deserves it."

I always tried to give everybody the benefit of the doubt, a weakness I suppose. That experience taught me to pay more attention to my environment. You can't get caught up and lose yourself to the point you forget who's around you, especially at that level in that game. I forgot rule number one to the hustle: Don't trust nobody.

Later on I started to come to terms with the meaning of the indictment as I read over it with Bruce Harvey. He was explaining to me, "You don't understand. You, right now, besides Larry Gleit, are the closest person to Steve Kaplan besides his wife and kids and they think you know more than what you're telling us. They are not going to make your life any easier than it is right now."

After the indictment, the waiting game of when the trial was going to start began. For two years we waited. Jesus, these people had my life on hold for two years.

Meanwhile, the other dancers became vicious. They would pick on me on principle: I couldn't fight back. If anyone called the police on me for anything I was going to jail. I wouldn't be seeing the light of day until the trial started.

It was payback. I was reaping the rewards of my actions, for being such a power control bitch in 1998. This was their way of getting back for all the times I fired, cussed them out or sent them home. In some way I probably got what I deserve.

There were girls who made it their job to tell customers, "That's the girl who was indicted. You don't want to sit with her."

My money decreased quickly.

I stopped dancing for awhile after we got indicted. I couldn't handle it. I went to promotions. After a while I got tired of it. I told Steve I wanted to go back on the floor. Back to dancing. My customers wanted me to come back. So I went back.

As 1999 went on and into 2000, it got harder and harder. By the end of 1999, the girls were making jokes about it in the dressing room. The girls were getting more vicious and telling more customers that I was indicted.

They took pleasure in small phrases like: You're going to jail.

Really cruel things.

Then as the girls realized the whole indictment thing was serious and real, some of them would come to me and offer support. "Hope you're OK and we got your back." There were a few girls that were still nice to me. But for the most part, I went from being the object of fear and awe to being the butt of dressing room jokes.

I was drinking more excessively than I usually did.

In February of 2000, I announced that I was retiring. I was on the brink of having a nervous breakdown. I was landing myself in the emergency room once a month, on average, for drinking myself into oblivion. The combination of stress, alcohol, heavy duty inhalants and smoke exacerbated my asthma to the point that I was having serious attacks. I was a basket case. But the whole time I kept working. Perhaps Norbie and Roy were smarter on that score: they took off months at a time and still got their salaries.

The housemoms threw me a retirement party with cake and food. A friend of mine who was a regular came and said, "I want you with us tonight." The tip was $1,500. They bought me champagne and sent me out in style.

They announced I was going to do my farewell tribute dance to all the dancers who ever worked at the Gold Club.

The guys in my Gold Room came out on the steps to watch and throw money at me. My farewell skit was S&M with my partner Shaney.

After it was over, I went up to the microphone and thanked everybody for all their support and love and concern. Then, because I couldn't let it go, I said, "And to all the people who have been dogging me out, at the end, when all this is said and done, I can't wait to come back, look you in the face and tell you to kiss my fucking ass!"

I went back to my Gold Room and finished out the night. That was my last dance.

Steve put me on salary and I worked the front door during the day, answered phones and ran errands with the daytime housemom, Allison.

Me and fear were friendly. I was afraid to fail at anything and when I did fail, it hit me like a ton of bricks. That was what was holding me down and making me depressed and what caused me to have a negative attitude all the time.

To me, nothing could go right because I was in this whole indictment thing and I couldn't understand how I got there.

Now I know how I got there. Some of the things I did were wrong. But a lot of the things I did weren't wrong so when I said to the media and the public, "I'm innocent," I was. What the government charged me with in the indictment was just plain bullshit.

* * *

Roy Cicola, the manager next to Norbie, intimidated me. He was extremely attractive, salt and pepper hair and one of the smartest men I've ever met. He was a computer genius with umpteen degrees. It took a year before I would even talk to him. He was a Harley guy who went to Florida for Bike Week. I thought he was mean because he didn't smile much and when he looked at me, he cut his eyes.

I was having a hard night and Norbie was busy with something else. I'd taken all I could. The girls were giving me a hard time and I wasn't making money and must have looked pretty down. That night after work Roy said, "Come here and talk to me." We chatted and he said his feet were hurting. I gave him a foot massage. Roy had been indicted, too. He said, " I know what you're going through. I go through it too but on a different level. I don't feel it as much as you do because I'm on salary. What you face is a lot different from what I face but I understand the heartache behind it. You can always talk to me."

We talked every day after that all the way through court.

The lease on the apartment with Elliott came up. We decided to go our separate ways. He was gone most of the time so it wasn't a big change for me or the children. I got my own apartment with the girls for another six months.

It was then that me and Joe decided that when school started up he would take the kids during the week and I get them on the weekends. It was simpler. There were times when I had to see my parole office or I was being called down for drug screening.

The last time the DFCS lady came up to my house, I told her about the agreement. She wrote a letter saying that I was a fit mom and that my ex-husband would take the kids until my life was back on track and then they could come back to live with me.

I believe they were getting ready to take my children. As she stood there, sanctimoniously screwing with my life, I asked her, "Why were you sent?"

"Somebody from District Attorney Art Leach's office notified us and then we came. That's how we found out." The government had sent DFCS after me.

During all this time there was more stuff coming from the Grand Jury: revised indictments with more charges. Many people were going downtown to talk to the Grand Jury. That summer, we didn't know it, but Jeff Johnson and Frederique were getting their deals ready, ready to turn.

Dancers are so naive. They make all this money and the boyfriends are sitting at home making them feel like they are the shit. Of course the boyfriends couldn't do it if they didn't cater to a certain degree.

These guys make the dancers think they've got a good man at home, who's supportive and thinks they're great but it's brainwashing. Frederique was one of those people. One of her boyfriends used to kick the shit out of her. Another, she helped to buy a sports bar and he dogged her out.

Just before she pled guilty and turned state's evidence, Frederique had gotten into this funky ass mood at work. We didn't know she was pregnant. She wasn't speaking to any-body. Everybody was to leave her alone. She thought every-body was against her. I said, "Frederique, we're both in this together. We got to stay strong. And you say you don't want to talk? Frederique, we're both under indictment together. We're facing this as two women."

She wouldn't speak to me. I was hurt. "I don't have to beg you to be my friend. I don't need you like that."

Then Frederique pled guilty. After that, she can never talk to me again.

It was a weird situation because when we found out that same day she turned, she called Steve apologizing to him, telling him she didn't have a choice. She said she had perjured herself in front of the Grand Jury, that she was afraid of going to jail and losing her child. She told Steve that she knew he didn't do anything wrong.

Frederique's betrayal hit the newspapers on Tuesday, August 22. As the article said, "Kaplan and 14 co-defendants had maintained a united front since the case was first indicted in November. But Pelnis becomes the first employee of the Buckhead club to plead guilty."

She was pregnant. The government had her believing all sorts of shit about what was going to happen to that child. She pled guilty to aiding a racketeering conspiracy. Usually she'd get up to five years, but since she turned and lied, her possible sentence was less than one year.

That's when Art Leach, the U.S. Attorney, started leaking all the celebrity sex stuff. They only used initials but it was pretty obvious who was who. Frederique told the grand jury that Steve paid her to have sex with these guys. She said a lot more later on the stand.

November of 2000 was difficult. It was just after Halloween. The decorations were still up. I was getting nervous because it was getting close to February 28th when the trial was originally supposed to start. I was depressed and scared, taking both Prozac and Xanax. That stuff depressed me even more.

My life was crumbling and I was losing everything slowly. I saw it but there was nothing I could do to stop it. One night when I was really drunk I drove home from work. I called a friend from the car, about five o'clock in the morning, and she said, "Get out of the car and stop driving around." I was driving around drunk as hell. I didn't care anymore. I was tired. I went upstairs and did exactly the same thing I did when I was 16. I emptied my medicine cabinet. Being an asthmatic

I had a lot of stuff in there with epidrine in it. Epidrine elevates the heart and can cause an instant heart attack.

After I took everything, my dog, Chanel, came around the corner. She just looked at me. She knew I was hurting. I called Elliott and I tried to talk to him and tell him I was having a really hard time. He said, "You're fucking drunk. I don't want to talk to you." And he hung up.

That was the final straw. I decided I was just going to lie there.

When my chest started hurting, I dialed 911 and crawled to the front door, unlocked it and waited for the ambulance.

They came and I was drunk and the pills were kicking in. I was apologizing to these guys. "I'm so sorry you have to come over here for this stupid thing I did."

They looked at me and recognized me from TV. One said, "Ma'am, I understand you're going through a lot right now. Just relax, we're going to take you to the hospital."

At the hospital, the nurse said, "You didn't mean to do this, did you?"

"No, if I'd been sober, I wouldn't have done it. I promised God when I was 16, I'd never do this again."

I left the next morning to go to an adult clinic for psychiatric help. I stayed one day and met with the counselor the next. She and I sat and talked and I told her I didn't need to be there. It wasn't the place for me. I needed to cut back on my drinking. I already knew the answer.

She said, "Sometimes when you're feeling like this, just don't be alone. Call somebody and go see them or have them come see you."

I had a neighbor I could have called that night, pounded on his door and he would have been there for me. But being selfish, all I was thinking about was my pain, and that everything was all about me. I worried. What if I had died that night? What if I had left my girls? What would they think of their mother? It was a cop out.

"My Mom killed herself." That was not something I wanted stuck in the back of their minds for the rest of their lives. When I sobered up, it was an eye opener and I realized what I had really done. I was so ashamed, I didn't tell anyone.

Second, I didn't need a suicide attempt to follow me with DFCS sniffing around. If they had known, they would have surely tried to take the kids away from me fully. So I said to myself, "All right, you dingbat, look what you did. Let's move on. You've got some serious problems in your life and you need to try and figure out what's next."

Rather than go to a shrink, I started praying heavily. It was the bottom. It was worse than being homeless because that was a condition I could work my way out of.

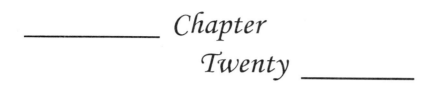

Chapter Twenty

My Mom came to see me and got a job waitressing at Ricky's. I was 18 years old at the time. Soon we became roommates again. I moved back in with her and Rock who had gotten another apartment across town. By now Rock was paralyzed, shot in a robbery for money and drugs. He made the best out of the situation, talking about his days in Vietnam, about a tree log he saw in the road there that turned out to be a giant snake. He was years from pimping, from being a player, but in his heart he remained wild.

We had a neighbor, Greg, who used to come to the house, watch football games. I worked at Greentree Nursing Home up the street, planning menus and prepping food. One day I was getting ready to walk to work. It was very cold and I was headed out the door and was coming around the corner. There weren't any sidewalks. Greg yelled out from his apartment upstairs, "You want a ride up the hill?"

"Sure," I said gratefully. Snow blanketed the ground and I could feel the icy wind slicing my face.

"Gimme a minute. Let me throw something on," he called down and then he buzzed me up.

I went up and sat on the couch, listening to him talking as he got dressed in the other room. He was telling me about going to University of Wisconsin Milwaukee. I said, "That's great."

Then he came running out of the room, punched me in the face, grabbed me by the hair and dragged me down the hallway. He pushed me into his room and tore at my clothes. He hit me in the face again and my lip busted. Blood went everywhere. He hit me again and my nose busted. He was trying to get my pants off.

I lied and said, "Greg, please don't do this to me. I just had surgery and you can kill me." That made him snap back. "I'm so sorry," he said, dazed, moving away from me. "I ... I don't know what I'm doing. Come in the bathroom and let me clean your face."

I was trying to be nice as he cleaned my face with luke-warm tap water and a rag. "Greg, what is wrong with you?" I asked gently.

"I don't know. I'm so sorry. You're so beautiful I want you."

"You don't have to go about it like this," I said soothingly. "I'm going to go home and go to my room. I'm not going to say anything to my mother."

He believed me. I got out the door and ran to the apartment, flew to the phone and dialed 911. By the time the police got there, he was already gone but I gave them a description and the address of another friend of Greg's. He was a normal guy, tall, golden brown hair with a short fro, brown eyes.

They looked for him for a week. Later we discovered Greg had not only tried to rape me but had actually carried out a rape against a lady a few nights prior to me, across the street.

Greg got 26 years. For a while, after that, I wouldn't leave the house. I quit my job. My Mom was worried about me.

* * *

I met Eric the following summer. I was nineteen. He was a hustler, a drug dealer. He was gorgeous, 6'3" light-skinned black guy with brown eyes who wore his hair in a low box cut fade. He had a thin muscular build. We dated about a year. At the same time I met Eric and Greg Jackson, they introduced me to Greg's sister, Paula.

Paula was one of the downest, realest bitches I've ever met in my life. She didn't take any shit. She didn't lie. She was a hustler who knew instinctively how to make money. After we met, we clicked and became inseparable. She taught me how to walk and how to carry myself. She was 5'11" with cocoa brown skin and hair that was never in the same style two weeks in a row. Back then, she was a hustler, a dancer and a drug dealer. Together we were ghetto fabulous, unstoppable. She didn't let anybody hold her down and she was always going to be all right.

Eric dealt cocaine and weed. Before long, I started dealing coke as well, selling about 2-3 keys a week. A kilo of coke cost about $8,000-10,000. If the going price was $8,000, I'd charge $8,500 and make a nice profit. Making about $5,000 a week between dancing and dealing, I was taking care of my little sisters and brother and giving my stepmom money. I took trips and was spending just to be spending because I had it.

I'd do coke occasionally but I didn't really care for it because it made your cheeks numb and your brain paranoid. Besides, my life as a drug dealer was short-lived. There was a guy I dealt with about twice a week who did me in.

We always met down at the lakefront of Milwaukee at the Rocks. It was an area called Northpoint on Bradford Beach. I got out of the car and greeted him as usual and he pulled a 9mm and told me to give him all my money, drugs and jewelry That day, I had two keys on me I was supposed to deliver. In exchange, he was bringing me a duffel bag of money. I had $3,000 cash, $20,000 in jewelry and the two keys of cocaine. I was scared to death. This man was going to blow my head off. I kept thinking, if I make it out alive, I'm getting out of the game. It's just not worth it.

The guy took it all and let me go.

Chapter
Twenty-One

The next big thing to come along in the case just shows how fucked up things were. Steve's ex-girlfriend, Debbie Pinson, shows up in the papers. It's February of 2001. Debbie had been talking to the grand jury from the beginning back in 1999. Steve knew about it and that Debbie had it in for him.

To find out what Debbie was saying, Steve hired a private investigator, Robbie Burton, to go out to Las Vegas where she worked at the Hard Rock Casino. Debbie knew Robbie Burton from before and trusted him. Anyway, he went to lunch where she worked and tipped her a hundred bucks to meet him somewhere.

At the meeting, Burton's tape recorder was running. He told Debbie he was worried about what might happen to him regarding stuff that happened when he worked at the Gold Club.

Steve's attorneys entered the tape, with all her bitchy comments, as evidence that she was out to get him. The media, who were all over the Gold Club story 24/7, found out about the tape and naturally wanted a copy. Debbie had talked about athletes getting their dicks sucked, along with the other bullshit of interest. Sports Illustrated and CNN teamed up and got their lawyers to file a motion with the Judge to get the tape unsealed.

The Debbie Pinson tape went public on February 23. She was on the record for saying that Steve told us—the Gold Club employees—how to commit credit card fraud. To that she added, she'd never actually seen the credit card scam committed. Debbie also volunteered that there was some scam that Steve ran about Delta tickets but she didn't know how it worked. She said that Steve was prostituting us but she had no knowledge of criminal activity at the club. Which is it, bitch? I thought when I heard about her grand confession. Debbie probably shot herself in the foot when she got personal. She ranted on about what a shit Steve was to her and how she hated him.

No sooner had the Debbie Pinson tapes been released, then the Feds decided to tie Steve to the mob—to the Gambino family, no less. In the sense that Steve's kids and John Gotti Jr.'s kids went to the same private school on Rhode Island—$50,000 a semester—they were tied together. So that made them, what? PTA affiliates? I don't care where you go, you're going to know somebody. That's just the way it is. But you can't be guilty by association.

Michael DiLeonardo was supposed to be Steve's "Gambino guy." At first, he wasn't in the indictment with us because they knew the case wasn't strong enough. Also, the Feds figured if they threw the mob thing in it would look more glamorous, and make Steve look more fucked up because he and Mike DiLeonardo were such good friends.

They accused Michael Dileonardo, a.k.a. "Mikey Scars," of being a Gambino captain. For the money laundering charge, the Feds said the cash that went up to the Gold Club corporate headquarters in New York every week was actually to pay off the Gambino family. Once a week, according to the Feds, the Gold Club was using every penny of its profits to pay off the Mob.

Meanwhile, the Feds had John Gotti Jr. put away in a Federal pen in New York for 77 months on extortion, fraud, gambling and bribery charges. His old man was, and is, in the pen for life. Somehow, prosecuting attorney Art Leach thought Mr. Gotti's son was going to cooperate with him.

Going on that assumption, he had John Gotti, Jr., transferred down to the Atlanta Federal Pen, close by. The move created a media feeding frenzy. While they were waiting for the real dirt, they wrote stories about the infamous Atlanta Federal Pen. Step right up! Former home to Al Capone!

By then, I was guilty by association, too. People even looked at me as if I was guilty and my life flipped upside down overnight.

From this experience, I realized society was made up of two types of people and not much in between. The first type believed that I was innocent until proven guilty. Then there was the other half of society who figured, if I was being charged, I had to have done something. The Feds wouldn't pick on me for no reason.

My face was in the papers and on television constantly so even when I left the courtroom, I couldn't go any place in public without people feeling it was okay to judge me there, too. Seemingly normal people would recognize me in the street and call me a "whore," "Steve Kaplan's little bitch," "Mafia girl" or "Heidi Fleiss." I had all sorts of nicknames.

One day me and Heather were out in traffic on the way to drop the kids off at their Dad's and this taxi pulls up next to us at a stop light. The cabbie was waving to get my attention. Our windows were down. He called over to us, "You are the woman! You go, gold girl!"

In the grocery store, people asked for my autograph. There wasn't any place I could go where people didn't have some sort of emotional reaction or comment to make.

I found out who my friends were in the worst way. Before the trial, I was A-list Atlanta. I was invited to all of the big functions—parties with the mayor, local media personalities, dignitaries. Before the trial, thousands of people welcomed and accepted me—at least to my face. During the trial, only a handful were left.

Things were really starting to close in. Steve had been taking care of me. Although I was still working, my money was running low. I wasn't making the bucks I used to. I had expenses. A lot of them—three kids, a car note, insurance, and medical insurance, along with the fact that my lease was up and I couldn't afford to get a new apartment.

"If you're found guilty, God help you," my lawyer Bruce Harvey warned me, "the court can take everything you have for restitution."

I started making plans to put stuff in storage when a friend decided to spend some time in New York and I got his place for a while. Meanwhile, me and Joe were working out the best thing for the kids, because it looked as if the trial was finally going to start.

I was damned if the court was going to take my stuff so I started to sell it off, but then ended up giving it away. I decided I'd give it away before I let the government steal it. It was sad. We even had to give up our dog, Chanel. We found a good family with children through the Humane Society. My car note got to be too much to handle and I had to let it go. Then I moved in to Steve's Dunwoody house.

At the same time the trial was warming up, I had other things I was working on. I had had my chance to think about what I wanted to do with my life. I wanted to be the Diva I was, but the Diva that inspired others.

Once you are Diva, after all, there's no taking it out of you. It's an attitude, more or less, the way you carry yourself. You can be 65 years old and wrinkled but as long as you're dressed to the hilt and you've got your head held high, that's the true Diva. A Dominating, Independent, Vivacious, Adult. That's what that word stands for.

I couldn't just sit there and play the victim. I had to push forward in any way I could—and then the opportunity presented itself. There was a tanning salon in Buckhead called Sunday's where all the girls at the club had a great membership package. That's how I met the owner, Richard Rubin. We became friends. Three years prior, I had noticed little plaques around the salon and asked what they were for. It was then I became involved with Richard's pet cause—Project Open Hand—which had a meals on wheels program for AIDS patients. It also provided the funds for the delivery of three meals a day to the elderly, people on dialysis, others who were shut away. Right away, I wanted to get involved.

Every year Project Open Hand did some type of charity event to raise money. That year, we had planned a photography auction at the tanning salon. I was grateful to have something useful to do to take my mind off the trial.

The media was lazy. That investigative reporter stuff doesn't mean shit. There were a few who worked hard but most would only report what they heard or saw in the courtroom, and get it ass backwards. The day before the trial started, I did a 15-minute interview with a local TV anchor. It was aired the night before the trial. For the first time, the people who had been following the Gold Club got to see who I was. They got to see me smile, cry, and laugh. They even saw me angry. I got my nerve up and asked the anchor on-air if she would MC the auction for Project Open Hand. The answer, of course, was Yes.

That TV interview may not have shifted public opinion, but it did help me to relax that trial eve. All of us—me, Steve, Russell, Jimmy, Norbie, Heather, Mike DiLeonardo—were sitting around the TV at Steve's Dunwoody house and watching me on the news. Steve was on his feet clapping and screaming and hugging me. "You are the woman! You are so strong!" he cheered. The approval felt good.

The first week of the trial, April 30th thru May 4th, John Gotti Jr. was finally brought down from New York to that Atlanta Federal Pen. He pleaded the fifth, wanting to have nothing to do with this.

During the second week, the jurors were chosen. Out of 98 possible jurors, both sides whittled down to the needed 12 regular jurors and six alternates. The newspapers were reporting that the trial would last three months to five months. Reporters were salivating, wondering what jock was going to be named as having his pants down and his dick out.

Steve Sadow and our lawyers looked hard at the jurors' attitudes, whether they were backwards, judgmental assholes or not. They wanted people who understood what life is like. The defense questioned jurors as to how they felt about religion and the mob and strip clubs. We had a defense block of a devout Jehovah's Witness. We blocked a member of the Mothers Against Drunk Driving group. A man who listened to Christian radio. The prosecution, on the other hand, kept a man off who believed in legalized prostitution.

It took them two weeks to come up with the 12 and six: seven men and five women. Steve Sadow said that was the best jury panel in twenty years in federal court. We had a diverse jury. There were so many different people, it made it easy for them to get along and listen to all the evidence and build bias at the same time.

* * *

Chapter
Twenty-Two

There was a place across the street from Ricky's in Milwaukee called Hoops that had just opened. It was beautiful, just huge, on the scale of the Gold Club. Their stage had a runway that was gigantic so I went over there and auditioned. The owner said, "Oh, you're the one from across the street. You're hired, I need you in my place. I heard about your drink sales over there. You're incredible."

In addition to the drink sales—which are important to any club owner—I put on a really great show. I didn't prance. I danced. I didn't pose. I would bend and move like a fantasy. I could be sexy without being vulgar. I knew how to catch a guy's attention. You have to really look at a person when you want them to look at you. You get their attention and then express to them why you want them to look at you.

With the great setup, and the runway and stage to work with, I started putting on skits with costumes and themes from movies like "Flashdance." I had my lighting set up with the lighting guys and brought in pyro techs for my explosions.

I had so many regulars it was hard to go around and speak to them all, I couldn't.

My Mom came over to Hoops and started waitressing there. The next thing I knew, I had convinced her to do a mother/daughter thing. Mom was twenty years older than me, 98 pounds soaking wet, and still had her beautiful long red hair.

There was a main stage and then another smaller stage behind the bar. I said, "Mom, work the small stage first, I'll do the main stage and they'll announce us as the mother-daughter team. Once you get comfortable you can come up on the main stage with me."

We did one really nice choreographed show of Purple Rain that was very tasteful and made a crapload of money—$500 just in tips. She never did it again but she was still very proud of the way I carried myself and that I was a dancer, not a stripper. My Mom sat down with me and explained. "There is a difference, Jackie," she said. "Anybody can take off their clothes. It's another thing to entertain."

I felt like I was coming alive. I entered and won Miss Teen Wisconsin pageant. I paid for the table for my family to come see me right up front but nobody came. Afterwards, I stopped by Dad and Jeannie's. She was sitting on the couch and eying my crown. "You won?"

"Why didn't you guys come?"

"Your Dad said he had something else to do." She put her head down. She couldn't say anything.

At twenty, I got pregnant—again—with Joe—again—and my dancing career ended. I danced until I was four months at which point the baby busted outta nowhere.

My Dad made us get married.

Joe, who was by then in the Marine Corps, came home on leave for Christmas. My Dad called the pastor at my stepmom's church and set our date. Everything was moving so fast. I paid for my own wedding—for all of it. I was so miserable I didn't even have my own wedding dress—it was an aunt's old bridesmaid's dress—not how I envisioned getting married the first time.

Dad gave me Sue Dagey's credit card, in front of Jeannie, for Joe to take me to dinner and for us to get a hotel. I just looked at him and shook my head. Fine.

In spite of the circumstances, I was happy to be marrying Joe because that's what I wanted. I thought that marriage was the right thing. Lo and behold I did not know. Ten days after we were married he had to ship off to the Mediterranean for six months on the U.S.S. Roosevelt, guarding nuclear weapons on the ship. So it turned out, Joe wasn't there for the last six months of the pregnancy. He wasn't there to see our first child be born.

The pregnancy went on, with my cousin Clarence and my Mom and sister Marquita for support, while Joe was on a six-month deployment to the Mediterranean Sea. Every day after work I could count on Clarence coming from that bus stop to our grandmother's house and he would rub my belly for me because I was miserable. He found out during the same period that his girlfriend was pregnant, too.

I was almost ten months pregnant. Labor went on for three weeks during which I was induced seven times. On the eighth appointment to be induced, my Dad was outside barbecueing.

I said, "Dad, I got to go to the hospital."

"Yeah? What are you telling me for? The hospital is five blocks up the road."

"Dad, I'm having contractions. They are worse then they've ever been."

He insisted I should just get in the car and drive myself.

I grabbed Marquita, who was about 14 years old, and made her drive me to the hospital. She parked the car, came back, but they wouldn't let her in for labor or delivery. So she had to walk home. I said, "Don't walk. Take the car."

After some cajoling she drove again, scared to death she was going to crash or get stopped. I wanted natural childbirth.

I didn't want any pain medicine. It got to be about five o'clock in the afternoon, two hours from my inducement appointment at three. Everybody in the hospital knew me.

About eight o'clock I couldn't stand being alone anymore and called my Mom at Ricky's. I said, "Mom, this is it. I'm in the hospital. I've been in since one and I don't wanna be by myself no more."

She started screaming through the phone, "Paul! I'm leaving! Jackie's having the baby!" All you hear in the background is the bell ring, the bell that signals two for one drinks. In honor of me having my baby, ding ding ding! Two for one! Jackie's having the baby!

My Mom arrived: She kicked open the hospital room door and came flying in, all dramatic. "Got here as fast as I could. How are you doing? How are you feeling?"

My mother was rubbing my hands in hers and I could smell their sub sandwiches, nauseating.

My Mom said, "Why don't you get some pain medicine?"

"No, Mom, I want natural childbirth. I don't want my baby drugged-up when she comes out of me."

Around midnight my water broke and I got excited. The hours kept ticking by until it was morning. The lady across the hall was throwing things, she was in so much pain. I'm thinking, "I can't believe that woman's only been in that room for about an hour and she's losing it and I've been here since yesterday at one o'clock." I yelled across the hall, "Bitch, shut up!"

She yelled back, "Fuck you!"

My Mom is over in the chair, dying laughing.

About 3:16 in the afternoon, Breanna came by c-section. She was nine pounds, twelve ounces, and 22 inches long. She looked like Frankenstein.

Joe called four days later while I was still in the hospital. Breanna was crying because she was hungry and he got to hear her for the first time. "Did you hear that?" he breathed like he'd heard an alien just landed from outer space.

The last day in the hospital they had a dinner for the new parents. I was living with my grandmother at the time so I called her and said, "It would be an honor for you to come and have dinner with me."

Grandma Ann got all dressed up and brought a pretty robe and house shoes for me to dine in and we celebrated the coming of this first child.

The next morning I got out of the hospital and my cousin Clarence came to get me, like the surrogate husband he had become during the last six months of my pregnancy. Clarence was so excited about having his own baby that when I came home from the hospital, I asked him to hold Breanna but he would not touch her. "I want to hold my own child first before I hold my niece," he said.

He was hooked on crack. Before I left Virginia two weeks after Breanna was born, in the later part of 1989, I begged him to get some help for his addiction. "Please get off that stuff. You got a baby on the way." He promised he would find help and beat the crack but he didn't make it.

Two weeks after Breanna was born, I packed up and moved to Virginia. Joe was due to come in a week after I moved, and I was excited because he was going to see his daughter for the first time. Jimmy drove with me and the baby to help us get situated and then went back to Milwaukee.

I was so nervous the night before Joe was to arrive, I made myself throw up and had terrible diarrhea. It was so overwhelming. I stayed with my friend Betty until the day Joe got to the base. The military lets all of the new mothers go right out to the pier and our husbands were the first to get off the ship.

All of the new mothers were lined up with their strollers and the new fathers were lined up at the edge of the ship. As they pulled in, I saw Joe waving wildly.

I had gained 82 pounds during the pregnancy but miraculously lost every ounce and was back down to my regular clothes.

Joe picked up the baby and held her at a distance like she might bite. "Oh, she's so cute!" he managed to say.

"Hold her close to you," I said, rearranging her in his arms. "She needs to feel you."

"You had this big baby? Where's all the baby stuff?"

I was skinny. My stomach was flat as a board. My six pack was even back. So Joe and I launched into life in a wonderful marriage.

Two weeks after Joe had come home, I got a note on my front door from the office saying to call home immediately. The phone had not even been turned on yet. I walked to the pay phone, with Breanna lying in a harness on my chest. My uncle's girlfriend answered the phone at my grandma's house.

"I heard something's wrong. What is it?" I asked, on pins and needles.

She said, "How are you?"

"What is wrong? I just got this message. Tell me what is wrong."

She started crying, "I don't know how to tell you this." Then I heard silence as she passed the phone off to my Aunt Brenda, one of my father's sisters.

Her voice cracked but then steadied. "You have to come home."

"What?"

"Clarence is dead. He got shot to death last night after stealing a car."

My sweet cousin Clarence, hooked on crack, got high and stole a car. A neighbor that saw the whole thing said it was racially motivated. Most of the cops were white, there was one black cop that got there after the fact. The neighbor saw my cousin get out of the car with his hands in the air. Clarence said, "I'm going to get my wallet out," and when he reached for it, the cops started shooting, calling him "Nigger! You crackhead!" and other things like that.

As my Aunt Brenda gave the details, we both cried. It couldn't really register. There was no way Clarence was dead.

Aunt Brenda said, "I got a plane ticket for you at the airport. Go home and pack a bag."

I was in a daze walking home. I packed, set my bags by the front door and called a cab. I had completely forgotten about my husband. He came in, saw the suitcases, and thought I was leaving him. "Where are you going?" he asked.

I had this dazed look and Breanna still on my chest. I had never taken her off. I fell to the floor crying, "Clarence is dead."

Joe rose to the occasion. "I got the next six days off and I could take four more days. Let's go home." It was the Fourth of July. With Joe at my side, we drove and canceled the plane ticket. We saw the fireworks in the distance. My cousin's gone. I couldn't get my mind around the facts. I drove the whole way home, 7-1/2 hours for a ten hour drive from Virginia.

At my grandmother's house, Joe said, "Look, I'm going to take the baby and go to my Mom's so we can lay down and get some sleep because it's obvious you're not going to be sleeping."

As they drove off, I walked in to mass confusion. People were cooking and my grandmother was down on the floor with a hammer tapping down a runner. I was standing behind her. "Grandma Ann?"

She looked up and said briefly, "Oh, you're home," and continued tapping as if it hadn't registered, my arrival.

Three beats later, she jumped up and started crying and screaming and fell into my arms. And I looked around and asked, "What is going on? Where is he?"

"He's dead."

"No, I don't want to believe it." I looked at my aunt, Clarence's mother, my Aunt Barbara. She couldn't cry, she couldn't do anything.

"Well, my son is in heaven. We got things to do." She was smiling. She looked at everybody else crying but she could not cry. His sister was a basket case.

My brother Jimmy was outside with friends and grabbed me as I came out. "You're home. You're home. When did you get home?"

"I just got home. I didn't know you were out here."

"It's my fault …. " Jimmy began, looking at me through blood shot eyes filled with pain.

"What!?"

"If I had stayed with him, he wouldn't did that."

"Jimmy, don't do this to yourself. C'mon now, it's not your fault. You didn't tell him to go steal that car. He was high. He wanted to go sell the car and make some money and get his drugs." Grandma had finally cut Clarence off financially. She would take his paychecks from him and distribute money to him a little at a time. But my grandfather put his foot down and said, "No more. You take his check and you keep it and if the mother of his children needs anything, then you give her the money, but don't give him any more."

It was tit for tat. Either you give him the money and let him do the drugs and he's saved. Or you take the money away and then this happens. Either way, Clarence was headed down the wrong road.

I looked down at the casket, and the body lying there didn't look like Clarence. I kept saying, "This is not my cousin lying in that casket. Who is this guy?"

They didn't have his hair fixed the way he would usually wear it. His little scraggly mustache was gone. He was all trimmed up with makeup. I collapsed right there on the floor in front of his casket.

The family asked me to speak the next day at the funeral because I was the closest one to him. He taught me how to drive. We did everything together. We went to the playground and I'd watch him play basketball at the park. It was me, Jimmy, Clarence and his sister Kim. He taught me not to take life for granted and that you can't dwell on the bad aspects of life like doing drugs, running the streets and going against the law because it doesn't work. I couldn't finish. I just broke down.

My husband was very good during that time. He was there for me. We buried Clarence and went back to Virginia. Shortly after, we got relocated to California.

San Diego, California, was beautiful and I loved it right away. The museums, the weather, the zoo, the people—I loved it all. On the way out, in Arizona, I got pregnant. It was a long drive.

In less than three weeks I got a job with the Mexican Chamber of Commerce out of San Diego and Tijuana. My boss's name was Carlos Martinez. He worked out of his house, right around the corner from us. I started out as his Administrative Secretary and quickly became a board member. Mr. Martinez thought I would do better on the board than working as his secretary. We voted on issues that went on in the city of San Diego, like conventions.

When I went on maternity leave we got base housing at Camp Pendleton in San Clemente and we were too far away for me to work for the Chamber. Also, with two kids and Joe gone much of the time, it was too much to balance and I stopped working all together and became a full-time house mommy.

I had friends, other military wives at the base. There was a sweet girl named Gabby who had a little daughter Joey, and a girl named Amy King who later became a flight attendant and was sadly on the second plane that hit the World Trade Center. There was Melissa and Than, a little Vietnamese girl.

I spent my days cleaning house, cooking, looking after the kids and shopping. Me and Gabby would go back and forth to each other's houses because there was really nothing to do but visit with each other on the base.

Joe was in the field back and forth. They were training for the Gulf War that started a year after we moved. The Marine Corps knew a year before it started. Half of Joe's platoon was shipped over to Saudi Arabia and spent seven months there, building an American city over there to use as a military base. He was gone a lot so it was just me and Breanna and my friends.

I had this thing when I was pregnant with our second child. I could tell when there was going to be an earthquake. I'd get nervous, start pacing the floor. Toward the end of my pregnancy, Gabby spent a lot of time with me because her husband was in the same platoon as Joe.

At night, every now and then, I'd start pacing, she'd say, "Will you stop that?"

I said, "It's going to happen as soon as I lie down, the house is going to shake." And it did. I lay down and the house shook.

Chapter
Twenty-Three

By the week of May 21, 2001 Judge Hunt said that prosecution had "misinformed" the court about the possible length of the trial.

FBI agent Robert Vandette got up and said the FBI had been trying to get Steve to turn on Gotti for months back in 1996. Vandette's job was to get Steve to turn informant. Steve told him the truth, he hardly knew Gotti. He couldn't inform on what he didn't know. It was more than a coincidence that the court learned that one month after Steve turned down the FBI—in April of 1996—they started investigating the Gold Club.

It was like reading a Mario Puzo novel, learning the ins-and-outs of Mafia culture. The prosecution talked some more about Mike DiLeonardo being a "capo"(a captain) in the Gambino family. The prosecution even brought a whole eraser board full of mob terms so everybody would know them.

The biggest hole in Leach's case was the fact that the Feds didn't tape anything. They set a nice stage for a Mafia connection and the witnesses were certainly Mafia-bred, but there wasn't any evidence to back up what they said. Another FBI agent, named John Steubing, said it was standard for them to have wiretaps and bugs.

Steubing got called to the stand and talked about how the FBI paid their witnesses and informants. The Fed's informants and "cooperating witnesses" didn't have to say how they spent the money—they could do anything they wanted with it. "Cooperating witnesses" are the criminals who turn and then become available to the court for testimony at anytime. "Confidential informants," on the other hand, stay in the middle of whatever scam they're in and the Feds give them money for information. Nobody has to sign any receipts. The FBI agents are simply told to make expenses "reasonable." A full-time cooperating witness could have all of their living expenses paid by the FBI. Even if the guy is already in prison, the Feds put the money in his commissary account.

Dino Basciano, for instance, received $188,000 from the Federal Government once he began testifying. They moved his family four times and gave them money to live on while he was in prison. In addition to the money, Basciano got out early.

In return for the money the informants get, none of the information required to be recorded—they just regurgitate it from memory.

So that was it. All the testimony about Steve's connection to the mob and his mob payoffs came strictly from paid gangsters without one scrap of evidence to back them up.

We had to sit and listen to more government witnesses. This one guy got up there and smiled and bragged about how he used to torture people to steal their money and drugs and whatever else was in their houses. It was an evil art. One victim was taken into the bathroom, sat in a chair, and then the gangster slit his scalp open and peeled it back. There was ten million dollars hidden in the house somewhere. One guy would not tell him where the money was. He said, "Please kill me. I want to go be with my daughter." His daughter had gotten killed a month prior and he wanted to go be with her. The guy says, "Why should I let him die? He didn't give me what I wanted. All I asked for was the money." He dumps him in the Everglades. It's like a popular graveyard for these guys.

This guy was in the witness protection program. He got $100,000 to move him and his immediate family to a safe location. They changed his identity, his name, everything—guys like him testified in front of big cases like ours because they really were involved in organized crime. They're considered to be good people to testify because they've been in the Mafia and know what it's all about, so they can come in and make up stories about people and go live their lives and get paid to do it by the government.

As the FBI agents began to testify, I started recognizing some of the guys I'd been seeing for months. One was John Iocavelli. He walked in the door and I said, "That is the same person I've seen at the mall! Ain't this a bitch?"

Everywhere I went it seemed like I was running into him. I passed him on the mall escalator and when he looked at me he turned his head as if to scratch, because he caught me looking at him. I kept seeing him all over the mall. When he walked in the courtroom I knew it was the same guy. He had on jeans and a shirt and tennis shoes like an average schmoe on the street. I told my lawyer, "I remember him. He used to follow me sometimes."

You couldn't miss this guy because he has pointy ears, salt and pepper hair, high cheekbones and his eyes are a cross between Asian and Italian. I was stunned when I first heard him speak; he had this high nasal annoying voice, not the deep, voice you would expect.

There was another one, John Simmons, who also liked to follow me. He looked like your average white man—sandy blond short hair, 5'11" or so. Nothing distinct. My lawyer told me about him. When I saw him in the courtroom and knew who he was, I thought, "You bastard. I hope you got what you were looking for."

All that time, he'd been like a ghost in the shadows watching me but I'd never seen him.

Then there was Agent Mark Sewell, an average to small-size guy with a high and tight Marine Corp haircut. His neck and face were always red and when he was angry, he got even redder. He looked like a rat with beady little blue eyes, not handsome, gipper little walk, pouty little mouth and big ears.

Sewell had installed a camera across the street from the Gold Club at the Wachovia Bank. He installed the camera, changed the tapes and monitored who was coming and going. He made tapes for ten months.

When I found out my phones were tapped, I was furious. Who do these people think they are to just come into my life like this, listen to all my phone conversations, follow me wherever I go, take pictures of me at the pool in Vegas? What do you want? Leave me alone. I felt violated. It made me mad to think they might be following my kids to school. There is no such thing as privacy, none, not when dealing with the federal government. I was nervous all the time.

I felt like cars were following me.

Feds drive Suburbans and Tahoes and F-350 extended cab pickup trucks, Blazers—normal nice cars you would never think are FBI—instead of the typical Caprice Classic Chevrolet or Ford Crown Victoria. Regular cop cars.

At one point I thought I was going crazy about being followed. I went to Steve at the club.

"Steve, are these people following us?" I asked although I knew the answer.

"Yeah, they are. I been going through this for years," he said matter-of-factly.

"Steve, I don't like this. Why do they have to follow us?"

"Because they want to see what you're doing at all hours of the day. If they think you're doing something wrong, they want to know where you're at."

This meant everytime we went out of town, there was probably an agent at the airport going through our luggage. A couple of times, on trips to Vegas and Miami, I noticed my stuff had been gone through. It wasn't the way I packed it. I was pissed. "There's nothing in my suitcase. What are you looking for?" I wanted to scream.

The first of June was the end of me living on my own. My kids were with Joe. All I had left were a few things like clothes and photo albums. I had no options. I didn't know what I was going to do and I didn't have time to think about it. I told Steve I was coming to live with him in his Dunwoody house. He said, "Alright."

Since Steve was like my father, if I wanted to move in the house, I could. I had access to any vehicle there if I wanted it. There were no restrictions for me.

Mike DiLeonardo and Jimmy Carillo were already holed up in the Dunwoody house with Steve. It was becoming like a safe house for the indicted.

The house was big and beautiful with five bedrooms, a two-car garage, and a Jacuzzi out back. When you came in the front door, a formal living and dining room were to the right of the foyer. Straight ahead, a grand staircase led up to mine and Steve's bedrooms. On that same hall were two more bedrooms and then at the end, another flight of stairs that led down into a great room. The kitchen was huge and state-of-the-art like everything Steve owned.

The purple velvet couches and the dining room set all matched, accented by deep purple carpeting. There was a big screen TV in the living room and a treadmill in the kitchen, where I exercised every day at 5:30 a.m. The living room was like our "vent" room: it housed a punching bag, a beating bag, some weights and a computer.

I tried to make myself at home and hung my own pictures

in my bedroom. There was one left that Elliott had bought me in a gold frame—a woman sitting on her knees naked with her head down and her hair covering her face. It was a silhouette and it looked different from every angle. It described me when I got depressed, when I needed my quiet time, just meditating and discovering who I was. Who I am.

The other picture I kept was like a walk in the park. A cement trail runs through the trees and flowers, my safe place.

The Dunwoody house, however, did not prove to be the safe place I had hoped it would be. The night I moved in, the FBI were parked at the turn, watching me. I was standing outside smoking a cigarette after unpacking and taking a bath, when I saw a pick-up truck slowly pull into the subdivision. It stopped at the end of the hill on the other side of some bushes. The lights went off and then it crept over to the other side of the street. Someone got out with a camcorder—agent Mark Sewell. I couldn't believe it. It scared me so bad I dropped my cigarette in the bushes and ran upstairs into Mike DiLeonardo's room.

"Mike! Mike!"

"What?"

"Mark Sewell is down at the end of the street with a video camera in his hand. I was out there smoking a cigarette and saw him."

"You're kidding?!"

"No, I'm dead serious. They're parked right down there."

He went to look. When I ran into the house, they got in the truck and drove off. I thought, I can't even smoke a cigarette without worrying that these fucks are going to be sitting out in front of the house. Steve was irate that night. Mike told us all, "Your life will never be the same again." He had been going through this for years. Once they get hold of you, he said, they eventually have to catch you doing something.

"Yeah, they will be watching us from now on," he said, shaking his head, tired.

It was a sick thought.

Two months into the trial, Sewell and Iocavelli were out in front of Steve's house. When they saw me and Steve they drove off.

All of us at the house had this pattern during the trial. I'd get up and do my cycling at 5:30 a.m. to get ready for court. Me, Steve, Jimmy, and Mikey—we'd all go in the van to the courthouse. A lot of times Steve's wife, Mona, would call Steve while we were driving. He had a clipping service in New York so he got all the newspaper articles from *The Post and The Daily*. Mona used to read them to us.

They were talking about me a lot in the New York papers. The sketch artist who worked the Gold Club trial made everyone look like a transvestite.

Mona said to Steve on the phone, not knowing I was in the van, "I hope this Diva girl does not look like this because if you're telling me she's the most beautiful girl in the Gold Club, baby, I don't see it. She looks like a transvestite." Everybody started laughing and Steve snatched the phone off the hands-free kit.

The next day we went golfing after court and Steve called Mona back. He started the conversation with, "Mona, Jackie's in the van. "

"Hi, Mona," I chimed in.

She says, "Sweetie, I finally saw a real picture of you. You are so cute! I didn't know you were in the van that morning. I'm sorry."

"That's okay. That sketch artist sucks."

"He's fucking horrible!"

By the fifth week of the trial, Ziggy copped a plea and took the stand. I'd been waiting for this. I knew he was the biggest stink in this pile of shit. Ziggy didn't even take a plea agreement until the day he went on the witness stand and he had known for two years what he was doing. He should have made his plea and been sentenced but he didn't cop his pleas until the day before he was due up. A lot of them didn't because they were waiting for the best deal.

Ziggy had been feeding the Feds since 1999 on a deal to plead guilty to three charges: the Delta scam, interstate prostitution and income tax evasion. That wasn't because he was necessarily guilty. He just got his nuts caught in a wringer and had to sell somebody out.

By June, when Ziggy finally talked in court, his charges were cut down to one: concealing he knew crimes were committed. He could've had three years on the three charges. But the more he gave the Feds, the less time he got.

He testified in closed court. He couldn't stand to look at us while he lied.

Leach called Ziggy "an insider who knows all." And he was, too, all the bull crap he could pull out of his pea brain. Backstabbing son-of-a-bitch.

Ziggy says Steve set up all of the sex for athletes and prostituted us at the club and on our trips to Vegas and Miami. It was where a lot of the shit they had against me came from. Ziggy said he saw Steve give money to the Gambino family. He saw the weekly bag of money go to New York to Steve's business office, just like any business. Steve just didn't send it FedEx since Jimmy Carillo was coming and going every week anyway. But if Ziggy had been telling the truth, he would have explained how Steve had the Brinks service every day.

Ziggy also took poetic license and made up a fantastic story about Larry Johnson coming in "begging" for Steve to give him a girl. Ziggy plays the part of the upstanding prude and says something like, "I'm so sorry, Mr. Johnson, but we don't do that sort of thing here at the Gold Club." Steve Kaplan, the evil villain, then says, "That's what we need to do here at the Club. We can make these guys bow down. That guy's a superstar. You see he was on his hands and knees to you? Do you understand the power of this club?"

Of course, it was very theatrical, maybe for everyone but me. I knew Larry Johnson and the fact was, he didn't need some small-time pimp to set him up with beautiful classy women nor did he need to pay anyone for sex.

Anyway, Ziggy went on supposedly quoting Steve Kaplan, evil villain, as saying, "We'll use this to draw stars and athletes and that'll draw more people."

The lesbian sex shows along with the sex in the Gold Rooms, again, were Steve's brainchild. Well, other than the fact that the lesbian sex shows were always there, before Steve even bought the club. And they aren't illegal.

Ziggy then started in on the celebrity athletes. Andruw Jones, (who was subpoenaed later to testify), Patrick Ewing, Antonio Davis and guys from the Knicks, Hornets and Pacers who all paid for sex set up by Steve and Ziggy. Antonio Davis later went on to sue Ziggy for $50 million for defamation of character.

Me and Frederique were supposed to be the women who gave out the most sex. Ziggy called me "the Michael Jordan of sexual activity at the club" and Frederique was the "Scottie Pippen." Well, I was "Michael Jordan" at what I did—making men feel comfortable and happy and they paid me out the wazoo for it. Frederique was the sex machine.

Then, Ziggy got around to the first night I saw Dennis Rodman at the Gold Club and we went back to his hotel room at the Ritz-Carlton. Again, he said Steve paid me to have sex with my friend. I knew it would come back and bite us on the ass. I told Steve that at the time. I don't trust Ziggy.

More interesting than anything I did, was that John Starks of the New York Knicks told the grand jury Ziggy had been running girls out of the club to have sex with athletes. There was some trip to Charleston where it was all supposed to have happened. It was unfortunate I wasn't even around then so Ziggy couldn't include me.

The problem was, Ziggy had his own little pimp business on the side and he said it was Steve instead to take the heat off himself. He was about to get nailed when he decided to use the opportunity to get back at the people he hated.

I was at the top of the list, right there with Steve Kaplan. Ziggy couldn't say enough about me being a prostitute. I told the press and public I was innocent, because on the prostitution charge, I was. And because everything else they charged me with in the indictment was bullshit.

The media blew the prostitution piece out of the water and loved every minute of it. Maybe I came across as one of those archetypes—a prostitute with a heart of gold. The media didn't publicize the fact that I was charged with racketeering, conspiracy to commit racketeering, money laundering, extortion, and credit card fraud. I wasn't looking at prostitution charges alone. I was looking at a trumpload of charges. I was looking at 100 years in prison.

All the trips we took with Steve—trips for him to say thank you for all your hardwork and determination—turned into prostitution trips in the court room. In fact, one of the prostitution charges was for the Miami Super Bowl trip at which there were 30 Gold Club employees. Heather did meet Tyson Beckford at a nightclub there. But it wasn't our fault she went back to a hotel with him and had sex. We were out there to have a good time. That was a big 1998 bonus trip.

If the Feds had only charged me with prostitution, it would have been a state case and a misdemeanor. They actually tried to get me on prostitution as interstate commerce, which meant somebody used their credit card to pay me to have sex in and out of the Gold Club. The trips were interstate commerce because we left town and I suppose we got paid to have sex while we were out of town on the credit card.

The Feds also decided that if a customer gave me Gold Bucks at the Gold Club and then we had sex, that was interstate commerce, too, because it was on the customer's credit card wire transfer. The fact is, even if I did (and I did) give a guy a blow job from time to time, big fucking deal. It's not against the law. You have to have intercourse for it to be prostitution. A guy could give me $50 million on his credit card, and I could suck his dick all night long, but it still wouldn't be prostitution.

What the prosecution tried to do with the jurors was to enhance the fact that so much oral sex and so many lesbian shows were going on. The jurors would then draw the conclusion that with all that, there must be some intercourse somewhere. The fact still remains, I never had intercourse in the Gold Club. I didn't have to. I had Frederique and others to do it for me. Why would I risk contracting AIDS?

My lawyer, Bruce Harvey, gave the jurors the laws and rules of adult entertainment and told them to read them thoroughly to understand what was law and what wasn't. Bruce emphasized in his opening statement oral sex and lesbian sex shows aren't against the law in the state of Georgia. They are not crimes. Intercourse for money? That's a crime. But if you have no proof of intercourse, you have no crime.

I never had intercourse in the Gold Club. There were, however, girls who did on a nightly basis. A lot of times, they weren't using condoms. It was just the heat of the moment and they did it. When they got caught, it was, "I can't believe I'm doing this."

Personally, I made more money with my clothes on than with them off. At the Gold Club you didn't even have to take your damn clothes off. If you had just a little intelligence and a mouthpiece, you could talk your way into thousands of dollars. But some girls just didn't have the intelligence, the tact or drive to work that hard to make the money. They felt they had to prostitute themselves. But they didn't and they don't. I'm living proof.

One night, I came in in Ralph Lauren blue jeans, a sweatshirt and boots, and made $3000 sitting in a room not doing a damn thing.

The stupid part about it was, once a girl let a guy screw around with her, then the guy loses respect and figures he can just tip her whatever he feels like. He's done his dirt and the damage is done. If a girl was freelancing like that usually she was going to get burned. I've heard girls in the dressing room say things like, "I let him finger me and all I got was the minimum, two hundred fucking dollars and then we got into an argument." Of course they couldn't go saying anything.

When Steve Sadow took over the courtroom Ziggy just fell in on himself. First Steve got him to admit to the plea deal and the testimony about his prostitution ring. Bruce took part of the cross examination since most of Ziggy's testimony was about me. He got on the trips to Vegas and Miami. He got it out of Ziggy that we, especially me, could earn up to $30,000 in tips per night without having to have any kind of sex.

Bruce says, "You don't have to give sexual favors to get a big tip?"

Ziggy stuttered. "No, you don't."

Bruce then introduced the evidence of my friendship with Dennis Rodman, and how he gave me a diamond bracelet and earrings for my birthday.

Bruce asked Ziggy directly, "Did you see Steve Kaplan give Diva money?"

"No, I didn't," Ziggy answered but then he added Steve told him it happened.

I heard Steve Sadow say forty-five hundred times during the course of three months, "Well, how do you know that?"

"Well, Steve said."

How did Steve say all this shit when half the time he wasn't in Georgia? I'd like to know that my damn self.

Art Leach and his boys worked on their witnesses like they were masterpieces. They'd prep them for weeks at a time to say exactly what they needed them to say. We could see all of the effort they'd put into it. As the prosecution fired questions, it all came out like clock work. It just flowed.

When the witnesses were cross-examined, they got tongue-tied and screwed up their answers. Art Leach was in his chair getting mad, throwing hissy fits.

After Bruce Harvey and Steve Sadow were done with Ziggy, Norbie's attorney Bruce Morris kicked Ziggy's ass on that thing that Norbie took bribes for overlooking sex at the club. Ziggy said that Norbie was going to New Jersey to work as punishment for letting sex stuff happen on his shift. Finally Ziggy had to admit the truth, New Jersey had nothing to do with sex at the club.

Then Morris started in on the police corruption. The Atlanta cop on trial with us, Reginald Burney, was supposed to have taken bribes from the Gold Club to tell Norbie when the city permit inspectors were coming by. Like Larry Johnson, I also knew Reginald Burney personally. He was just this upstanding, model police officer type, really good at his job. He was found "not guilty" on all charges.

The Feds said that because Reginald got comped when he came in, he was somehow guilty or in collusion with us in spite of the fact that it's considered common courtesy among club owners to comp law enforcement as a sign of respect. You don't charge them.

In fact, poor Reginald was the subject of three different Ziggy stories. They were just variations on the same theme.

The police permit officers came in and testified that it wasn't possible for anybody to call ahead and say somebody was coming to your establishment that night because they themselves don't know.

The club's records were entered in as evidence. In the eight years that Steve Kaplan had that club, he never got a violation. Reginald Burney was only around maybe a couple of years. What about the other six? Maybe we were clean because Steve ran a tight ship.

Ziggy folded on this too. Morris got Ziggy to admit he only knew of one time during the five years he was at the club that one of these tip-offs took place and he didn't even know what year. Further, Ziggy didn't know about it himself. He said, Steve told him. (And I swear I was about to pull my hair out if I had to hear the words Steve said one more time.)

But more than the permits, there was the more serious charge of money laundering. Nobody could believe that Steve was making that much money legitimately. Steve thought up ideas that made money and were good for our customers like our promo passes, which made admittance free. Steve figured if he gave up 80% of the front door versus the money he made inside the club, he was doing really good. He had a courtesy bus that used to go out in Buckhead and pick guys up and bring them to the club. If they needed to go back to the hotel, they could. If you were a VIP member, they had a chauffeur and limousine. If you got too drunk or just wanted a ride, they would pick you up. If you were an exclusive platinum VIP and flew into town, our limousine would pick you up to take you to your hotel. If you wanted to go out to dinner the limousine would come and take you to dinner. Or take you to the club and take you back.

Stuff like that worked to sell the hell out of memberships. Steve was making a shitload of money but he was also spending a shitload of money. The cost of the shuttle bus alone was $150,000. There was the cost of a limousine, maintenance, upkeep and salaries. He was making millions but there was a lot of overhead. He forked out a lot of money.

For weeks five and six, Ziggy continued to talk shit. Finally, he denies that he's prostituting girls, it's Steve. And on that note, Bruce Harvey spelled out the word "PIMP" on the eraser board and asked, "What does this make you, Ziggy?"

The judge was sick of Ziggy. He fought with the attorneys about everything. A lot of the time when Sadow asked him a question, Ziggy would turn his back to him. Judge Hunt literally screamed at him a couple of times for not answering the questions and fighting with the lawyers. He said, "I think it's clear to everybody that the jury has had it up to here with this man's testimony." The judge lifted his hand about a foot above his head when he said it.

The same day, Ziggy was sued for $50 million by Antonio Davis. Antonio said Ziggy was lying when he said Antonio had sex with the dancers under the prostitution part of his testimony.

Off the stand, Ziggy told the reporters that Steve was "like O. J. Simpson because he beat his case. You know what this is all about? Greed. But I'm not going to go to jail for Steve Kaplan's money."

After Ziggy, somewhere towards the end of week six came a parade of ex-girlfriends. To be exact, Steve's, Norbie's and mine.

First Debbie Pinson got up. She went on about what a shit Steve is, how he "reveled" in us having sex with customers and how excited he was to prostitute us. She whined about how Steve was going to marry her and didn't.

I told the press the truth, "She's a liar and she's heart-broken. He wasn't going to leave his wife. To me, she's just bitter."

Art Leach got Debbie Pinson to talk about how she started the skits and then she said Steve let everything get nasty and it was just too much for her to work there. She said, "The girls were dancing lewder. From nasty dancing comes more touching, and from more touching comes a whole lot of nasty stuff." She said Steve let girls do drugs and wouldn't call an ambulance when they fell out and foamed at the mouth. And that we paid the Gambinos and that Steve actually walked around with hundred dollar bills stuffed up the arms of his jacket.

She talked about being told to pour out the champagne on the carpet when customers weren't looking so they'd order more. And how we had to rip out the carpet every few months because of the smell. (I must have missed that meeting because at one point, if you gave me a blood test, I think it would have come out Cristal.)

We had the tape of Debbie Pinson discussing her grand jury testimony and how she wanted to ruin Steve. She was so low—she called Steve a bully and a wolf in sheep's clothing, preying on sweet little innocent girls like her.

By now the jury was getting sick of all these "witnesses" Art was running up there. There were a couple of jurors who always looked at me when someone would say something that just didn't sound right. I'd just look back and shrug my shoulders. They knew what was going on.

Norbie's turn was next. His ex-girlfriend, Jennifer Romanello, said our gentle Norbie threatened to "whack" her if she talked about all the shit he was supposed to be doing. It was like Norbie was a movie guy all of a sudden who "whacked" people. It's amazing how she claimed that he was going to whack her if she ever said anything against him about the Gold Club when in her testimony she claimed this was in Florida—the Club Boca days—long before Atlanta.

* * *

Even after hearing all of this testimony, I still had other things on my mind. I had a charity event I was planning and on June 10th, the Project Open Hand auction came to fruition. In spite of the trial—or maybe because of the trial—I had worked my hardest to help make it happen.

But from Project Open Hand, I looked at my life and saw even with the indictment and all the shit I was going through, I was really blessed. I didn't have AIDS or an elderly grandparent who couldn't get out of bed. Yes, I had suffered and been through a lot but I didn't have those things. I looked at these people and I saw my own grandfather committed to a hospital bed, never to sleep beside my grandmother again. I saw my own friends who were lost to AIDS. It's not a pleasant thing to die from. It is very painful towards the end. It's excruciating. You can't get out of bed or do anything. It's hard to eat because of all the medication you're on. Then for someone to come in with a hot meal makes a big difference.

The evening of the event, everyone was dressed very elegantly. I was wearing a gold thigh-length backless dress with spaghetti straps with gold strappy Gucci heels to match. My hair was up in a French twist with curls and my lips glistened with gloss, the only makeup I was wearing. The atmosphere was exciting and uplifting. Everyone was eating and drinking and talking and enjoying the artwork along the walls of the salon.

Richard Rubin and I were arranging everything for the auction to begin when one of his employees came up and said that she had a group of friends that would be singing for the auction. The group was called Mane Tane. Two local anchors, alongside of myself, began the auction.

The pictures were selling fast—$150-$300. We took a break from the auction to introduce the singing group. On cue, the group stepped out, four guys, singing acappella. They were in black slacks with silvery black tops, sharp. If I doubted their worth, I was corrected the moment the first note came out of their mouths. They opened up with "Don't You Remember" by Luther Vandross and ended with "End of the Road" by Boyz II Men.

I couldn't help but notice one of the singers. His skin was milk chocolate. He had sweet sincere eyes and lips that would make any woman want to walk up and kiss him. He was tall with a distinct fro, very clean cut. I noticed him all night, not realizing he was noticing me, too. I felt as if each time I was looking, he was looking somewhere else and I guess when I was looking somewhere else, he was looking at me.

One of the other group members approached me first but he wasn't my type. I had another member in mind. I finally got the opportunity to break free from my duties to go speak to him. I walked up and touched his face ever so gently, pulling his ear to my mouth and whispered, "You are gorgeous."

He thanked me shyly and introduced himself. His name was Stan—Stan Lackey.

I got called away and didn't get to finish the conversation. Little did I know that he'd written down his phone number and tried to find an opportunity to give it to me without everyone seeing. But he didn't get the chance.

Being the intelligent man that he is, Stan called back on his friend's phone and asked her if I was still there.

I got on the phone and we exchanged numbers and said we'd talk later.

In week eight, they got to me. They put Amanda Pappas on the stand. It broke my heart what they did. I had only been with Amanda for six months. She started doing Ecstasy and I couldn't deal with it. Not a girl with a drug problem.

Amanda wasn't at the Gold Club long enough to really do anything. She never went in front of the Grand Jury. The truth was that her boyfriend got caught up in this Ecstasy case in South Florida that had something to do with one of our witnesses. The Feds found out that she was my ex-girlfriend through this boyfriend.

Amanda's new boyfriend was looking at 97 months. Her baby was already disabled because she was on Ecstasy during her pregnancy. This child's disability required her to be with him 24-hours a day. Because of that, when the Feds called her three months before the trial started, they told her, you testify and we'll let him off. He won't go to jail.

Amanda had to choose me or him. She chose him, of course, because he was the breadwinner.

It was a hard day for me. Amanda said I took a young, innocent girl and turned her into this wild woman. If that were true, why in the hell did she perform oral sex on Dale Davis the first night she met me? I think she might, perhaps, have been wild already. As if I made her do everything that she did. She was the one out partying all the time. People were telling me that she was sleeping around and I didn't want to believe it. Not my baby.

It didn't matter. The government told her what to say. They scripted it out. They worked with her for a few days until she had everything down pat. Everything she said was, Jackie told me this, or Jackie told me that. It was the same scenario as Steve said.

She said we frequently had sex with customers in Gold Rooms and that I showed her the ropes around the club and how to sneak and have sex with customers for money.

When Bruce did the cross-examination he asked her questions like, Who are these people? You said you were always with her and her regulars. Who were her regulars? So you mean to tell me you have sex with people and you don't even get their names? She could not give one name because she was never with any of my regulars. Amanda and I probably were in a room together a total of six times.

Amanda said that we were going to BellSouth Mobility giving blow-jobs to the owner for free cell phones. I gave my lawyer a copy of my receipts for my cell phone and my cell phone bills. "So let me get this straight," Bruce pondered the witness, "you would suck a dick for 2000 minutes at a cost of $39.95?"

I had had the same cell phone number for four years at the time, so Bruce asked the obvious, "What is her phone number?" Amanda couldn't remember.

She also tried to say that Dennis Rodman gave her $800 in Gold Bucks the night that she met him. The night that she went to the hotel with him. She tried to say that he gave her $800 Gold Bucks and I turned them in at work and gave her cash. She wasn't even working at the Club at that time. In fact, the night Amanda met Dennis, he only had two girls in our room—Nurse Cindy and her sister Jill. Those were the only two girls and he gave them each $1,000. That was all the money he ordered that night.

Amanda couldn't look me in the face. When she testified, she put her head down.

She told the courtroom that Dennis tried to snatch her top up. He had reached for her but I had slapped his hand and set him straight, that she didn't work for the Gold Club.

Bruce Harvey was cross-examining her and he said, "Would you say you were a little star-struck and a little intrigued by her lifestyle, that you wanted to be part of it that bad? Did anybody force you to come up to the Gold club that night to see her?"

"No."

"Did anyone force you to go to Dennis Rodman's hotel room?"

"No."

"Did Diva force you to have sex with Dennis Rodman?"

"No, I wanted to, it was Dennis Rodman."

She wasn't making herself very credible for the court-room. Steve Sadow got up and that's when they brought in the boyfriend's name. She got nervous, and started stuttering. She did not know that we knew that he had cut a deal with the government to testify. They saved the big guns for last, it was their trademark.

Steve Sadow was the man. He knew everything that needed to be brought out last, to be the clincher and just close the deal and get the jury looking at the witness like, Jesus Christ, why is it that every witness that comes before us that the defense has something that discredits them completely?

When they brought up who the boyfriend was and Amanda said he was an Ecstasy dealer who had been busted, they folded her on the stand. Bruce Harvey closed it with one last question that would bring tears to her eyes and choke her up as she spoke, "Didn't Diva tell you once that she loved you?"

Her answer was, "Yes. But how do I know she was for real?" And then she began to cry.

I was so enraged with her at that point, I started crying, too. She looked at me and she thought I was crying because she was testifying against me.

I was crying because I was so angry and I wanted to jump over the tables and go up and choke her. Both of us were crying and the jurors were looking at us like, ooooh, they're hurting for each other right now.

I got outside and the media was right on me. When I came out they asked, "Why were you crying, Ms. Bush?"

I told them, "Because this woman who I used to be in love with has sat here and lied and lied for a man that was dealing Ecstasy. Her child is disabled because that's the guy she was dating when she started doing Ecstasy and she wants to sit there and lie so I can go to jail and be away from my three daughters? I'm crying because I want to get up and choke her."

The media persisted, "Would you ever want to talk to her after this?"

"Are you kidding me? The bitch is trying to get me locked up for the rest of my life! I'm supposed to want to talk to her?" I don't think so. I couldn't believe the dumb-ass questions they were asking.

Amanda couldn't go on and the judge sent the jury home early. I said to the press that night, "I'm fighting for my life right now, my freedom. She tried to take it away." Amanda admitted she got paid for sex at the Club. I never did.

Chapter Twenty-Four

By 1990, my husband Joe started cheating on me and was never home. It was hell. Our daughter was two, the baby was going on one. He came in the house and said, "I have to get to the base right now. We got this training mission." Something told me to follow him outside, sure as shit, there was a woman waiting for him. He jumped in the car and drove off and didn't come home for three days.

When he came home, I was ready to fight. That was the first time he hit me. I called the police and had him arrested. The military bailed him out and said it was an accident, and they let him go. He was a corporal, a platoon leader and there was no way they were letting me press charges.

Three marines knocked on the door, and told me to drop the charges.

They came to my house and said, "You don't realize, if we wanted him to have a wife, we would've issued him one in boot camp so you need to straighten up and fly right. These men are under pressure and you need to realize that. You need to drop the charges right now."

"He didn't hit you," these uniformed hulks told me. "You just thought he hit you." It was more or less like me saying, "My husband doesn't hit me. I walked into the punches." That's basically the way I took it. I was so upset. I learned there was nothing you can do to the military when it comes to that kind of stuff. They will cover it up. Those are their people.

So I dropped the charges. I let fear get the best of me. It would become a trend.

I could have left but Joe swore that he would never do it again. He was so sorry. He was under pressure because he was getting ready to go to the Persian Gulf.

He continued cheating on me, however, with this woman. His excuse was he felt he was never coming back, he was going to die in the war.

Just having the baby, I thought, we got two kids, everybody makes a mistake, he's scared. That was my reasoning behind taking him back.

My mother and sister, Tina, came out for Thanksgiving and planned on staying through Christmas because Joe was never home. Just before they came he was spending a lot of time away telling me he was out in the field when he was really with his friend and his girls. I didn't know it because I was stuck at the house. Joe was elaborate with his stories, he even packed up his stuff like he was really going to the field.

For Thanksgiving I cooked a big dinner with only my mother and sister and the kids to eat it. The month passed and Christmas is upon us. Joe was still not home.

My Mom wanted to know what was going on. I lied and made excuses but my mother wasn't stupid, she knew, she'd been through it all before. She said, "Honey, you look miserable." I did. I weighed 105 and had dark bags under my eyes from being up all night staring out the window wondering when Joe was going to come home. It was really hard on me.

Three days before Christmas and still no tree.

Then Christmas Eve came and Joe was still nowhere to be found. The kids were sleeping and my Mom said, "Honey, I want you to come home with me."

"Okay," I said with little need of convincing. I was ready

to go home. That night me and my sister got in the car. I had my own checking account at the time for my own stuff but I didn't have any more money in the bank and didn't have any of Joe's checks. He had taken all of that stuff—even the ATM card.

Me and my sister found this Christmas tree lot but it wasn't open, so we stole the tree, threw it in the car and drove off. We stopped by the grocery store, where I bounced a check for Christmas dinner.

We had enough food for two weeks. Inside, I told my Mom what I did. "Honey, you didn't have to do this. I could've sent back home for money."

"No, Mom, I know you're on a fixed income." She was very upset with Joe. Four in the morning he comes prancing in the door, drunk.

I said, "Where have you been?!!"

Even though he was doing all this to me, his birthday was Christmas day and I'd bought him a birthday card with the bounced check. I had sat it in the Christmas tree. I didn't want my kids to wake up with just some wrapped toys with no tree.

Christmas morning we got up, came downstairs and got the babies down there to open presents. The little one didn't know what was going on, just tearing paper off, but the oldest was excited and understood.

My Mom looks at Joe and says, "I think you're a piece of shit I'm taking my daughter home." Joe took my Mom for a walk.

My Mom comes in the house, she says, "Honey, I can't make you leave your husband. Why don't you stay and work it out?"

Joe apologized. I was listening to my mother. I was young. I didn't know any better. I stayed.

On New Year's Day, Joe was deployed. The morning he left, I had to beg him to make love to me.

He spilled his guts. "I don't want to be with you anymore. I've been having an affair with three women," and all of this right before I take him to leave to go to war. I was torn up. My mother was gone and I was alone with the babies.

Joe should have let me go with my mother when I had a chance but he didn't want me to actually go, he wanted me there so he could control me. I was really bitter inside.

Some of his friends from Virginia got transferred to the base. They stopped at his platoon, found out where we lived, and came knocking on the door one night. I was so glad to see them. It was Ryan and J.T.

So we were sitting around talking. I told them everything that was going on. How could he do that to you? You are the perfect wife. Out in Virginia I made dinner for all his friends. I was the perfect little housewife. J.T. was really sweet. He would come over and bring diapers and stuff. Right before the war started, I was a basket case. I lost my husband. My mother and sister came back for another visit.

Joe called me one day and said the most hurtful thing over the phone. "I don't regret having any affairs." It was right after my Mom and sister had left again. I called my Mom, "I want to come home."

At that time I couldn't go home. War was going to break out and we were trapped on the base. The base was shut down. Everything was on the base anyway. So J.T. came over and one thing led to another and it was almost a revengeful thing on my part, to have an affair with Joe's best friend to get back at him. I thought, if he hears about this, he'll snap back and realize that he loves me. I was not thinking that having an affair with his best friend was probably the worst thing I could do.

It was the first time I'd ever done anything like that.

J.T. told me that he loved me and I fell for him. At the same time, I still loved Joe. It was scary: How do you love two people?

Joe called me two days before the troops went in to Desert Storm and I told him about the affair. Not four hours later I got a call from the chaplain in Saudi Arabia. "Ms. Bush, we have your husband under 24-hour watch."

It was a lie. Joe put one of his buddies up to it just to fuck with my head. The friend posing as a chaplain went on to say that Joe had tried to shoot himself in the head with his rifle because he was so distraught about "this ongoing relationship with you and his friend back there."

Meanwhile, two days later, on TV the ground war opens up and I had no idea what was going on with my husband. I was overwhelmed with guilt. Finally, I called the sergeant of his platoon. They always leave one person behind. I gave him all the information, asked him to find out what was going on. He said, "I talked to the chaplain, no such thing happened. Your husband had somebody make that call for him."

That bastard. From then on, I enjoyed my relationship with J.T. Then J.T. got called out to war and he walked out of my life.

The war ended and Joe called to tell me he was on his way back to the states and how much he still loved me. In spite of the infidelities on both of our parts, we were going to work things out, everything was going to be okay.

For a couple of months things were just beautiful, then out of nowhere he starts taking his attitude. He starts threatening me that if I tried to leave, he'd kill me.

One night he was beating the crap out of me. He had me in the closet on the floor kicking me wherever his boot landed. I got away and I went downstairs and took the cordless into the bathroom and called the MPs. They came to the door. Joe wouldn't let me come out of the bedroom as he went to meet them saying if I made so much as a peep, he'd kill me.

So when he answered the door, the MP said, "We got a call. Is everything okay here?"

"Everything's fine," Joe lied. "Who called you?"

"A lady named Ms. Bush, Jackie Bush, said that you were beating her and she was scared for her life."

Joe came to the bottom of the stairs to get me, saying under his breath, "I want you to come down with a smile on your face and act like nothing's wrong."

I was so scared, I did everything he said and the MPs left. As he closed the door, Joe said, "Don't you ever call the MPs on me again. Don't you know I can get in trouble?"

Meanwhile I was in love with this man. At least I thought I was. And at the same time I was scared of him. It wasn't long before he started back with the cheating.

One day, Joe had been gone for a day-and-a-half with some woman or another. When he showed his face, I was ranting and raving. I went upstairs to take a shower and he started in on me. I ran up and locked myself in the bathroom. The babies were sleeping.

He started dumping scalding hot water underneath the bathroom door. He said, "Open the door or I'm going to kick it in."

"I'm not opening the door. Go away. Leave me alone."

He kicked the door open. "Get undressed right now."

"What!?"

"Take off all your clothes!"

"No!"

He punched me hard in the chest. I took off all my clothes and Joe handed me a mop and bucket and said, "Clean up all this water in ten minutes. If not, I'm going to throw hot water on you."

He meant what he said. I didn't have it cleaned up in time and he came and threw hot water on me. I didn't know what to do. I was scared, stuck out in California with no family, nothing.

I finally got all the water cleaned up. He had gone up to

our bedroom and locked the deadbolt on the door and the garage door so I couldn't get out of the house.

I knocked on the door, "Can I please come in so I can get some pajamas and go lay on the couch and go to sleep?"

"No. Just sleep right there on the steps."

I was butt naked standing outside my bedroom door, asking if I could come in. I sat on the steps and cried. Finally he came out and he threw me a towel and some pajamas. "You can come through the bathroom to our bedroom and come out in the hallway." He unlocked the hall door but locked the bedroom door telling me to take a shower before he let me into bed. I took the shower, put on my pajamas and knocked on the door, "Can I please lay down? It's three o'clock in the morning. I'm tired."

He finally opens the door and I got a blanket. He immediately takes my pillows and the blanket. "You don't get any of these tonight." I didn't care. I just wanted to sleep because I had to get up in a few hours with the kids.

The next morning Joe woke up and tried to make love to me like nothing happened the night before. I said, "I don't want to. Leave me alone. Don't touch me."

"You're my wife," he ordered, "and you'll do what I say you do."

I just laid there waiting for him to finish and to get away from me. It kept going from there. He had an affair with a girl across the street.

Chapter
Twenty-Five

It was time for us to move back to Milwaukee because Joe's active duty was up and he didn't reup. He didn't want to stay in the Marine Corp. A week before we were supposed to go home, he disappeared. He didn't call, nothing. I was stuck at the house. No car, no money. There were only a few groceries left.

After three days I went over to a neighbor's and the wife went to the store and bought me some groceries.

With no sign of Joe, I continued cleaning and packing the things we could take with us in the car. The Marine Corps came and packed and loaded everything else on a truck. I was getting ready for the Marine inspection of our base housing, when Joe comes bopping in. It was the day before we were supposed to leave, towards the end of 1992.

I didn't say a word because I knew how it would end. The inspection people came, passed us, and we began the journey home. As we were driving across the country, in the back of my mind, I knew when we got home I was leaving him.

When we arrived, I took the children and went to my brother's. I called Joe. "I'm at my brother's and I'm staying here. You go to your Mom's. I can't do this anymore."

Two months later I was working two jobs trying to makea way for me and my kids. The first was a cashier job at

Cub Foods. The second job was at a mall, at a Lillie Rubin clothing store for women.

Meanwhile, Joe was trying to patch things up, calling me and telling me how much he loved me.

I was so bored, trapped between the jobs and taking care of the girls, that when an old high school friend called one night and asked me if I wanted to go out, I was more than ready. "Sure," I said. "I'll tell my brother if Joe calls not to tell him where we went, just that I'm not home."

What does my brother do? "Oh, she went out with some guy named Tony. They're down at Club Maryland."

Why Jimmy did that, knowing what a psycho Joe was, is beyond me.

Just as we had ordered our first drink, the first time I'd been out in years, Joe walked in the club and snatched the table away from us. Drinks went flying. He said, "Let's go."

Tony said I should go with him to avoid making a scene.

I said, "I don't wanna go."

He says, "Bless your heart but I can't get involved in this."

Joe escorted me out of the club holding the back of my neck.

We got in the car and he began the tirade. "You're my wife and you don't go out with any other man!" He had a knife and tried to cut my wedding finger off so that no other man would put a wedding ring on this finger.

The car was running low on gas. I tried to get out at the gas station but he grabbed me by the back of my hair and hit me in the face, busting my nose and top lip, spraying blood everywhere. He ripped my dress off, threw me back in the car and skidded out of the gas station, driving like a madman.

Finally we got to my brother's house. My brother saw the blood everywhere. He, too, was fighting with his girlfriend, and they were throwing blows at one another.

Joe took me upstairs to the bathroom to wipe the blood off my face. Then he dropped to his knees and started crying. He wrapped his arms around my waist and kept saying over and over again, "I'm sorry. Will you help me? I need help. I don't want to do this to you anymore. I need you. I love you."

What do you think after something like that? When he's screaming that he needs help. I think, What do I do?

We started family counseling and things started getting better so we got back together. We got a place of our own. For a while, we were happy together and then it started up all over again, the beatings.

On my sister Marquita's birthday she called and asked if I could go out with her and my other sister, Tina to celebrate. Joe was just as nice as he could be on the phone: "Sure! Happy Birthday. You guys have a good time tonight. Don't let her do anything crazy. Don't let her drink too much."

At first, I didn't trust it. I was scared to even go get ready.

He said, "You better go get ready. They're going to be here soon."

So I got ready and came out with no makeup, a turtleneck up to my chin and loose-fitting jeans. I tied my hair back in a bun.

Joe took one look at me and said, "Who do you think you're trying to be sexy for?" as if this whole other person was living inside of him. He swung back before I could answer and punched me in the face, knocking me to the floor. He went to the kitchen and came back with a butcher knife.

As I was lying there stunned, he cut the turtleneck open and balanced the tip of the knife on my throat.

He leaned on the blade with both his hands, looking at me like a psychotic, absolutely strange. "What if I slipped and penetrated through your throat?"

I laid there, stiff. I couldn't even cry I was so scared. Finally he got up and pulled the away. I called the police, they arrested him and took him to jail. I couldn't keep taking these chances. I got a restraining order.

Two weeks went by and he called to apologize. He started taking anger management course so I said, "Okay." And took him back like an idiot. I took yet a third job, working at Zales Jewelers because I was pregnant with our third child.

I continued going through all these beatings and changes. One day I came home from work and didn't have dinner done in time and he started hitting me. He kicked me in the side of the head with his boot which shattered the nerve and made me permanently deaf in my right ear. I was eight months pregnant.

On January 15th of 1993 in Milwaukee, I had the baby, Bethany. I had my tubes tied during the C-section and they kept me open too long, and a lot of air got into my system and it caused poisonous gas to develop in my side.

Eventually, I healed and got a job at a car dealership where I began making good money. Joe and I went through a calm patch but at the beginning of summer I started hemorrhaging. After many trips back and forth to the doctor, I was diagnosed with cancer of the uterus. Two months went by, bleeding, losing weight. The insurance company wouldn't approve the hysterectomy. My skin changed color. My brown eyes turned gray from blood loss. I was reliving my mother's illness from when I was sixteen. Finally Prudential granted the surgery.

There were complications and my skin turned bright yellow with jaundice. A blood clot had developed and I opted for a blood transfusion rather than a surgery which would have sliced a scar all the way up my side. Doing nothing would have meant a heart attack or stroke. I was 25 years old.

When it was all over, Joe walked in the room with our children.

The first words out of Breanna's mouth was, "Are you dying?"

"No, baby no, Mamma's not dying. No, mamma's not dying this is a standard procedure after surgery."

The questions kept coming. What's all this stuff Mommy? Why do you have blood?

"Mommy has to rest and we have to go," Joe cut in. He picked each one of them up for me to give them a hug and a kiss me. The baby was two years old. He said he was going to take the kids over to my mother's. Breanna was having a fit, convinced I was going to die.

When I was laying in bed, worrying about the blood clot in my side, smoke came from underneath my door and with the smoke I saw an intense yellow. I felt a cold breeze touch my forehead. As I was laying there, I saw Clarence standing next to my bed.

He touched the top of my toes and said, "You're going to be okay. You're gonna be fine." And then he just went away.

I fell asleep and the next morning went home. I called Grandma Ann to tell her what happened.

"Oh yeah, it was him," she said without hesitation. "Do you know he talks to his son?"

"Really?"

"All the time."

My little cousin, Clarence's son, was the spitting image of his dad from his weight to his mannerisms. Grandma Ann said sometimes she would stand in the bathroom outside the bedroom door and listen to him: "Yeah, dad I know. Yes, I promise I'm gonna take care and watch out for everybody ..." Just talking.

My grandmother walked into my little cousin's room one day and asked, "Who are talking to?"

"My dad."

"What?"

"He's right there standing right behind you."

"I don't believe you."

My little cousin said, "Ask me something to ask him that only he would know."

Grandma Ann told me this story of how she told little Clarence, "Ask Clarence what was his favorite breakfast."

Little Clarence asked. The answer came back: pancakes, fried pork chops, bacon, sausage, fried eggs and grits. This small child made a perfect list of foods my grandmother knew he couldn't know. She melted.

"He was standing right behind me in my own house. Clarence said he's here everyday."

I went home and started back with my husband. I was still working at the dealership who had kept my job for me. Things got to the point that Joe came up to the dealership with a shotgun in the van and put a shell casing on the dash and said, "This is for you."

I was sitting at my desk and I acted like my phone rang and picked it up and pressed zero which went straight to my manager. "My husband is sitting outside in that van with a shotgun and he's got a bullet on the dashboard and said this is for you."

I was smiling as if I were on the phone with somebody and he kept telling me to come outside. I asked my manager to please call the police, then, when I hung up the phone, to wait a couple minutes and page me.

You could hear the intercom outside, "Jackie come out to service." I met my manager in his office and I told him what had been going on and that I had been scared. He said the police were on the way. Joe figured out what was going on and left. The police escorted me home. I called my dad and he came over.

Joe wanted to kill me because I had asked for a divorce. Probably a big mistake on my part. A couple days later he came home in the morning and I didn't hear him come in and I woke up with an extension cord tied up around my neck. I couldn't breathe. I looked at him and told him with what breath I had, "Kill me."

Something snapped him out of it because he let go of the extension cord and walked out of the house.

I quickly packed up my daughters and went to my dad's house. Dad took me down to the courthouse and I filed for a divorce and got a restraining order all in one day. I stayed with my dad for a week.

The day I came back home, Joe called saying he wanted to come get his stuff. I called the police and when he showed up, they arrested him and I pressed charges and it stuck. He went to jail for about three weeks. It was only one of roughly eight times he did time for domestic violence against me.

It was ironic that it was my father, an abuser, who saved me from Joe. It was equally ironic that Joe, knowing how I grew up and all of the horrors I went through with my father, would do the things he did. I didn't understand it.

After the divorce, Joe took anger management counseling, he went into therapy. The psychiatrist said he had post-traumatic stress from being in the war. It was a strange diagnosis considering Joe had been beating me long before the war started.

My children grew and Breanna started kindergarten in Milwaukee at Engleburg Elementary. I went to the school everyday, helping out, doing things. I spent a year in a classroom program where I helped to prepare the weekly planner for assignments. After I completed the program, I taught first grade. They were semi-suburban classes, large, with a mixed racial population of children. Kids were bussed in from all over town. It was standard in Milwaukee for parents to send their kids to their school of choice rather than settling for the school in the immediate neighborhood.

Teaching was something I enjoyed and I would do it all over again. To sit with these kids and teach them and know that they were learning, coming to me for advice, made me feel so good. The job took me away from the problems I was having at home with my husband and my family life. It was my escape away from everything.

When I found out that I was going to be teaching my daughter's class, it was incredible. It gave me a fulfillment, a sense of contribution that is indescribable. I didn't show favoritism, nor did she want me to. She said, "Mom, I want you to treat me just like the other kids in class. No special privileges."

I laughed. "Ha ha," I said. "I wasn't going to treat you special."

I even sat in my middle daughter Brittany's class for about three months.

I got awards for being a Milwaukee Public School volunteer.

We would hold programs, like 'Thanksgiving with the Pilgrims' and the kids would dress up. We'd have the Indians and Pilgrims and a feast. One year I baked two turkeys and brought them in. I baked pumpkin pie, chocolate cake. I was a part of my children's everyday school life. On their birthdays, I baked cupcakes. Sometimes I would send snacks to school just on general purpose.

I was very domesticated when it came to my kids' school. It was important to me to become a part of their education and watch them learn. The neighborhood was very close-knit. Everybody was involved in school. Field trips, chaperoning.

I wanted to give my children what I didn't have. I didn't have that drive and push and support from my family. I didn't want my kids to be in school and not have a parent there showing their face and letting them know, "I care about your education."

I didn't ever want my kids to think, "Mommy doesn't care enough to just go to school." It's easy to shove your kids out the door and not be involved in their lives. That's the way I grew up. Missing that probably contributed to some of my actions and bad choices. Filling that role for my children was also filling a void in my life.

Without an example of how a good parent behaves, I went in with guns blazing. I never questioned my ability to do something new. I had learned that negative voice only set me up for failure. Well, maybe I used to question myself on a personal level but never when it came to my kids. I always knew what the right thing was.

It showed in my kids' smiles. If I was in school, I would walk past their classes and just stick my head in the door just to see them look up and know, "Oh, there's my Mom. I know she's here." Now my kids have big goals. The oldest wants to be a surgeon and the middle one wants to be a pediatrician and the baby wants to be an actress.

When I started stripping to pay the bills, I didn't lie to my daughters but I did qualify my actions, saying, "This is not something that I want you guys to even think about doing when you get grown, because you have the avenues to get the things that you need to be successful women. I want you to be independent, have your own house, car. I don't want you to rely on anybody for anything."

* * *

After I got divorced, I wanted to find out who I was. I felt free for the first time in years. I wanted to experiment with different things, see different things. I was tied down from age 20 to 26, not able to go anywhere or do anything. I felt I had missed my 20s. I didn't experience what my friends did when they were single and going to college. I didn't get to do that. I was a housewife, stuck at home. Going through the relationship—abuser and abused.

So when I was finally free of Joe it was time to live a little. So I went back to the Encore. I was having fun, making pretty decent money, $3-400 a night. I dated Vin Baker of the Milwaukee Bucks at that time. I slept with Glen Robinson who played on the same team.

There were two girls at the club that I really liked and thought were uniquely sexy. Niko had tattoos all over her body. She had straight black hair parted down the middle and a beautiful face. She was into alternative music. The other girl I had a thing for was Candace who was tall with short, bobbed blonde hair. She had beautiful breasts and was very muscular. The way she danced was as if she was moving in slow motion. Her body just flowed. It was the most intense thing I could watch. She turned me on in a way that scared me because although I'd always liked women, I had always been with men.

I had this regular named Jim who was the vice president of a big company back home. We got a hotel room at the Phister and me and Niko were hanging out with him drinking champagne. Jim knew I liked Niko which is why he set the whole thing up for me, so I could be with her.

"I hope you're not uncomfortable and I hope you understand why I asked you here," I said to Niko timidly.

"I think I do. I think you're afraid to tell me."

"What is it?"

"You like me, like a guy would like a girl, don't you?"

"Yeah I do but I'm scared because I've never done it before."

"There's nothing to be scared of," she said drawing me close to her, and my first, uncertain experience with another woman unfolded.

Jim stayed in the living room as we made our way to the bedroom. He didn't watch us. He wanted the experience for me.

It was like making love for the first time, every touch magnified a thousand times, every caress. Niko took it slow, sensitive to the fact that I had never been with a girl before. It was the most beautiful thing I could have done because it opened me up to who I really was. I felt more beautiful as a woman, complete for the first time in a long time. I had finally done something that had always been inside me that I hadn't been able to let out because other people couldn't accept it. More importantly, the first experience with Niko marked the beginning of my acceptance of myself and not caring what other people thought.

At first, I was living with my little sister Tina and dancing part-time, three nights a week at the Encore. Me and Elliott were having a long-distance romance our first year together. We had had a falling out over the phone and broke up for a couple months at which point I met another NBA player, Vin Baker, with the Milwaukee Bucks. At first, I wouldn't give him the time of day on the strength that Elliott was a basketball player and I thought Vin would be leaving me all the time. I already knew I didn't want that. Finally my sister said, "Girl, do you know who that is? That's Vin Baker from the Milwaukee Bucks and he plays right here in town."

So I gave him my number and we started dating. He had every girl in the city of Milwaukee flocking after him. I didn't tell him I danced because I didn't think it was any of his business. All he knew was that I worked at the car dealership.

One night I was on stage and he walked in. I almost fainted. Oh shit, I panicked, what do I do now? It was the beginning of my first song of three songs. I was in a white lace teddy with white t-backs and a white bra, white lace thigh highs and high heel shoes. We had this pole that went up to the ceiling but then out to the side as well. My songs were all romantic, slow, and seductive. Whenever I wore that outfit, I glowed under the lights. As I began my dance, Vin's flunky, came to the edge of the stage and started peeling off $100 bills. He threw six of them up there.

I came to the edge of stage and said, "Stop. Knock it off."

I latched onto the pole with my thighs and let my body hang back vertically, hanging there in mid-air. I loved dancing with the pole doing acrobatic tricks.

The club was cramped and so it was easy to spot a big 6'9" guy like Vin Baker. One of the girls came over with a tip from a guy she was sitting with and asked, "Who is that?"

"That's my boyfriend," I whispered.

"You are so lucky! That's Vin Baker! And those are $100 bills!," she sighed looking down on the floor.

I was not impressed. I kept dancing and by the time I finished and was down to my bottoms, the flunky shows up again and peels off another six $100 bills. "Tell Vin I said knock it off!" I hissed. I was embarrassed as I picked up all of my money at the end of the set. I didn't do my walk. Then, I didn't need to.

The walk was standard procedure. Girls had to walk the room after they came off stage. Go to each guy. We all went on stage ten times during a shift and had to go to the same guys each time for tips, a couple dollars everytime you came around.

I went in the back and sent one of the girls out to tell Vin I'd be out after I freshened up and changed.

When I emerged, his first question was, "Why didn't you tell me you were a dancer?"

"I didn't think it was necessary," I said getting my back up. "Why is it important?"

"Well, it's not but it would have been nice to know. You're phenomenal! I saw you do things on that pole that I didn't think were humanly possible."

Vin was fascinated. "What time do you get off?"

"About one thirty."

"Well, see can you get off early."

"You just give me $1,200." I didn't think I needed to take any more money from these girls, so I went to Debbie my manager and said goodnight. She was in awe. It wasn't the kind of money girls were used to in that place so the word spread as if I'd just hit the lottery jackpot.

We left and went back to his loft on the lower east side overlooking the lakefront. The windows were floor to ceiling and the walls were made of glass. His bedroom was probably 200 square feet, huge.

We dated for about four months, then he did the same thing everybody else did, he cheated. I walked in on him with two white chicks who were groupies.

I walked out and Vin chased me but it didn't matter. Three of them butt-naked getting it on was enough for me. I was very cold after my divorce. I didn't want to hear any excuses. You cheat, that's it, it's over.

Vin kept calling and I didn't keep my promise to myself. I forgave him and gave him another chance. It wasn't until it happened the second time with another girl at the club that I couldn't ignore the truth and let him go for good.

Chapter
Twenty-Six

Amidst all the chaos, of the trial I found a free evening to go on a first date with Stan. We met at Puff Daddy's restaurant, Justin's, in Buckhead. It was Friday night, the place was packed it was an hour-and-a-half wait. I walked up to the podium and the manager greeted me warmly. "Good evening Diva. You need a table for two?"

He immediately seated us. We had Long Island Tea with 7-up instead of Coke. We started talking about the trial. Stan sensed I was under a lot of pressure and that I was in a serious situation. I was straight and laid it all on the table. I told him what I was facing and left the decision to him, based on that information, if he wanted to see me again. I also let him know that I was one of those people who goes with the flow.

At that moment, I reached over the table and grabbed him by his wooden beaded necklace and gently kissed him on his lips. Being a polite Southern boy, he was taken aback in spite of the fact that he was still savoring the kiss as he leaned back in his chair and said, "Thank you. What was that for?"

"I just told you. I do what I feel and I felt like kissing you." From that moment on, we both knew, that there was something special between us. Not long after I'd gone back to court, Stan and I made a pact not to see each other until the trial was over. But that didn't mean we couldn't talk. We spent hours on the phone every other night getting to know each other.

Stan liked the fact that I was smart and he said it was a turn on to learn from me. I liked the way he was able to get his point across, to really express what he felt. He was honest. He could talk about anything openly and without reservation.

By the ninth week of the trial, on June 25th, it was Steve and Mike's turn to get blasted. Craig Carlino, a former manager of the New York Strip Club Scores, testified that the Gold Club was a "whorehouse" and that Steve had promised to help him keep his job with his Mafia connections.

We all listened to hours of FBI tape recordings of conversations that were supposed to tie Steve and Michael DiLeonardo to the mob. Not once on one tape recording or video-tape did we hear or see Steve and Mike DiLeonardo talking or even together. It was like somebody got a new camcorder and was crazy to shoot just anything.

Finally, we all got a break for the Fourth of July. Me and Richard Rubin and the kids got a deli picnic which we took to his high rise apartment to watch the fireworks. A severe thunderstorm rained out the show so we went back to the Dunwoody house, made popcorn and watched movies. It didn't matter what we did, anyway, as long as we were together.

When we returned, one of the Gold Club dancers testified that she was raped in a limousine by club manager Russell Basile in 1997. Nothing happened to him. Then one of the limo driver's, Anthony Butina, testified that Steve told him to lie to police about the rape. Since I wasn't there, it was all news to me. It was a lie. As evidence, the girl had written on the back of a business card both of her numbers along with "I love you." The way their intimacy became "rape" was that her boyfriend caught her getting out of the limo. Butina was made out to be a liar when the evidence was brought out that he was the limo driver for the South Carolina New York Knicks sexual escapade with Ziggy.

The credit card fraud was a recurring theme, hitting different defendants from different angles. It didn't have anything to do with me and it certainly wasn't news what The Vultures had been doing all along. Bruce kept that point at the forefront.

In week twelve the celebrity shit cranked up again when former club manager George Kontos took the stand. I didn't know George. He was also there before me. He talked about Madonna coming into the Gold Club and leaving with one of the dancers, Baby, whose picture was on the front of the complimentary passes. That got the press all perked up. They were all up in our faces again. I liked the reporters that bothered to check out what they were told. That wasn't the majority.

Andruw Jones, of the Atlanta Braves, testified in the thirteenth week. He said he had sex with dancers at a hotel party that the Gold Club invited him to. He and a girl went in a room and did it. Not illegal. Andruw said he came to the club about thirty times and he would go out and party with the dancers but there was no money involved. He came to get what the Gold Club had, the least of which was a few free drinks.

There were all these athletes who kept saying they were at the Gold Club and maybe some said they had sex, but most of the time it wasn't at the Club and it wasn't for money. The prosecution couldn't find the evidence necessary for the RICO indictment to ring true. Proving athletes have sex with girls sometimes, or girls throw themselves at them and they get it for free, well shit. It wasn't anybody's business except for the two, three, four people who were involved.

It got to be a national joke. On NBC's "The Tonight Show" Jay Leno said, "After one particular outing in Atlanta,

Patrick Ewing reportedly told the press: 'It's going to be a long season, and we just have to take it one illegal sex act at a time.'" Jon Stewart, the host on "The Daily Show" on Comedy Central made the athletes the butt of his jokes, saying, "Here's how hot and unpleasant it is. It was so hot today in New York City, the strippers were getting under Patrick Ewing just for the shade."

Steve said, "There are times that ball players might have come in the club and I might've done something stupid every once in awhile. But if you think that every customer comes in here and [is] having sex with a girl and I'm fucking condoning it, you're out of your mind, okay?"

Steve Sadow said, "It has been our position from the very beginning that the only reason that the pro athletes and other celebrities have been dragged into this is that it gave the prosecution something to talk to the media about. No one is suggesting for one second that these athletes or celebrities need the Gold Club or anyone else to attract women. If there was anything that went on with any of the entertainers, it was done with consent. It was done without money exchanging hands, it was done without the help of Steve Kaplan. In fact, in my opening statement, I said in reference to Dennis Rodman, I didn't think he needed Steve Kaplan to get Carmen Electra. And Jackie Bush already knew Rodman. They were friends."

Then Frederique got her moment in the limelight. She was pregnant and for a drama queen, it was a really good deal. She got out of everything and got on the news too. By the end of this week they started getting into the credit card fraud really deep.

The FBI threatened to take Frederique's unborn child from her and she got really, really scared and freaked out. So she turned state's evidence and said whatever they wanted her to. It was pretty sad, it broke my heart to see her like that.

What didn't she say? She said that Steve was sort of like a pimp to everybody and that he took us on trips for prostitution. She said everything that the government wanted her to. I guess she felt like she had to ... it was a weird situation.

The defense presented the tape of her apology to Steve the day she turned states evidence in the courtroom. It made her a total ass, just unbelievable. She denied that it was even her voice but did not deny the fact that she had called him that day to apologize. She said that I gave oral sex to Patrick Ewing one night. My lawyer presented the evidence that I wasn't at work that night but rather in Milwaukee. I wasn't even in town.

Frederique rolled her eyes at me but she was very predictable. I'd nudge Bruce Harvey everytime she got ready to cry, and whisper, "Watch, here come the tears." All of a sudden he's sitting there laughing his ass off. It was crazy.

Rather than discount everything Frederique said that was a lie, I'll just say the only truth in her testimony was regarding me sleeping with Billy Baino, the head coach for UNLV (University of Nevada Las Vegas). It wasn't really my fault. I couldn't help it. He was gorgeous!

But then Frederique's version ended up with me and three other girls having a foursome with him. I wanted to jump up and scream, "Nobody was in the room when I was with this man! What is she talking about?"

She said that I told her because she didn't want to participate since she was sick. She furthered her story, when she said I actually told her I'd tell Steve she was part the foursome so she'd still get paid.

She talked about Dekembe Mutombo and Terrell Davis. Her blowjobs became my blowjobs and so on.

I had a connection to one of the jurors, one of the women. She sat in front of the jury box and she would look at me when she didn't believe what one of the witnesses said. During this last bit of Frederique, I returned the look, shrugged my shoulders and shook my head. The juror flipped her hand back like she was blowing it off.

Frederique would have done better and been more credible if she had at least somewhat told the truth but she just came up with shit that was totally not believable. She said Steve Kaplan knew everything that was going on in the Gold Club at all times.

I learned more about the lying ways of people in one day in that courtroom than I had learned in my whole life. People will say any shit to save their asses, and the more worthless they are, the more they want to try to take other people down with them. It was a whole courtroom full of sick motherfuckers everyday.

Consider this. A million people came through the Gold Club in five years, taking in around $50 to $60 million. The government said $125,000 of that was fraudulent. And if it was, why did the government decide to spend time and money going after something that little? Don't they have some other shit to fix?

None of my credit card bills came up doubled. I never even had a chargeback in the Gold Club, not once. I never tried to deceive any man by saying give me this or that, or telling the girl to order extra. Whatever a guy said, that's what I got. Thank God, the Gold Club kept such detailed records.

But the credit card fraud was basically done by Bank's girls and Alicia Mitchell, the Gold Bucks lady who handled the actual processing of the order. She would go downstairs to the computer terminal, swipe the card, run an order, then swipe the card again and run another order.

Along those lines, the witnesses were the ones that would wake up the next day and look at their receipts and say they wouldn't pay. Many of the people on the credit cards showed up whining after the indictment. They couldn't get to the Feds fast enough to tell them they were ripped off.

There was this developer from South Georgia, Russell Todd Arline. He said he thought seven-zero-zero was seven dollars! He was defrauded of $10,000. When they showed the bills in the courtroom and the jurors looked at them, the defense said, "Can you please tell me how you thought seven hundred meant seven dollars? There's no decimal point or anything?"

"I thought it was seven dollars or thirteen dollars, or eleven dollars."

Everybody in the courtroom is dying, looking at this guy like, No you didn't. You were drunk. You had a good time and when you realized how much money you spent, that's when you changed your mind.

Steve Sadow asked, "Isn't eight drinks in three hours enough to get you drunk?"

"Not a big boy like me," he says.

He didn't go against his bill until after a year and couple months later. He was there the night before we got raided in 1999. That was the only reason he disputed the charges. He thought because the club had been raided that he could get his money back. The defense brought that out and blew him out of the water.

"So the only reason you disputed the charges is because the Gold Club had been raided the next day and you saw it on TV in your hotel room and you decided this was a quick way to get this money off your credit card?" Steve Sadow continued.

He says, "Yes."

The prosecution was pissed. They were so mad at him.

The credit card customers claimed they were lost in a fog, having out-of-body experiences and that they were drugged by these girls and this was how they spent so much money. When they got on the stand, these guys confessed that they were drunk as a skunk and forgot what the hell they were doing. Two of the customers I had actually been in a room with:

279

Dwight Allen Kent and Michael Mitzen of Tallahassee, FL and his business partner Keith Rackly with a piddly $6,500 bill for three or four girls in a room for a couple of hours along with champagne and food. Both Mitzen and Rackly were married. It was like they were saying we were slipping them mickeys when the only thing slipping was them.

Of course, it turned out it was one of the Gold Bucks girls that was running that ring and Steve didn't know about it for a while. But so because he didn't fire her when he found out, he had to pay back thousands of dollars in charges.

The last of the credit card fraud witnesses was this guy, John DelNegro of Virginia. He was at the Gold Club for several hours in October of 1999 in a wedding party that had been drinking since two o'clock in the afternoon. He was plastered when he got to the Gold Club. His bill—for him and three of his friends—came to $13,615. He says although he couldn't remember what he thought at the time, he now thought it was too much.

Nick, Roy's lawyer, asked him if he thought the room and dancers were free. DelNegro couldn't even remember getting his Gold Bucks even though he signed the credit card receipt and put his thumbprint on it. At the end, he admitted the truth, "I had a good time and I was stupid. I was drunk."

Then we had Anthony King. He was a former assistant manager at the GC. Anthony was a really sweet guy. Good looking, little choppy haircut, dressed real nice all the time, he's funny. He got fired because he had a drug problem, Ecstasy, GHB. He used to get high at work sometimes.

He was still a pretty good manager. He was adamant about letting other managers know if stuff was going on, if a girl was having sex, if a girl was giving a blowjob. The other managers would go in and discipline her. The government thought Anthony was going against the defense. Art Leach was getting upset. You could see him literally getting mad because Anthony wouldn't answer the questions the way he had anticipated, the way they had coached him.

Anthony didn't cut a deal. He was subpoenaed to testify and went over his testimony with the government ahead of time. He would tell them whatever they wanted to hear in the backroom just to get through the process of going over the testimony but when he got in the courtroom, he told the truth. I was very proud of him because he let them know yes, girls were having sex, girls were doing drugs. And it was true. On a daily basis, every night something was going on at that club. He stressed the fact that Norbie and Roy Cicola conducted drug searches, became furious at drug usage, always stopped sexual activity in Gold Rooms and disciplined most dancers involved. And they did. There were locker searches in which they shut the locker room down and you could not get in there to go to the bathroom.

King said the only dancers who were seldom disciplined for violating rules against sex were "Steve's Girls." Like he said, we were making too much money.

The title was probably overrated. "Steve's Girls" be-came—for the purposes of the courtroom—me, Frederique, Hannah, Desiree and Banks.

That last Friday, July 27, was usually hot, humid and hazy in Atlanta. The club was still open and patrons were still getting table dances and partying in Gold Rooms, but we didn't know how much longer. I would go there sometimes at night. It was hard to be there and know how fucked up everything was.

The last week of the trial, everybody knew the Gold Club was closing. I was up there hanging out and next thing I hear is, "Next on the stage we have Rose."

Rose went up on stage and got butt-naked and was dancing. She was drunk. I went up on stage with her and she held my hand up in the air like we were boxers. She said, "Who knows Diva?"

I didn't realize half the guys in the club knew me. They're cheering and yelling "Yeah, Diva!" Somebody yelled out, "S&M!"

I walked to the edge of the stage. The music got quiet. Rose gathered up her money—$600 that night.

I made a little speech: "I retired in February and swore I wouldn't come back to the stage and I'm not. Whoever yelled S&M God bless you because that was one of my favorite skits and I'm glad you like it enough to ask for it again. I'm sorry. You all have seen me on TV and you know what I'm going through. I just want to thank you for cheering for me, for your support."

Guys were coming up to the stage handing me money, "You're beautiful! You're beautiful! We love you! We're going to miss you!"

Then noise died down again and someone called from the crowd, "Is the club really closing?"

"Well, it's up in the air. I can't say for sure. You don't know from one day to the next what's going to happen. For now, everybody grab your drinks, raise 'em high and party on!"

I walked off the stage and me and Rose went to the dressing room. She was crying, "Do S&M, do S&M."

"I can't."

Shaney wasn't at work that night but Rose egged me on so I started getting undressed, drunk as a skunk. They called Jimmy Carrillo, who was living at the Dunwoody house with us. Jimmy was running the club for Steve. He came all the way up to the club to the dressing room.

He says, "You're not going on stage."

"Fuck you, who do you think you are?"

"I thought I told you to go home a long time ago."

"You know last time I checked I was 32 years old and my parents stopped telling me what to do when I was 17. So do you think for one minute you can step in and tell me what the fuck I can and cannot do? You can kiss my ass. I ain't got time for your shit."

Then Jimmy's girlfriend, Alaysia, stepped in my face and said, "Don't you realize that you're on trial? You've got to set an example."

"Bitch, you don't need to remind me that I'm on trial. Do you think this is something I don't already know? You know what? I am taking the heat for every bitch that ever did anything wrong in this fucking club. I'm the one in that courtroom everyday of the week. None of you know what I'm going through right now. So you and the rest of these phony-ass bitches that are smiling up in my face right now can get the fuck out of my face. Aren't you the one that stole $20,000 in Gold Bucks? Aren't you the one who probably should be arrested right now and on trial?"

Jimmy got pissed because I called her out like that. He says, "Fuck you Diva."

I said, "That's your problem." I went on about how I was glad we'd never worked together, how he would have never been able to call my shots, but it didn't matter. The moment had gone. The mood was spoiled.

I got dressed and went to Heather's. I didn't even go home that night. The next day in court Jimmy was telling Steve, "Yeah, Rose was on stage last night and Diva was going to go up."

"Yeah, Steve, I was going to go on stage last night. I was going to do a farewell S&M skit because a couple of customers called out while Rose was on. What can happen? I'm already on trial. It's already there. They can't do anything to me that they haven't already done."

* * *

By the first of August, a Wednesday afternoon, we had worked out a deal. Steve Kaplan and Steve Sadow really did it. They called a recess suddenly. It wasn't what anybody expected and the media did not report the story properly.

Just for the record, the government didn't give us a deal. Steve Kaplan gave them a deal, and said, "If you don't accept this we're going to go ahead with this trial."

We didn't have to sit there and wait for them to come back to us with a plea bargain. We did all the negotiating ourselves. We told them what we wanted, and if we couldn't have it, there was no deal. On the news Rick Dean said, "We basically got what we wanted. The club is closed. We got $5 million restitution and he (Steve) is going to jail and we got five of the other defendants to plead guilty."

The fact was, Steve Kaplan was tired and he didn't want to run the risk of any of us being found guilty on any charges, so it was easier for him to say he'd do up to three years in prison and give them money in exchange for them letting the rest of us go. Don Samula, Larry Gleit's attorney, called what Steve did "heroic."

Steve knew the government wasn't going to accept the deal if he didn't do any jail time. But he would rather sacrifice his freedom for a little while to make sure that the rest of us didn't have to do 20 years, because that was the minimum we were facing.

One of the female reporters said to me towards the end of the trial, "I've been in this courtroom every day with you guys for months now. It's made me realize that nobody's safe. This could happen to anybody. You just never know. I have lost all faith in our government after watching what has transpired in this courtroom."

* * *

The next day, Thursday, August 2, 2001, was the end—the last day. The press knew some of what was going down and they covered the plea like it was a rocket launch, minute by minute.

Atlanta Journal-Constitution reported on "Two hours of courtroom drama."

After a long morning of fidgeting on wooden pews, a packed courtroom gallery was cleared for lunch shortly before noon Thursday, to reconvene at 1:30 p.m. About 1:25 p.m., lawyers, defendants and observers begin to trickle back into the Richard B. Russell Building's room 1708.

1:40 p.m. Former Gold Club owner Steve Kaplan walks into the courtroom and sits at the defendant's table.

1:45 p.m. Bruce Harvey, attorney for former dancer Jacklyn Bush, pops a piece of mint gum into his mouth. He tells Bush: "My breath is refreshed now."

1:50 p.m. Kaplan and his attorney, Steve Sadow, leave the courtroom through a side door.

2:00 p.m. Defendant Michael DiLeonardo, who did not plead Thursday and still faces trial, walks through the courtroom, shaking hands and making small talk.

2:05 p.m. Bush notes all the activity of lawyers and defendants arriving and then leaving. She turns around to her entertainer friends in the gallery with a rendition of the familiar piano tune "The Entertainer" "from the movie "The Sting"— "Do, do, do-do, do-do, do-do." When she's signaled out of the courtroom by an attorney, she laughs and to her friends says, "We changed our minds!" (He didn't get this right. What it meant was we were all sitting there talking and one of the attorneys called me out to tell me to tell one of the reporters to come outside. Everybody was looking at me like, why did that attorney call you? I was joking and said, "We changed our minds." (As in we are not pleading.) Reporters started scrambling. The whole joke about the Entertainer was that one day in court my cell phone went off and the music playing on it was the Entertainer. It happened to me twice. The court Marshall said, "If your phone goes off again we're going to have to take it from you." So we had this ongoing joke about my cell phone. One day the court Marshall's radio went off. Everybody turned around. Me and Bruce Harvey pointed at him and said, "It was him, Judge! It was him!")

2:10 p.m. Prosecutors, defense attorneys and defendants take their seats.

2:12 p.m. U.S. District Court Judge Willis Hunt enters.

2:15 p.m. With Kaplan and his attorneys about to enter a plea, court officials realize the court reporter is not in the room.

2:16 p.m. Court reporter in place, U.S. Attorney Art Leach tells the judge that Kaplan will enter a guilty plea to a count of racketeering, which included interstate prostitution, credit card fraud and defrauding Delta Air Lines of up to $50,000.

2:28 p.m. Hunt tells Kaplan he will accept his guilty plea and he is free to leave until further notice.

2:35 p.m. Club manager Norbert Calder pleads guilty to "misprison of a felony" relating to interstate prostitution, credit card fraud and tax violations.

2:49 p.m. Club manager Roy Cicola pleads guilty to "misprison of a felony"—meaning he knew a crime was committed but did not report it.

3:02 p.m. Former dancer Jacklyn Bush pleads guilty to "misprison of a felony."

3:20 p.m. Hunt calls for a 10-minute break.

3:30 p.m. Club chief financial officer Larry Gleit pleads guilty to a misdemeanor tax charge.

3:40 p.m. Judge Hunt formally accepts Gleit's plea. Court is adjourned.

* * *

At first Steve was going to have to do 30 months, no challenge. In his deal he could get up to 36 months but he could ask for a lesser term; Sadow said he intended to argue for a year and a day. Steve was giving them five million bucks and the club, plus $38,400 they took the night we were raided. The first deal had him paying 7.5 million and still losing the club. He had to pay restitution of $50,000 to Delta, and $250,000 to the credit card people. But he was facing up to ten years and losing everything he had including all of his other businesses which were worth about fifty million.

The last day of court was also the last night at the Gold Club. It was the weirdest damn night ever. Part of the plea deal was they could change the locks on the club immediately and take control in seven days. They got what they wanted right away.

It was about people losing their jobs at this point. If we made money we sure as hell paid for it. Heather and I got there a little after ten to find a whole host of employees, regulars, and lawyers drinking and saying their final good-byes. Rose was trying to comfort the crying dancers. As I walked up the stairs to the VIP lounge, I heard shouts of "Diva!" Some of the girls ran up and hugged me tight and thanked me for bearing the brunt of everything. And said good-bye.

Steve came in and was mobbed by a crowd of grateful dancers and friends. Jimmy Carillo was walking around telling everyone it was time to go. He was a fly in the ointment. Just then, the news came on. We all crowded around the TV on the main floor. We watched, waitresses and entertainers on TV cheering and thanking Steve on local television for all he did for them and for the money they made. One of the waitresses said, "If you ever want to know how to make money, look Steve Kaplan up. He'll teach you."

Then they began chanting his name.

At 11:30 as we walked out the front door and turned off the lights, hot tears, dammed up for weeks, began to spill over my cheeks in a torrent of sadness and relief.

At midnight the Federal Marshalls put a chain through the door handles and padlocked the Gold Club.

My sentencing was Tuesday, October 23rd. Eight of us were sentenced, one at a time. The atmosphere of the courtroom had changed. Tired is the best word to describe it. The judge was tired. The lawyers were tired. Even the media was showing signs of exhaustion. We all got fines ranging from $1,000 to $2,000 with community service hours ranging from 40-80 hours. My sentence was the lowest of them all.

Chapter
Twenty-Seven

I had been penniless, living on the edge since the day the trial ended. But the weeks in between also gave me time to re-think my life—once again.

I had a chance to consider the anger in my life and decided, it's just an evil I don't need. Intellectually, I've always known that—my life has shown me nothing if it hasn't shown me about anger. And that's primarily why I've had to work hard to forgive the government and to forgive the people who turned on me when I was down. Forgiveness gives me some relief.

After all, I always check my kids, if I heard them say, "I hate that." I'm quick to point out, "No, you don't, you don't like it." Hate is taking it to another level and then violence follows closely behind.

I got some good advice from my lawyer friend Neal Howard. It was something I was thinking anyway. I told him I was kind of bitter after I pled guilty.

He said, "Can I tell you something, Diva? Never forget where you came from and never forget where you are. Always remember that people are going to be people and they don't know how to handle a situation like this. They can't handle chaos. When you get in trouble with the law people run scared because they don't want to be drug into it. Their jobs, their families, they got shit to do. Just because they detach doesn't mean they don't care about you. It's for their own protection. Versus you saying to them kiss my ass or not speaking when you do run into those people again—greet them with a smile, let them know you're okay now, and that you understand that sometimes you got to do what you do for your own benefit." I listened and I've tried to heed those words.

And maybe I believe that God stepped in and put me through this whole indictment and trial and taking everything that I owned, that I worked so hard for at the Gold Club. I lost everything—my house, my car, my dog, my kids, my furniture and all my money. I think he took all that negativity away from me on purpose so that I could start from scratch and get my money and respect and admiration from people the right way, the correct way. I also think God presented the idea to write this book as an outlet to search my soul, find out what hurts me on the inside, deep-rooted over the years, aggravations, and let-downs and despair. He's letting me feel that all over again so that later on, once the dust has settled and my life is better, maybe I'll value it more and truly enjoy it.

I know how I feel about God and I don't need other people telling me how I'm supposed to feel. Don't tell me how to pray. I know how to pray. I always have.

Well everyone has moved on with their lives, as for me I am taking steps to restore a comfortable atmosphere for my children, and I am looking towards the future. I will continue to participate in community service work and eventually head up my own non-profit organization. I want to get into movie directing and producing, and I hope to be the next Julia Roberts of Hollywood.

I guess you're wondering what happened to everyone, and where are they now?

Steve Kaplan—is serving his 13-month prison sentence in upstate New York, he'll be released in the Spring of 2003.

Thomas (Ziggy) Sicignano—on the day of Mr. Kaplin's sentencing, we were informed that all the charges against "Ziggy" were dropped and he is a free man.

Heather Rellinger—and I are no longer friends because she has not changed and she is currently a cocktail waitress in Midtown Atlanta.

Patrick Doggrell—still resides in Georgia, as far as what he is doing, I haven't been in contact with him.

Dennis Rodman—and I still keep in contact. He is residing in Newport Beach, CA and has opened a restaurant.

Joesph Bush—has made great changes in his life, he is no longer a violent man, and is the world's greatest father. He and I are best friends and all is forgiven.

Micheal DiLenoardo—is currently under a new federal indictment in the Southern District of New York City. He was acquitted of all charges here in Georgia.

Mitchell Lafleur—is serving his prison sentence here in Atlanta, GA at the federal prison camp.

Norbie Calder—resides in New Jersey and is part owner of Rosa's Pizza in Penn Station, New York.

Roy Cicola—still lives in Georgia and is doing well.

Jimmy Carillo—is currently running Steve's Business in New York until he is released from prison.

Lyle Goodman—currently has a night club in Philadelphia.

Greg Sage—currently reside in Florida where he works as a professional photographer.

Russell Basile—is married with two children and works for Steve at Penn Station.

Stanley B. Lackey—and I have broken up, but are still friends. He needs time to get himself together, and so do I. Who knows what the future holds!

Elliott Henderson—is still playing basketball overseas and he is still single. He's currently in Switzerland.

Jana—Frederique—well, she's working at a day care center taking care of other people's children. Enough said.

Amanda Pappas—is probably somewhere in Florida taking care of her child. I guess we all gotta do what we gotta do.

Richard Rubin—is still a good friend and remained so throughout. We're still hanging together planning future charity events. He still has a tanning salon and is doing quite well despite the financial loss which resulted from the closing of the Gold Club.

Larry Gleit—is still in New York and remains the CFO of all of Steve Kaplan's businesses. Why fix it if it ain't broke?

Reginald Burney—was also found not guilty and is now running his security company in Atlanta.

Bruce Harvey—my lawyer, is still pulling his court room shenanigans hoping to one day go down in history. Unfortunately, his career as a dancer was short lived.

My mother, Karen—once she got away from my father, her life took a turn for the better. Without him, she didn't need to be a crazed drug addict. She could be her wonderful generous self. She's in her early fifties these days and has acute arthritis and bursitis and can't work anymore. For the past five years, she took charge of two of her grandchildren. I vowed to take care of her for the rest of her life and I think it tickles her to be loved so much. She finally decided to leave Milwaukee when I called her and told her to pack everything and come down to Atlanta. I just couldn't take it anymore. I needed her. She brought two small bonuses—my niece Desiree and my nephew Dorian—who now live with us and brighten everyday with their independent views on life. They're okay.

My father, James Lewis—hasn't changed one bit. He got caught sleeping with his current wife's niece. This time he paid a price, it cost him his marriage. His wife, of course, left him and is doing okay. He is still unemployed.

My three sweet girls are still in between me and their father but we're working things out. I'm saving for a new house, one that we can keep. I imagine it'll be the same house that sees them off to their first proms and later to college.

As for the rest of the Gold Club employees, most of the entertainers have gone to several different clubs around Atlanta. The rest are bartenders, waitresses and bouncers at regular nightclubs. B.A. and Boyd, the old promoters for the Gold Club, now own a popular club in Buckhead called "Chaos," and a few of the Gold Club employees now work for them.

And me? I am taking it one day at a time, putting my life back together. I am telling my personal life story in hopes that it will help others. I pray that my story will serve as a deterrent for those who are contemplating taking the wrong path in life, as well as light for those who feel trapped in the darkness of life. I hope that my story will serves as a "Life Jacket" to those who feel as though they are drowning in sin and have lost hope for restoration, and have no peace within.

I thank God for the love he placed in my heart for my mother. My mother was not able to take care of me as a child, and contributed to my taking the wrong path in life: due to the fact that she was not there for me emotionally or physically. Today, I am happy to have the opportunity to take care of my mother and to do for her what she could not do for me. I truly love my mother with unconditional love.

I consider myself to be a good mother—not a perfect mother. And I pray that my daughters will not withhold their love from me for the pain and suffering I may have caused them during my ups and downs.

I am able to move forward because I have forgiven myself and others. I believe that we all fall down in life. However, the tragedy does not lie in the fact that we fall down, the tragedy lies in the fact that we do not fight with all our might to get back up.

I'm sharing my life and the lives of my family members in order to make a positive difference in the lives of others.

I am a free woman today, and I refuse to allow my past to hold me hostage. I consider myself blessed to have had a Romans 8:28 experience. The verse reads as follows: *And we know that all things work together for good to them that love God, to them who are called according to his purpose.*

I am now walking in the path that God originally intended for me. My goals are to help in restoring wounded hearts and to restore love between parents and children. I have a dream and I have purpose and if I can change a few lives, I know that my struggle was worth it all and my living is not in vain.

BOOK AVAILABLE THROUGH

Milligan Books, Inc.

An Imprint of Professional Business Consulting Service

"The Gold Club" The Jacklyn "Diva" Bush Story $15.95

Order Form

Milligan Books, Inc.

1425 W. Manchester Ave., Suite C, Los Angeles, CA 90047

(323) 750-3592

Name_____ Date _____

Address_____

City_____ State____ Zip Code _____

Day Telephone _____

Evening Telephone_____

Book Title_____

Number of books ordered___ Total ....$ _____

Sales Taxes (CA Add 8.25%)....................$ _____

Shipping & Handling $4.90 for one book..$ _____

Add $1.00 for each additional book...........$ _____

Total Amount Due....................................$ _____

☐ Check ☐ Money Order ☐ Other Cards _____

☐Visa ☐ MasterCard Expiration Date _____

Credit Card No. _____

Driver License No. _____

Make check payable to Milligan Books, Inc.

Signature_____ Date_____